THE EROTIC IMPULSE

Also by David Steinberg
*Erotic by Nature: A Celebration of Life,
of Love, and of Our Wonderful Bodies*
(editor)
Fatherjournal: Five Years of Awakening to Fatherhood

This New Consciousness Reader
is part of a new series of original
and classic writing by renowned experts on
leading-edge concepts in personal development,
psychology, spiritual growth, and healing.

Other books in this series include:

Dreamtime and Dreamwork
EDITED BY STANLEY KRIPPNER, PH.D.

Fathers, Sons, and Daughters
EDITED BY CHARLES SCULL, PH.D.

Healers on Healing
EDITED BY RICHARD CARLSON, PH.D., AND BENJAMIN SHIELD

Meeting the Shadow
EDITED BY CONNIE ZWEIG
AND JEREMIAH ABRAMS

Mirrors of the Self
EDITED BY CHRISTINE DOWNING

Reclaiming the Inner Child
EDITED BY JEREMIAH ABRAMS

Spiritual Emergency
EDITED BY STANISLAV GROF, M.D., AND CHRISTINA GROF

To Be a Man
EDITED BY KEITH THOMPSON

To Be a Woman
EDITED BY CONNIE ZWEIG

What Survives?
EDITED BY GARY DOORE, PH.D.

SERIES EDITOR: CONNIE ZWEIG

THE
EROTIC
IMPULSE

Honoring the Sensual Self

EDITED BY

DAVID STEINBERG

JEREMY P. TARCHER/PERIGEE

Rockwell Kent ornaments and part-opening illustrations used courtesy of
The Rockwell Kent Legacies.

Jeremy P. Tarcher/Perigee Books
are published by
The Putnam Publishing Group
200 Madison Avenue
New York, NY 10016

Jeremy P. Tarcher, Inc.
5858 Wilshire Blvd., Suite 200
Los Angeles, CA 90036

Published simultaneously in Canada

Library of Congress Cataloging-in-Publication Data

The Erotic Impulse: honoring the sensual self / [compiled by] David Steinberg.
        p.   cm.
    Includes bibliographical references.
    ISBN 0-87477-697-X
    1. Sex.   2. Sex customs.   3. Sexual excitement.
    4. Erotica—Psychological aspects.   5. Erotica—Miscellanea.
    I. Steinberg, David, 1944-.
    HQ21.E76   1992
    306.7—dc20   92-7810
                                                                        CIP

Design by Lee Fukui

Printed in the United States of America
1   2   3   4   5   6   7   8   9   10

This book is printed on acid-free paper.
                    ∞

Confusion is a word we have invented
for an order which is not understood.

Henry Miller
Tropic of Capricorn

Contents

Introduction   XV

PART 1
THE NATURE OF THE EROTIC IMPULSE

Introduction   3

Summer Brenner
Let Me Tell You How It Feels   7

Jack Morin
The Four Cornerstones of Eroticism   9

Rollo May
Love and the Daimonic   21

Greta Christina
Are We Having Sex Now or What?   24

Michael Ventura
The Porn Prince of Decatur Street   30

Joan Nelson
Lighting Candles   36

Allen Ginsberg
Song   37

James Broughton
Sermon   40

PART 2
EROTIC INITIATION AND PASSAGE

Introduction   43

Lonnie Barbach
Bringing Up Children Sexually   46

Henry Miller
Discovering the World of Sex 49

H. M. Ruggieri
The Girl Next Door 54

Gore Vidal
A Warm Emotion Which He Could Not Name 58

John Berger
How Did It Happen? 64

Rachel Kaplan
Another Coming Out Manifesto Disguised as a
    Letter to My Mother 71

James Joyce
On the Beach at Fontana 75

e. e. cummings
i like my body when it is with your 76

PART 3

THE EROTIC IMAGINATION

Introduction 79

Camille Paglia
The Roving Erotic Eye 83

Richard Goldstein
Pornography and Its Discontents 86

Barbara Wilson
The Erotic Life of Fictional Characters 97

Statements by Erotic Writers, Photographers, Poets, and Artists
On Eros and Erotic Art 101

Michael Rubin
Horseman, Pass By 107

David Steinberg
The High Priestess 108

Lenore Kandel
Seven of Velvet 109

PART 4

EROTIC DIFFERENCES BETWEEN MEN AND WOMEN

Introduction   113

Anaïs Nin
Eroticism in Women   117

Susie Bright
What Turns Her On?   124

Paula Webster
Eroticism and Taboo   129

Nancy Friday
The Masculine Conflict   142

Thomas Moore
Eros, Aggression, and Male "Shining"   148

Nan Goldin
The Ballad of Sexual Dependency   152

Robert Bly
The Horse of Desire   154

Carolyn Kleefeld
I Could Die With You   156

PART 5

THE SUPPRESSION AND DENIAL OF EROS

Introduction   159

Robert T. Francoeur
The Religious Suppression of Eros   162

Marty Klein
Erotophobia: The Cruelest Abuse of All   175

Carol Cassell
Still Good Girls After All These Years   181

Carole S. Vance
Photography, Pornography, and Sexual Politics   187

Ellen Willis
Feminism, Moralism, and Pornography   192

Sallie Tisdale
Talk Dirty to Me   199

Scarlet Woman
Radical Femme   211

Anne Sexton
Us   213

PART 6
EROTIC FRONTIERS

Introduction   217

Betty Dodson
Going Public   220

Carol A. Queen
Erotic Power and Trust   225

Tee Corinne
Dreams of the Woman Who Loved Sex   235

John Preston
How Dare You Even Think These Things?   244

James Broughton
At Beck's Motel on the 7th of April   256

Ron Koertge
This is for every man who licks   257

PART 7
EROTIC TRANSCENDENCE AND SELF-DISCOVERY

Introduction   261

Kevin Regan
The Prayer of Conjugal Love   265

Marco Vassi
Bodhi Is the Body   269

Margo Anand
The Tantric Vision   277

Robert Moore and Douglas Gillette
The Lover in His Fullness   284

Robert Bly
The Humming of Eros   289

Sy Safransky
Some Enchanted Evening   290

Deena Metzger
The Work to Know What Life Is   296

Leonard Cohen
Beneath My Hands   298

Lenore Kandel
Eros/Poem   300

Epilogue   301

Contributors   303

Permissions and copyrights   309

ACKNOWLEDGMENTS

It is hard to know where to begin in documenting the influences and support that collectively form the soil for any labor such as this book. Realistically, this book is both the outcome of and input to the strange and delightful path that, very mundanely, could be referred to as my personal process of erotic and sexual discovery. To be thorough I should begin, years back, with Anaïs Nin and Henry Miller, erotic parents opportunistically discovered during my uncertain adolescent unfolding, who gave form, both feminine and masculine, to my budding sexuality, as well as to the particular form of envisioning that was to become my writing. But then I would have to go on to acknowledge literally hundreds of erotic muses along the way, direct and indirect—an interesting exercise, really, but more than is called for here.

Pretending for a moment that this book can be meaningfully separated from what comes before and after, I want to thank the people at Tarcher, where the idea for this book began—particularly Robert Welsch for the initial connection; Connie Zweig for her thoughtful and subtle editorial insight and perspective; and Jeremy Tarcher for his direct honesty, for so quickly seeing me for who I was, and for his flexibility in embracing my vision of this book even though its was initially more than a little different from his own. The opportunity to stay caring and human with each other through the delicate process of birthing a book, and to maintain emotional and intellectual integrity in the face of the demands of an often inhuman world, has been as important to me as the specific decisions about what this book should and should not be.

Thanks to Michael Hill, as always, for his enthusiasm and support, for believing in me even when I seemed to be going off the deep (or shallow) end, for believing in this book that is in many ways more a reflection of our differences than our common journey, and for reading the draft manuscript with care and giving me his perceptive reflections; to Joani Blank, my forever friend and shepherd, for her continuing support and love through all the ups and downs; to Marty Klein for reaching out and caring about me across all the reasons not to; to Andrea Ossip for seeing more of me than I could see myself; to Tom Starkey and Kenton Parker for working with me through all the changes; to Marcia for supporting and honoring my erotic path year after year even when it made her life most difficult, for clearing space for yet another somersault in our life together, and for responding with love and care to the various insanities this book has generated; and to Dylan for his love and appreciation, and for accepting with grace and perhaps too much understanding the ways this book has interfered with our increasingly rare time together.

INTRODUCTION

What happens when you follow the erotic muse wherever it may lead, follow with your eyes open but with complete trust, lust, love, and wonder? What happens when you fully open yourself to the erotic life force, even when it leads you into territory that is as unpredictable as it is delightful, as unsettling as it is exciting? What if you give the erotic impulse the right-of-way, only defining as perverted whatever blocks its flow? What if you reject the pervasive notion that there is something wrong with your erotic feelings and desires—something wrong with being interested in erotic matters at all or being fascinated by the erotic too much, too strangely, or too differently from what other people consider proper? What if you make erotic existence your art, your path, an organizing principle for your life, and refuse to apologize for the consequences? What if—at certain times, in certain places, with certain partners—you surrender yourself completely to the erotic waterworld, surrender deliberately, with innocence, wisdom, and open-ended expectancy, and let yourself discover the depth and complexity of what this essential life force is trying to say to you and through you?

We are told that if we surrender to the erotic impulse, if we indulge our erotic desires, if we engage the erotic world in any but the most carefully controlled and perfunctory ways, terrible things will happen to us. We are told, and we come to believe, that welcoming the full strength of erotic existence will make us crazy. We imagine that if we open this Pandora's box we will run amok, find ourselves doing bizarre, disgusting things to ourselves and to others. We imagine that relaxing the reins of erotic control is the same as relinquishing all influence over our behavior. We fear that if we listened and responded to our erotic impulses our lives would disintegrate; we would no longer be productive members of society; we would lose our jobs and shatter our primary relationships. We imagine that we would be dismissed by our friends as foolish and childish, or weird and disreputable. We believe that we would become degenerates: morally unworthy, unlovable, and unloved.

We are told repeatedly, and we come to believe (so deeply that we don't even recognize it as a belief system) that if we acknowledge, honor, and embrace the erotic impulses of our sensual selves we will destroy the order in our world and be cast into chaos. This terrifies us. We turn against desire itself, against our own erotic impulses and feelings, as well as the erotic expressions of others. We set ourselves the task of keeping the erotic impulse down at all cost.

Keeping erotic desire under control, keeping it within the narrow boundaries acceptable to our reason-loving, puritanical culture, is a continuous, life-denying endeavor which, in the end, is emotionally exhausting. We are, after all, declaring war on one of the most powerful and fundamental aspects of who we are. Eventually, we become angry at the impossible task we have taken on, usually turning that anger on erotic existence itself for threatening our stability, our security, our very sanity.

If we understood this issue more we would focus our resentment where it belongs: on those forces that try to deprive us of this wonderful aspect of being fully alive human beings. But because we have so internalized the anti-erotic premises that surround us, we come instead to despise the objects of desire that inspire the erotic feelings we are desperately trying to deny and ignore. The more powerful the repression—the tighter the lid on the cauldron—the stronger the denial, fear, confusion, and anger we feel toward anything that threatens to stimulate our repressed erotic natures.

This is the erotic shadow, the price of erotic denial. In its more extreme forms it operates as a dangerous cultural and political force, threatening our most fundamental values of freedom and diversity. Those who most misunderstand and fear the power of the erotic impulse label eros the work of the devil, a satanic force to be resisted, subdued, and transformed. The task of suppressing or eliminating sexual expression in all but a few sanctioned forms becomes, for them, a holy war.

Despite the well-publicized preaching of terrified censors and moralists, the erotic world is hardly an invitation to chaos. It is a world as thoroughly ordered, sane, consistent, wholesome, and subject to reflection and understanding as the worlds of science, logic, and reason. To be sure, the erotic realm is neither scientific, nor logical, nor rational. But the rational/scientific paradigm is but one way of ordering the universe. It is only because we have so lost touch with our erotic natures, because we have become so alienated from experiencing ourselves and the world around us in erotic terms, that we feel the need to impose rational order *everywhere.*

The process is cyclical: the more we assert the hegemony of reason, the more we dissociate from and fear the erotic life. The more we become divorced from eros, the more ferociously we turn to reason for meaning and stability.

It is one of the premises of this book that there is a non-rational, yet profound and primary system of order that is inherent to the world of eros. Only when we see how differently the erotic world is organized from the worlds of physics, biology, business, or production—only when we stop oversimplifying the erotic by trying to make it fit the premises of the rational mind—only then can we begin to understand, trust, and honor the erotic universe on its own terms. When we see that embracing our erotic feelings involves moving from one form of order to another, rather than throwing ourselves into chaotic self-destruction, then we can begin to appreciate eroticism and sexuality as expansive, powerful, creative expressions of the best of who we are.

We live in a culture that idolizes control. We are taught, almost from birth, how to control ourselves, the material world, and the people around us. Men are taught the importance of controlling both their inner emotions and the world around them. Women are given more room than men for emotional expression and loss of control, but the woman who loses control of her erotic desires is subject to vilification unique to her gender. Women who allow themselves the range of sexual expression taken for granted by men are likely to be seen, metaphorically, as witches, whores, and sex-demons, and may well (again, metaphorically) be burned at the stake.

The converse of our cultural infatuation with control is that we are woefully ignorant about the emotional and spiritual significance of *losing* control—of surrender, abandon, turning yourself over to the power of the unknown and unknowable. Because loss of control is seen only in negative terms we do not learn how to lose control skillfully, intentionally, or artfully, as a means of personal growth and self-discovery. We do not develop discipline, consciousness, or grace in loosening our habitual restraints. We do not learn how to create circumstances in which personal surrender can be safe and enlightening, or how to distinguish safe contexts from those in which surrender would be reckless or dangerous. When we do go out of control, we often do so unconsciously or rebelliously. If we get hurt in these times of blind release, it only reinforces the moralism that condemns personal surrender in the first place.

In our obsessively rational culture, erotic feeling, erotic desire, and sexual arousal are inherently heretical. The experience of surrendering to desire, which could be welcomed as the sweetest of meltings, becomes intrinsically suspect. Ecstasy, indeed any feeling of uncontrolled and intense wonder and amazement, is condemned as dark and dangerous. Loss of ego boundaries, dissolution of the discrete, discernible self—a core component of deep sexual experience—is perceived not as an emotional, spiritual, or even religious opportunity, but as something to be feared and resisted.

These attitudes are applied to all forms of erotic experience, but they come into particular significance when we look at the experience of orgasm. Orgasm requires precisely the ability to let yourself go out of control, to let go of the need to limit and direct, to lose your mind, both figuratively and literally. In orgasm, we relinquish for a moment the reins of control and order, trusting that we can enter this transient state of abandoned ego-dissolution because orderly existence will recollect itself, spontaneously and without need of our conscious intervention, once the wave of release passes.

People obsessed with control often have difficulty being fully orgasmic, and this is not just an issue for women. A half-century ago, Wilhelm Reich discovered that almost as many men as women among his patients were nonorgasmic, once he separated male ejaculation from the deeper experience of full-body orgasm.

The same issues of order and control that make the erotic world frightening to some people are, for others, the basis of erotic intensity, excitement, and fascination. What some fear as chaotic, others welcome as an opportunity to move beyond the restrictions of our over-civilized society, to explore facets of ourselves that are more unruly, spontaneous, and closer to the primal forces of nature.

We have taken on the technological mission of overcoming and subduing nature. As a result, our lives are safer in many ways; we are less subject to the ravages of weather and disease; we are surrounded by creature comforts beyond the imagination of anyone a mere century ago. But we also tend to be profoundly bored with the routines of our lives, the predictability of our existence, the blandness of our emotions. We wonder where the fire has gone, the engagement, the passion, the intensity—if, indeed, we ever had any fire at all.

Somewhere in us there remains an erotic yearning for wildness, an intrigue with unpredictability, an infatuation with spontaneity and uncertainty. If we are afraid to include these energies in our actual lives, we may well sublimate these erotic desires into worlds of fantasy—film, pornography, or romance novels. We may find ourselves powerfully drawn to romantic flings or extra-marital affairs—erotic firestorms that often break down under the heavy collective burdens of guilt, inflated expectation, and rebellious anger.

The desire to breach conventional limits of order and civility are apparent in the widespread appeal of the image of the wild man and, increasingly, the image of the wild woman. The innocent, pristine image of the ideal woman—once the very mainstay of socially defined femininity—seems to be losing its appeal for both men and women, replaced by a more unapologetically powerful, unpredictable, and openly sexual female figure who is attractive not only as a sexual partner, but as a dynamic life force as well. The increasing popularity of fierce sexual play, and of sadomasochism, body piercing, and tattooing—subcultures that are already becoming part of the cultural mainstream—also speaks to a rising urge to reconnect with the primitive, animal, passionate aspects of our natures. It is as if we are looking for ways to bring some of our lost erotic wildness back from exile.

Bringing eroticism more centrally into our lives, however, is as tumultuous and difficult a process as any other form of personal, social, or political revolution. Overturning deeply entrenched patterns of thought and behavior involves more than simply seeing the light and moving forward in a blissful state of enlightened liberation. The partisans of the French Revolution learned this as they watched their noble principles disintegrate into the Reign of Terror. Russian Marxists saw their vision of the "society of the new man" deteriorate into Stalinism. Gandhi watched heartbroken as his principles of nonviolence were washed away in the bloody rivers of nationalism and religious intolerance.

Forces that have been confined under intense pressure for generations cannot be released suddenly without explosive consequences. Our erotic desires and feelings have been pushed and shoved, condemned and distorted for decades, indeed for hundreds of years. All our lives we have been suffering from the conflict between our erotic natures and the pervasive systems of morality, judgment, and condemnation that strive to keep all erotic feeling under control. Inevitably, we have become deeply invested in the very systems of control we also want to overturn. There is much we have internalized that we need to question and restructure.

For example, we generally think of sexual matters almost exclusively in terms of what is *right* and what is *wrong*. Most of us will judge our erotic urges in moralistic terms before we even take the time to fully experience what we feel or to define what we want. Most of us are inclined, automatically and unconsciously, to find objectionable any but the most narrow range of erotic and sexual desires and thoughts. If we find ourselves aroused by an image, person, or circumstance that surprises us, we usually challenge not our system of judgment, but the feeling itself. "I shouldn't be turned on by that," we say guiltily. "I shouldn't want to behave in that way. There must be something wrong with me."

Similarly, if another person's sexual feelings or practices are substantially different from our own, most of us think there must be something terribly wrong with that person—as if we should all have the same feelings and desires. Most of us still feel that there is some objective way to determine what is normal and abnormal, and when it comes to sexual matters, the range of what we consider *normal* tends to be extremely narrow. *Abnormal* becomes everything else.

Thus, someone who wants or thinks about sex often is considered oversexed, obsessive, or now, all too commonly, sexually addicted. (A person who spends his time running marathons, painting, or playing classical music, on the other hand, is simply called passionate.) Enjoying oral sex is dubious to some; anal sex is disgusting to many. Homosexuality and bisexuality are regarded nervously by most, and thought positively vile by more than a few. Sadomasochism, regardless of how consensual, is still almost universally condemned as downright perverted. Even a person who has unusual desires or fantasies with no intention of acting on them often battles internal demons of self-doubt, confusion, and shame.

When we ask ourselves, "Is it right to feel this way?" before we even ask, "What is this feeling?" we become unable to know with any clarity who we are as erotic beings. Yet developing erotic self-awareness, acknowledging the reality and complexity of our true erotic yearnings is where we must begin if we want to substitute an understanding of erotic order for our habitual fear of erotic chaos.

When we know what we really want (as opposed to what we *think* we want, or fear we *might* want), the world of erotic engagement can be transformed from a frightening territory of demons to an exciting realm of personal exploration and fulfillment.

While the erotic is not essentially a demonic world, it is important to acknowledge that we do have real erotic conflict within us. We have long-simmering resentments, emotional wounds, memories of painful humiliations, confusions, fears of inadequacy and rejection—all of which we must deal with when we enter the world of eros. As we open ourselves to our erotic natures, we will find that we are often divided against ourselves—our feelings versus our judgments, our desires versus our fears, culturally designated icons versus our individual imaginations—no matter how diligently we try to keep ourselves whole. It takes time to develop clear vision when we have been blinded and misdirected for so long. It takes time to develop the confidence to believe in our erotic individuality when that individuality so often conflicts with who we have been taught we are supposed to be. As we expand our erotic consciousness, we may well allow ourselves new forms of erotic exploration only to be tortured by guilt and shame afterward. We may pursue a form of erotic expression we have always fantasized about, only to discover that what was delightful in fantasy is unappealing or even unpleasant in practice.

Given all the uncertainties and ambiguities, the best compass to guide us through the turbulent sea of erotic emergence is the simple ability to recognize honestly and acknowledge openly who we are and what we truly want—situation by situation, moment by moment. What we experience during these times of erotic expansion is almost certain to surprise us. This is why erotic self-awareness requires the ability to suspend judgment, preconception, and even logical definition, long enough to experience the intensity and the nuance of what is really going on.

The essays, stories, and poems in this book represent a broad spectrum of information and points of view. The 51 contributors speak with a variety of voices—journalistic, personal, literary, scholarly, humorous, spiritual, psychological, sociological, and political. Hopefully, they address the erotic impulse in ways that will be meaningful to readers of different ages, lifestyles, sexual orientations, sexual preferences, ethnic backgrounds, and psychological dispositions.

Some readers may find individual pieces to be emotionally challenging, controversial, or provocative. This is inevitable when addressing the charged issue of eroticism in more than a superficial way. It is not my intent, however, to fan the flames of sexual controversy, or to gratuitously shock any person's sensibilities, whatever their sexual orientation. There is already far too much writing and imagery that manipulates our sexual insecurity, confusion, fear, guilt, and shame for one purpose or another. Rather, I hope to present new and thought-provoking perspectives on various issues of eroticism and sexuality, writing that is emotionally and factually honest, thoughtful, imaginative, unusual, and complex as a way of expanding the breadth of erotic possibilities available to us all.

It is also my intent, with all the selections in this book, to celebrate and affirm the wonder of the erotic impulse as a complex, powerful, paradoxical, and potentially transformative life force, even while appreciating its more difficult and painful aspects. Perhaps by addressing the erotic world seriously and unsensationally, this book will help shift the ways we talk and think about the erotic impulse in a positive, truthful, and tolerant direction.

Despite the current backlash from well-financed moral crusaders, I am convinced that a curious, lively, and accepting erotic sensibility continues to grow among most people in this country. I believe there is a deep hunger in most of us—a hunger that cuts across boundaries of gender, age, income, geographical region, and political persuasion—for information that can help us stay grounded in our individual erotic natures during this time of rapidly shifting values, a hunger for information that acknowledges and encourages our full range of erotic feeling and desire. Above all else, it is my hope that this book will help people better understand and embrace the full complexity of their erotic existence, as well as the diverse erotic expressions of others.

1

THE NATURE OF THE EROTIC IMPULSE

INTRODUCTION: PART 1

What is the nature of the erotic impulse—the feeling of being erotically engaged, the tug of desire, this way of feeling especially alive and aware? What is its source? What is it trying to express? What core energy does it animate within us? What sorts of stimuli set it in motion or stop it dead? How do we work with it, use it (or let it use us) to enhance the quality of our lives? How do we come to grips with its intensity and depth in a way that encourages growth and empowerment?

Understanding what lies at the heart of erotic experience is not a rational or scientific matter, though some would like to reduce it to that. Erotic experience, arising as it does from the very core of the psyche, extends far beyond the conceptual limitations of the intellectual and logical perspectives to which it is so frequently subjected. To understand and appreciate how the erotic force moves within us and between us, we must transcend logical analysis, go beyond our cultural infatuation with reducing all life to what is measurable, scientific, and literal. Without a doubt, there is much we can learn from submitting the erotic world to rational scrutiny. But to engage the erotic universe on its own terms, we must also bring a sense of mystery and poetry, an appreciation of uncertainty and ambiguity, for these are as much a part of erotic life as anything more definite and concrete.

We are immersed in a culture that desperately wants to minimize and trivialize all things erotic and sexual, a culture that persistently tries to reduce the power and complexity of eros to something as simple as the physical release of sexual tension. We live in a culture that desperately wants to turn this profoundly deep and mysterious primal urge into something that can be easily understood, regulated, predicted, and controlled. And yet, whether we like it or not, the life force we call eros, the movement we feel as erotic impulse, again and again defeats our best efforts to control, civilize, tame, or confine it to our imposed boundaries of propriety.

While the erotic impulse clearly relates closely to the world of sexuality, it equally clearly extends well beyond the sexual act itself. One could say that eros informs almost every aspect of our lives in one way or another. It is a continuing and continuous part of being alive, an ongoing plane of existence. It is expressed in how we walk, how we breathe, how we look at one another across a table, how we speak, how we touch (however casually or nonsexually). Erotic energy is stirred by watching a sunset or waves breaking against the shore, seeing a deer run or a lion stretch, feeling the wind in our faces, warm water around us in a bath or shower, the slip of our clothes on our bodies as we go about our daily business. It is part of the excitement of a thunderstorm, an athletic contest, or of rushing to catch a bus before it leaves without us. It is embodied in the harmonies and rhythms of music, in the pleasure of dance, in the exhilaration of appreciating a work of art, in the process of artistic creation. It is a prime ingredient in the electricity of connecting meaningfully with other human beings, whether that be by sharing a powerful experience, looking into the depths of their eyes, quietly touching their skin, entering or receiving their bodies with our own. It is central to the act of being born, of giving birth, of dying.

Yet all our lives we are taught that the erotic impulse is something to be feared, the enemy of order, the work of the devil, a threat to sanity itself. In a culture such as ours, devoted to rationality and the ability to control and order the world around us, we believe with almost religious fervor that we can submit all aspects of life to the axioms of logic. Not surprisingly, we try to fathom the mysteries of the erotic world with the rules of reason.

And yet, when we try to rationally approach and organize our erotic feelings and impulses, everything turns to ashes. We write books about eroticism and sexuality, read hundreds of manuals full of sexual techniques, only to find ourselves more mystified and less fulfilled than ever. We issue moral and legal proscriptions for various forms of erotic expression—extra-marital affairs, teenage sexuality, prostitution, pornography—even oral sex, anal sex, and homosexuality—but only manage to drive these behaviors underground where they flourish as before, albeit with new tinges of rebellion and guilt.

Indeed, this is part of what so strongly fascinates us, intrigues us, and at the same time makes us so afraid of the erotic impulse: that it so persistently refuses to subordinate itself to reason and control. One of the most significant qualities of the erotic impulse is that it is an expression of that part of us that senses the limitations of the rational world, the part that does not want to be logical and reasonable all the time, the part that wants to overthrow the hegemonic supremacy of this one-sided outlook on life and reality.

If we want to relate effectively to the erotic world, we must honor and engage it on its own terms. We need a new paradigm that transcends rationalism, that is more in tune with the inner workings of the psyche. We need a more subtle, imaginative, accepting way of looking at the erotic urge and all it represents.

The selections in this section create such a context, an introduction and overview to the subsequent sections which examine more specific aspects of erotic expression. Summer Brenner begins appropriately with a rich description of what matters most to her about erotic experience. Her evocative language and imagery direct our attention to aspects of erotic experience that we all too often ignore, encouraging us to approach the erotic world obliquely, paying as much attention to what we see in the corners of our eyes as we do to what lies in the center of our field of vision.

Psychologist Jack Morin adds a more analytical perspective, examining four themes that commonly underlie experiences of intense erotic arousal. He argues that erotic heat is commonly generated by the friction between our desire and the obstacles that stand in the way of satisfying that desire. He suggests that we make use of such factors as resistance, frustration, impossibility, and danger as means of intensifying our erotic experiences.

Psychologist Rollo May takes us into more mysterious and disturbing aspects of the erotic universe. Debunking romantic views of the erotic, he looks at how the erotic impulse is, at its core, a daimonic, wild force. Cautioning that "our effete cultivation of sex can make us so arbitrary and detached that the simple power of the sexual act evaporates," he encourages us to make use of the fiery nature of eros as a way of affirming our essential power and vitality.

In a more playful vein, Greta Christina takes on the seemingly simple task of listing her sexual partners, only to find herself confronting the surprisingly complex issue of how to distinguish *sex* from *not-sex*. As she tries to define the boundary between these two supposedly discrete universes, she finds herself increasingly confused, finally doubting whether the precise territory of sex can really be designated at all.

Writer Michael Ventura explores the process of his own sexual emergence—under the constellated influences of Marilyn Monroe, Dracula, Jesus, and Elvis—revering sexual expression as a ceremony of irrepressible individuality, a return to fundamental innocence, an opportunity to come home to oneself, beyond the homogenization and brutality of the external world.

Psychologist Joan Nelson addresses sex and sexual energy in their broadest sense, as fundamental life forces with the power for deep emotional, psychological, and spiritual healing. Two closing poems by Allen Ginsberg and James Broughton also acknowledge the full wonder and potential of the erotic impulse even as it eludes our best efforts at definition and control.

Summer Brenner

LET ME TELL YOU HOW IT FEELS

I'd love to tell you how it feels.

When it's riding you out to the sky, and your whole body is huddled in a point, and then it rockets away from you on waves. I guess something about the ocean says it best. The smell. The origin there. Conceived and then burst into a billion cells. I mean we have all been intimate with the deepest creative experience: we've all been born.

I think people who are lost, that's what they're most lost from. And sex. Well that is one of the simplest and most thrilling ways to get it back again.

Sometimes I think if I could make love once a week very awesomely, well that would really take care of it. But then when someone is around, I mean someone I love, then I want to do it a lot more. And then I think it's mostly for affection. Then the coming part is different. It's a level that can be thoroughly satisfying, but I don't have to have those stars. It's almost bureaucratic. If I don't *need* to come, I don't. Then there are days when I wake up, and I know that at a certain second someone's going to touch me on the shoulder, and I'm going to quake. It definitely gets easier. It never happened at all with my first lover. There are those degrees. Where it's a certain kind of thing that doesn't shake the sides. And then the one that grabs you so hard and takes you all the way there. I believe it's really the easiest way to understand the state of grace. And then when your lover begins to hoot and holler because he knows you've got it, then that's the best. I've only met a few men who could really gauge a wave.

I decided I didn't really care about making love with a lot of men because it takes so long to learn someone in that way. It always feels like such a big struggle, and then the best are always the ones you are going to love in manifold.

I used to be so afraid of being sexy. Now it really tickles me. I like to get to the part where I can wear a slip. It still takes me a while to get down. And I really only can with someone I like a lot. But then it's like the dance. And there's the step you do for yourself. And the step you do for your lover. And the step for the audience too. That's a push-up on white porcelain.

I guess certain people like certain things. I knew one who would grab my hair just above the wedge and make like he was going to touch that in the triangle there. I loved the feeling of the tease. It wasn't technique. He was learning to play an instrument well.

Men say the biggest thrill is to make it good for a woman. I can see how they'd come to that. I'd really like to know what other people feel.

Kissing is my favorite part.

I like to stop before it all explodes. Just lying together and breathing together. Connected by a stick and a hole. If I concentrate on what the space in my sex is holding, I can feel like I have a penis. We used to laugh that it was like being both sexes at the same time. And it is.

Society definitely makes us shy. Women I mean. I bet those reports about women's sexual peaks at thirty have to do with it actually taking a decade to overcome a certain kind of timidity.

Last year I saw this man at a party. We weren't introduced but I found out his name. I thought about him passionately for three days. Then I called information and got his number. Called him up and casually invited him to meet me, explaining about the party we had been at together the weekend before. I was practically throwing up. But it was so instructive to realize what the social dating procedure feels like. He was busy and disinterested. After the phone call, it lost its significance for me. Except for the fat understanding of what men have to go through all the time. Meet a girl, make a date, get laid. It's terrifying. And obviously drives them to wanting to *get a little* as some compensation for the uneasiness of the situation. Consequently, a woman is expected to submissively ride alongside, being sexually ignored and abused.

Until hopefully one day. She sees a clean sheet on the line with dry air blowing through it, and she decides that's the way she wants to feel.

Jack Morin

THE FOUR CORNERSTONES
OF EROTICISM

Ever since the seventies, I've been asking my psychotherapy clients, as well as hundreds of anonymous survey respondents, about their peak turn-ons. It's not the facts and figures that interest me, but the inside story-behind-the-story—what *really* happens when they're highly aroused. Most people know a lot more about what excites them, and why, than they normally reveal. We may be willing to discuss certain details of our adventures, but most of us guard our deepest erotic secrets like precious jewels. Because we don't usually tell each other the full truth about what excites us, most of us have a distorted view of how eroticism works. As a result we harbor unspoken doubts about the normalcy of our turn-ons since they don't match any ideal picture.

In peak sexual experiences, all the crucial elements coalesce—the partner, the setting, an unexpected twist of luck or fate. Even if we never tell anyone about it, we know that something close to the core of our being has been touched.

Peak encounters often have features similar to other events we recall vividly. Two *memorability factors* head the list: surprises and firsts. A tantalizing opportunity breaks through our routines and expectations. Letting go of inhibitions, we're launched into a world of new possibilities. That's what happened to this young woman:

> The first time I learned how to give a blow job was definitely an exciting moment. I was scared because my boyfriend and I had been seeing each other for five months—long enough for us to

have sex, but I wasn't completely comfortable with him yet. And besides, I just wasn't sure it was the right thing to do, or if I could do it right.

I don't know why, but all of a sudden I had this thirst for knowledge that *had* to be quenched. We were in my bedroom when I surrendered to my curiosity. He was very loving and patient as he guided me. He showed me exactly where it felt best, almost like an anatomy class. He let me experiment on his cock and balls with my lips and tongue. His moans told me I was on the right track. I felt adventurous and—it was weird—kind of in control. The combination of spontaneity and nervousness created an arousal all its own, especially when I saw my boyfriend's face as he came.

Peak turn-ons express, in bold relief, the key operating principles of our eroticism. Hot sex can teach us how to have more of it. And since eroticism is the interaction of our inborn capacity for arousal with the central challenges and concerns of living, directing our attention to the inner world of the erotic also can be an adventure in self-discovery.

THE EROTIC EQUATION

Sexual arousal, whether it involves romance or pure lust, is highest when there is a tension between the attraction pulling us toward the partner, and one or more barriers standing in the way. The formula for hot sex is

ATTRACTION + OBSTACLES = EXCITEMENT

The obstacles necessary for high excitement may be external or internal, conscious or unconscious. They can arouse us whenever something makes it difficult to get together. Or the chemistry between the partners can bring its own obstacles into the encounter. Overcoming barriers is a testament to the strength of the attraction. Thus geographic obstacles turn up the heat in long-distance relationships, keeping erotic interest high over long periods of time. And there's the situation of Romeo and Juliet, where both families forbid the relationship, thereby assuring that it would be irresistible for the star-crossed lovers.

The erotic equation predicts that the hottest sexual experiences usually won't be the sanitized affairs most of us were taught to idealize. On the contrary, starting very early in our lives, we weave into our experiences of arousal aspects of living that involve overcoming obstacles. As we each develop a unique, internal blueprint for excitement, we build into it the personal struggles, conflicts, and risks facing us at the time. Converting the messy uncertainties of life into the triumph of sexual excitement *is* the erotic process.

There are certain life experiences so fundamental and universal, and so inherently fraught with obstacles, that they are more likely than any others to become erotically significant. I call these the four cornerstones of eroticism.

LONGING AND ANTICIPATION

It is part of being human to be able to picture in our minds something or someone we desire but don't have. We use this ability each time we long for a person who isn't present, or who's not present in the way we want, or as often as we wish. In sexual longing, the real absence of the object of our desire is the obstacle. Our attraction increases as we focus on the most desirable aspects of the person we miss. We look forward to opportunities to be together, relishing any communication that circumstance permits.

Longing has a natural affiliation with romantic love. It's difficult to imagine experiencing limerence (the feeling of being in love) without wistful preoccupation filling the hours when the lovers are apart. Almost all romance novels are based on longing. The most extreme case is "unilateral limerence," the state of being head-over-heels in love with someone who seems to feel little or nothing in return.

Usually longing is most intense when we foresee at least some possibility of fulfillment or, better yet, when we've actually tasted what we crave and are aching for more. Longing reaches its zenith under conditions of partial or intermittent gratification. Just an occasional crumb of response reinforces the yearning. Sexual encounters fueled by longing tend to be explosively exciting and memorable.

Anticipation is a variation on the same theme. Anticipation, however, is less painful since fulfillment seems within reach. Where the emphasis in longing is on the absence of the desired one, anticipation is almost totally focused on the desired goal.

The interplay of longing and anticipation is obvious in a story told by a thirty-year-old man who spoke of his wedding night as the setting for an ultimate turn-on. For starters, he and his fiancé had to be apart for nearly six months before their wedding, making most of their plans by phone:

> We decided that we would stay overnight in a hotel before our honeymoon. I had just one request: that she wear garter belts. At first she laughed, but she admitted that she already had some surprises in mind. I couldn't wait.
>
> The consummation of our marriage was constantly on my mind, even during the ceremony. I kept looking at her, thinking how beautiful she was, that we would be together at last.
>
> Later, in our room, I was so aroused I could hardly keep my pants on. But we undressed each other slowly, very tenderly, taking all the time we needed to fully enjoy each moment. I felt like I would explode! Our sex that night was the absolute best I've ever had. What made it so great? I'd have to say it was the celebration, our deep feelings for one another, and being apart for months beforehand.

In this idyllic tale, longing and anticipation star as aphrodisiacs. But what happens next, when longing yields to fulfillment? Must the longing barrier be preserved so that future encounters will also be hot? It's a classic dilemma faced by most long-term couples.

Anything that encourages partners to take each other for granted is the enemy of longing. You can kiss anticipation goodbye if you get into one of those over-close, clingy relationships where the partners give up their rights to be separate individuals, blending into an amorphous *we-ness*. Sooner or later, one or both of the fused partners will long for freedom rather than for each other.

Conversely, anything that makes it difficult to take each other for granted invites longing and anticipation. Sexual intimacy requires a balance between involvement and separateness. Individuality is one of the best aphrodisiacs. Time apart, vigorous disagreements, and occasional fair fights all reestablish individuality and can fan the flames of desire.

Sexual teases are another effective means of bringing anticipation into an encounter, even after all barriers and contact have been overcome. Skillful sensualists learn to touch in ways that build anticipation rather than reduce it. The recipients often sing the praises of such lovers, like this woman in her fifties:

My husband has a tendency to go directly for what he wants, even if it's me. I'm glad he's still interested after all these years, but one morning he decided to take his time. Without a word, he started stroking my back and then my butt and legs. I was in heaven and really getting wet. He would do things like run his finger up my thighs, gently brushing against my pussy. When he turned me over, he touched my nipples so lightly with his tongue that they were screaming for more, but he would only do it for a moment and then touch me somewhere else. I don't know what got into him that day, but he teased me into one of the most intense orgasms of my life.

Violating Prohibitions

Every society places limits and restrictions on sexual behavior. These prohibitions are important means of enforcing the ideals and mores of the community. But sexual regulations have another function, which is usually not consciously intended: they provide natural barriers that anybody can use to intensify arousal. This effect is especially pronounced in societies like ours that seek to suppress childhood and adolescent sexuality.

The erotic equation predicts that people who grow up immersed in sexual restrictions are likely to discover the erotic potential of violating them. Through a simple learning process, arousing experiences and fantasies become associated with feeling naughty, dirty, guilty, or afraid of punishment—all significant barriers to be overcome, and all of potentially tremendous erotic significance.

During adolescence, it's not just raging hormones motivating those horny teens. This young woman recalls pulling out all the stops:

My boyfriend took me home after I watched him play in his band. Earlier that evening we were messing around so we were still pretty horny. We parked in my parents' driveway. The back seat was filled with his band equipment so he crawled over the stick shift and sat on top of me. He undid my bra and I unbuttoned his pants. We kissed and touched until we couldn't stand it anymore.

We switched places so I was on top. My pants were all the way off and his were around his ankles. With my legs sprawled apart, I sat down on top of him so his penis could penetrate deep inside me. Bobbing up and down, kissing passionately, and looking over our shoulders in case someone came outside to greet us—

it was all very exciting. It was daring to make love with my mom and dad inside. They totally hate my boyfriend! They think he's trying to seduce me.

It only took a few moments for both of us to come, calm down, and get our pants on. We looked at each other, laughed, and kissed as he walked me to the door. We said good night, both looking quite satisfied.

Adults find opportunities to enjoy the same naughtiness factor. Take this forty-year-old man:

One of the most memorable sexual experiences of my life took place while I was living and working in a London public house. I had an affair with the owner's wife. One day I had to go down to the cellar to change a barrel of beer. She happened to be there too. Even though the pub was very busy, we started fooling around right there. We were both afraid someone might hear us from the kitchen, so we moved on top of the barrels. But it was too cold, and too easy for us to be caught red-handed.

Eventually we moved under the stairs where we could hear the door being opened. If someone came down, we would at least have a few seconds to get apart and straighten our clothes. We might look suspicious as hell, but at least we wouldn't be caught outright. What made this encounter doubly exciting was the imminent danger of discovery and the fact that her husband was directly above us pulling pints for customers.

Everything about this encounter is forbidden: the partner, the setting, the timing. The risk of discovery and the irresistibility of forbidden partners are two themes people return to again and again. One woman told of an adventure she had with another woman. Not just any woman, though—she picked the ex-partner of her own current lover.

I found it very arousing to know them both intimately. I felt *between* them, so to speak. It was nasty to rent a private room in a hot tub place, sort of like paying for sex by the hour. I imagined that everyone could tell instantly why we were there. In my normal life I'm quite conservative and traditional, so it was stimulating to feel unlike myself. We had rough and wild sex with lots of screaming, biting, and scratching. I enjoyed making a lot of noise and letting myself go.

She sat on the edge of the hot tub and I went down on her. She is the type of woman who ejaculates when she comes. There

I was, standing in the hot tub going down on her while she was coming all over my face and into the water. I felt like a real slut. We made a very sexy mess, and it was an added bonus that we didn't even have to clean anything up!

The imagery of passion gone wild permeates this story. At every opportunity, she paints a picture of sleaze and dirtiness with big, bold strokes. Lesbians and gay men are particularly inclined to refer to forbidden pleasures in their stories. Since same-sex desires are so strongly prohibited, the inevitable feelings of naughtiness often become permanent features of lesbian and gay eroticism. Those raised as Catholics are the most likely of all to mention breaking the rules in their peak encounters—further proof that growing up in an atmosphere of intense sexual prohibition produces unmistakable attachments to rule breaking.

Luckily, it's not necessary to take serious risks or cheat on your lover to enjoy the naughtiness factor. One fifty-year-old woman told of the dilemma posed by a family vacation and the sparks that resulted. She and her husband stayed in a too-small cottage, where it was impossible to get away from their two young children. "We were forced into celibacy," she complained. It took four days until she and her husband got around to taking a walk *alone.*

It was a wonderfully romantic night. The park was beautiful. In no time we were kissing and hugging, all the while looking anxiously around to see if anyone was coming. I was frustrated *and* completely excited. My husband suggested we find a sheltered place.

At first I thought he was kidding, but I soon found out otherwise. We picked our hiding place, laid down on our jackets and had a marvelous time giggling and playing passionately. My breast sticking out of my half-open blouse really got my husband's attention. And when I opened his zipper and his rock-hard penis bounced out, I almost came on the spot. But we never stopped listening for approaching strangers.

SEARCHING FOR POWER

The history of childhood is, to a large degree, the story of our attempts to move from the total powerlessness of infancy toward a clear and strong sense of self, able to stand our ground in a less-than-ideal environment. Without some success in our search for power, we would be forced to live in a state of perpetual, submissive dependency.

There are two basic strategies we can use to help us overcome powerlessness. The first involves direct action. By the time we are two, we have developed such power tactics as stirring up a fuss to get our way, threatening or using retaliation measures when we are denied what we want, and going on a sitdown strike when all else fails.

There's another strategy as well. By yielding to a stronger force, we can join with or even co-opt that superior power. When this strategy is highly refined, "giving in" can provide the "powerless" practitioner with almost total control of the situation.

Either way, expressing power involves pushing against obstacles. The odds are that our search for power will eventually intersect with experiences of arousal, adding an extra spark to our turn-on. If it does, we will probably try it again. That's why the enjoyment of power games is an unmistakable feature of adult eroticism.

The power scenario most frequently mentioned by both men and women is surrendering to a super-aroused, aggressive partner. When done voluntarily and enthusiastically, the results can be extremely gratifying, as they were for this guy whose girlfriend taught him a thing or two.

> I had just stepped out of the shower when she rang the bell. I wrapped a towel around my waist, invited her in, and followed her to the couch. It was exciting to be sitting there nearly naked while she was fully clothed. The tension was rising.
>
> She said, "If you're not careful I'm going to rip your towel off." I didn't say a word. In a moment she made good on her threat. I was totally naked and she was still fully dressed. There was something completely unnatural about this, but also very exciting.
>
> She took total control. Without warning, she turned me on my belly, draped me over the couch, stuck her finger up my anus, and masturbated me with her hand. It was as if my whole body became a giant penis and she was massaging the whole thing. After orgasm, I shivered for ten or fifteen minutes while we held each other.

He's technically the "bottom" in this encounter, yet he certainly seems to get a lot out of it, which always seems to be the case when sexual surrender is part of a peak encounter. For one thing, the passion of a forceful partner, whether male or female, demonstrates the value and desirability of the one who submits. Then too, the bottom is usually getting the lion's share of attention. So who's *really* in charge?

One of the advantages of at least appearing to surrender to a more powerful other is that by giving up control it's also possible to disclaim responsibility for what follows. This is especially helpful for women. Sexual submission can be used to circumvent the intense messages almost all girls receive warning them not to be lustful.

Many memorable encounters involve seduction, the process through which the seducer uses his or her powers to draw out or ignite desires that the seducee is holding back, either as a ploy or from genuine reluctance. It is a primordial erotic power dance. When carried out with style and integrity, the interplay of the tantalizing possibilities hinted at by the seducer and the reticence of the seducee becomes a perfect manifestation of the erotic equation.

There's another kind of story, usually told by a woman:

> A bunch of us were hanging out in the park on a Saturday night. I ended up talking with one guy for hours before we slipped away to a romantic corner all alone. There we made love on the grass by the water. He was very gentle and I orgasmed every time he came.

Lots of women describe the men in their hottest encounters as either gentle or "strong, yet gentle," while relatively few men emphasize the gentleness of women. For women, gentleness is not just a sign of caring and sensitivity; it also describes a power relationship in which the partner is *not* rough, harsh, or violent. I believe a collective female awareness of the potential for unwanted male aggression lies behind this focus on gentleness. But when safety is assured, many women love opportunities for powerful surrender.

> I had a stormy relationship with this guy for almost two years. Sex was on his mind all the time. A couple of times I even used a "headache" to avoid sex, but usually I wanted it as much as he did.
>
> One time, he was obsessed about his job for two weeks. He'd get home late and be asleep in minutes. I was climbing the walls. It was a warm night, so I watched him sleep naked, the nightlight reflecting off his gorgeous body. I started caressing his penis, watching it rise. He was still asleep. I used a little massage oil, very slowly masturbating him. Soon he started to squirm.
>
> He was about to come when all of a sudden he woke up saying, "So you want to play, huh?" He pushed me onto my back, climbed on top, and held down my arms while he fucked me hard. I loved every second of it. I sure brought him back to life!

OVERCOMING AMBIVALENCE

It doesn't seem logical that mixed feelings in a sexual situation would be exciting, but since eroticism is the interaction of arousal and the challenges of living, ambivalence can weave its way into our turn-ons. Rare is the person who has not been hurt by love, beginning in our earliest family relations. The warmth, comfort, and security we crave is inevitably accompanied by the pain of being misunderstood and the fear of rejection and abandonment. Erotic situations often reactivate this conflict. We feel both desire *and* reticence; our emotions create obstacles for us to overcome. Under the right circumstances, the result can be a very memorable turn-on.

Peak encounters often occur at the critical juncture when ambivalent reluctance gives way to passion, as it did for this woman:

> My boyfriend kept asking me to try anal sex but I always refused. I was curious, but I just wasn't sure if it was the right thing. Besides, my friends all told me it hurt really bad and I believed them. Anyway, I decided to try, but I couldn't help wondering if I was making a big mistake.
>
> We used salad oil as a lubricant. I liked the way it felt as my boyfriend relaxed me with his finger. For the first five minutes I was too scared to get into it. Then I finally asked to be on top. It was such a pleasure to try something new, and I felt a lot safer. Penetration felt deep and wonderful. Believe it or not, anal sex is now one of my favorite things. I was surprised to learn how wrong my friends were. I've never felt any pain at all!

It's interesting to note that ambivalence is mentioned as an ingredient of excitement more frequently by those who are attracted to men: bisexual women, gay men, and straight women. Partners often mention traditionally masculine qualities that are both arousing *and* distasteful.

> There was this big, muscular hunk in my office who was always trying to put the make on me. His attitude toward almost everything disgusted me; even the way he propositioned me was so tasteless that I had to refuse. But just thinking about him made my vagina wet.
>
> Once, after an office party, I let him drive me home. We made out in the car. Unfortunately, he was a terrific kisser. I invited him

in. Rarely have I felt so excited. In bed he was aggressive, but totally aware of what I wanted. His body was even better naked.

I've been refusing him ever since. He's still a pig at the office, but I'll always enjoy that memory.

Those drawn to women rarely mention ambivalence in their stories. But those who do usually tell stories involving an "unwanted" partner.

I was trying to break up with my girlfriend because she allowed her ex-boyfriend to constantly interfere in our relationship. I avoided her calls and went out a lot, trying to forget her. One time she got hold of me and begged to see me. I felt sorry for her and said OK. When she picked me up I felt so irritated with her that I wanted to leave.

She tried to explain everything. Even though I insisted I still wanted to break up, deep down inside I knew I loved her. She kept holding me while I kept pushing her away. I had so many mixed emotions that I walked out the door, but she pulled me back inside and started crying and kissing me. I felt so weak and I listened to my heart.

She rubbed my back and my side and finally my rear end. She unbuttoned my shirt as her lips moved slowly down my neck. She stripped me down and I did the same to her. We made passionate love like in the movies. That moment was so intense I'll never forget it.

At those special moments where the chase gives way to passion, ambivalent liaisons are hard to beat for sheer, knock-your-socks-off intensity. Anyone who's ever been involved in such a romance knows how totally exciting, even obsessive, they can be.

These four cornerstones are not *necessary* for arousal; they just give it an extra kick. Think of them as building blocks which, in various combinations, can be used to construct an erotic scene in fantasy, or as opportunities present themselves in real life. Individuals often reserve a special place in their eroticism for a favorite cornerstone or a special combination.

Think of each cornerstone as operating on a continuum, ranging from subtle to dramatic. I've selected examples with considerable drama to emphasize my points. But less can be more. When too intense, negative feelings associated with each cornerstone—anxiety or guilt, for example—can get in the way. Intense eroticism, it seems, is always a balancing act. Sometimes just a *hint* of naughtiness, a *tease* of anticipation, a *whisper* of domination is just the right amount.

It isn't necessary to be aware of the cornerstones as they work their magic. Sometimes awareness gets in the way, especially for those who are being excited in ways they wish they weren't. Consciousness can turn into self-consciousness; the spell is broken.

For others, awareness is crucial for full enjoyment of the cornerstone. If you don't actually *feel* naughty, how can you possibly enjoy *being* naughty? What's the point of unconsciously longing for someone? Why bother surrendering if no one notices?

By definition ultimate turn-ons stand out from the pack. Does that make regular, everyday sex pale by comparison? Sometimes it actually works that way, especially for people who are dissatisfied in a relationship, judge themselves harshly, or have a lot of performance fears. For these people, hot memories can become a source of disappointment, frustration, or pressure.

Luckily, most of us get to enjoy our peak experiences, even savoring the experience again and again through fantasy. The feeling of personal validation that accompanies satisfying sex stays with us in countless ways. The inventive pleasure-seeker uses peak eroticism as a map to the hidden sexual treasures of everyday life. Luckiest of all are those who remain open to erotic surprises, large or small. The capacity to be caught off guard, to find fresh possibilities in familiar surroundings—these are the key ingredients for a stimulating, imaginative erotic life.

Rollo May

LOVE AND THE DAIMONIC

Every person, experiencing as he does his own solitariness and aloneness, longs for union with another. He yearns to participate in a relationship greater than himself. Normally, he strives to overcome his aloneness through some form of love.

The psychotherapist Otto Rank once remarked that all the women who came to him had problems because their husbands were not aggressive enough. Despite the oversimplified sound of that sentence, it contains a telling point: our effete cultivation of sex can make us so arbitrary and detached that the simple power of the sexual act evaporates and the woman loses the vital, elemental pleasure of being taken, carried away, transported. The *love bite*—that moment of hostility and aggression, usually occurring at the point of orgasm but which may be an obligation all through love-making—has a constructive psychophysical function, as pleasurable, or more so, for the woman as it is expressive for the man.

There is required a self-assertion, a capacity to stand on one's own feet, an affirmation of one's self in order to have the power to put one's self into the relationship. One must have something to give and be able to give it. The danger, of course, is that he will overassert himself—which is the source of the experience shown in the notion of being taken over by a demon. But this negative side is not to be escaped by giving up self-assertion. For if one is unable to assert oneself, one is unable to participate in a genuine relationship. A dynamic dialectical relationship—I am tempted to call it a balance, but it is not a balance—is a continuous give-and-take in which one asserts himself, finds an answer in the other, then possibly asserts too far, senses a *no* in the other, backs up but does not give up, shifts the participation to a new form, and finds the way that is adequate for the wholeness of the other. This is the constructive use of the daimonic. It is an assertion of one's own individuality in relation to another person. It always skates on the edge of exploitation of the partner; but without it, there is no vital relationship.

In its right proportion, the daimonic is the urge to reach out toward others, to increase life by way of sex, to create, to civilize; it is the joy and rapture, or the simple security of knowing that we matter, that we can affect others, can form them, can exert power which is demonstrably significant. It is a way of making certain that we are valued.

When the daimonic takes over completely, the unity of the self and the relationship is broken down; a fact confessed by the person when he or she says, "I had no control, I acted as if in a dream, I did not know it was I." The daimonic is the elementary power by which one is saved from the horror of not being one's self on one hand, and the horror, on the other hand, of feeling no connection and no vital drive toward the other person.

A woman who had fallen in love with her garage mechanic reported to me that her husband had always "cringed around the house in the evening with a hang-dog expression waiting for me to come up to bed." Though we can understand why the husband was in this scarcely proud state, we can also understand that it was a great relief to the wife and a boon to her own need for abandon that the erotic aggressiveness of the mechanic was inhibited by no such ambivalence.

Biologically, a vivid expression of the daimonic in the male is in the erection—a phenomenon which in itself has bewitching, erotic seductiveness for the woman as she realizes it is occurring, if she is already interested. (If she is not, she is repulsed, which simply proves in reverse that the phallic erection exerts emotional power.) The erection itself is such a rich daimonic symbol that the ancient Greeks were led to decorate their vases with paintings of dancing satyrs, each with a proud phallic erection, performing in a Dionysian religious festival. Men have only to remember their own fascination as little boys in experiencing the magical quality of their penis becoming erect, possibly without apparent conscious cause, and giving them such wonderful sensations. A similar daimonic assertion, though perhaps less biologically obvious than in the human male, is present and necessary in the woman in her capacity to have outright desire for her man, to want him and to let it be subtly known to him that she wants him. Both man and woman need this self-assertion to bridge their separateness and to achieve union with each other.

Not in the slightest am I arguing here for a return to primitive sexuality. Nor do I want to comfort the still infantile man or woman who interprets aggression as blunt insistence upon his or her demands of the sexual partner. I am using aggression in its healthy sense as assertion of the self rooted in strength not weakness, and inseparably allied to the capacities for sensitivity and tenderness. But I am also arguing that we have amputated significant aspects of our sexuality in over-cultivation of sexual love, and so we run the risk of losing exactly what we set out to gain.

A curious thing which never fails to surprise persons in therapy is that after admitting their anger, animosity, and even hatred for a spouse and berating him or her during the hour, they end up with feelings of love toward this partner. A patient may have come in smoldering with negative feelings but resolved, partly unconsciously, to keep these, as a good gentleman does, to himself; but he finds that he represses the love for the partner at the same time as he suppresses his aggression. This is so clear that it becomes all but a rule of treatment. Dr. Ludwig Lefebre calls this the "inclusion of the negative"—which is essential if the positive is likewise to come out.

What is occurring here is more than the fact that human consciousness works in polarity: the positive cannot come out until the negative does also. This is why in analysis, the negative is analyzed, with the hope—which becomes true often enough to justify the rule—that the positive will then be able to come into its own. This is the constructive value in facing and admitting of the daimonic. For "eros is a daimon," we recall; eros has to do not simply with love but with hate also, it has to do with an energizing, a shocking of our normal existence—it is a gadfly that keeps us forever awake; eros is the enemy of nirvana, the breathless peace. Hate and love are not polar opposites; they go together, particularly in transitional ages like ours.

Greta Christina

ARE WE HAVING SEX NOW OR WHAT?

When I first started having sex with other people, I used to like to count them. I wanted to keep track of how many there had been. It was a source of some kind of pride, or identity anyway, to know how many people I'd had sex with in my lifetime. So, in my mind, Len was number one, Chris was number two, that slimy awful little heavy metal barbiturate addict whose name I can't remember was number three, Alan was number four, and so on. It got to the point where, when I'd start having sex with a new person for the first time, when he first entered my body (I was only having sex with men at the time), what would flash through my head wouldn't be "Oh, baby, baby you feel so good inside me," or "What the hell am I doing with this creep," or "This is boring, I wonder what's on TV." What flashed through my head was "Seven!"

Doing this had some interesting results. I'd look for patterns in the numbers. I had a theory for a while that every fourth lover turned out to be really great in bed, and would ponder what the cosmic significance of the phenomenon might be. Sometimes I'd try to determine what kind of person I was by how many people I'd had sex with. At eighteen, I'd had sex with ten different people. Did that make me normal, repressed, a total slut, a free-spirited bohemian, or what? Not that I compared my numbers with anyone else's—I didn't. It was my own exclusive structure, a game I played in the privacy of my own head.

Then the numbers started getting a little larger, as numbers tend to do, and keeping track became more difficult. I'd remember that the last one was *seventeen* and so this one must be *eighteen,* but then I'd start

24

having doubts about whether I'd been keeping score accurately or not. I'd lie awake at night thinking to myself, well, there was Brad, and there was that guy on my birthday, and there was David and . . . no, wait, I forgot that guy I got drunk with at the social my first week at college . . . so that's seven, eight, nine . . . and by two in the morning I'd finally have it figured out. But there was always a nagging suspicion that maybe I'd missed someone, some dreadful tacky little scumball that I was trying to forget about having invited inside my body. And as much as I maybe wanted to forget about the sleazy little scumball, I wanted more to get that number right.

It kept getting harder, though. I began to question what counted as sex and what didn't. There was that time with Gene, for instance. I was pissed off at my boyfriend, David, for cheating on me. It was a major crisis, and Gene and I were friends and he'd been trying to get at me for weeks and I hadn't exactly been discouraging him. I went to see him that night to gripe about David. He was very sympathetic of course, and he gave me a backrub, and we talked and touched and confided and hugged, and then we started kissing, and then we snuggled up a little closer, and then we started fondling each other, you know, and then all heck broke loose, and we rolled around on the bed groping and rubbing and grabbing and smooching and pushing and pressing and squeezing. He never did actually get it in. He wanted to, and I wanted to too, but I had this thing about being faithful to my boyfriend, so I kept saying, "No, you can't do that, Yes, that feels so good, No, wait that's too much, Yes, yes, don't stop, No, stop that's enough." We never even got our clothes off. Jesus Christ, though, it was some night. One of the best, really. But for a long time I didn't count it as one of the times I'd had sex. He never got inside, so it didn't count.

Later, months and years later, when I lay awake putting my list together, I'd start to wonder: Why doesn't Gene count? Does he not count because he never got inside? Or does he not count because I had to preserve my moral edge over David, my status as the patient, ever-faithful, cheated-on, martyred girlfriend, and if what I did with Gene counts then I don't get to feel wounded and superior?

Years later, I did end up fucking Gene and I felt a profound relief because, at last, he definitely had a number, and I knew for sure that he did in fact count.

Then I started having sex with women, and, boy, howdy, did *that* ever shoot holes in the system. I'd always made my list of sex partners by defining sex as penile-vaginal intercourse—you know, screwing. It's a pretty simple distinction, a straightforward binary system. Did it go in or didn't it? Yes or no? One or zero? On or off? Granted, it's a pretty arbitrary definition, but it's the customary one, with an ancient and respected tradition behind it, and when I was just screwing men, there was no compelling reason to question it.

But with women, well, first of all there's no penis, so right from the start the tracking system is defective. And then, there are so many ways women can have sex with each other, touching and licking and grinding and fingering and fisting—with dildoes or vibrators or vegetables or whatever happens to be lying around the house, or with nothing at all except human bodies. Of course, that's true for sex between women and men as well. But between women, no one method has a centuries-old tradition of being the one that counts. Even when we do fuck each other there's no dick, so you don't get that feeling of This Is What's Important, We Are Now Having Sex, objectively speaking, and all that other stuff is just foreplay or afterplay. So when I started having sex with women the binary system had to go, in favor of a more inclusive definition.

Which meant, of course, that my list of how many people I'd had sex with was completely trashed. In order to maintain it I would have had to go back and reconstruct the whole thing and include all those people I'd necked with and gone down on and dry-humped and played touchy-feely games with. Even the question of who filled the all-important Number One slot, something I'd never had any doubts about before, would have to be re-evaluated.

By this time I'd kind of lost interest in the list anyway. Reconstructing it would be more trouble than it was worth. But the crucial question remained: What counts as having sex with someone?

It was important for me to know. You have to know what qualifies as sex because when you have sex with someone your relationship changes. Right? *Right?* It's not that sex itself has to change things all that much. But knowing you've had sex, being conscious of a sexual connection, standing around making polite conversation with someone while thinking to yourself, "I've had sex with this person," that's what changes things. Or so I believed. And if having sex with a friend can confuse or change the friendship, think how bizarre things can get when you're not sure whether you've had sex with them or not.

The problem was, as I kept doing more kinds of sexual things, the line between *sex* and *not-sex* kept getting more hazy and indistinct. As I brought more into my sexual experience, things were showing up on the dividing line demanding my attention. It wasn't just that the territory I labeled *sex* was expanding. The line itself had swollen, dilated, been transformed into a vast gray region. It had become less like a border and more like a demilitarized zone.

Which is a strange place to live. Not a bad place, just strange. It's like juggling, or watchmaking, or playing the piano—anything that demands complete concentrated awareness and attention. It feels like cognitive dissonance, only pleasant. It feels like waking up from a compelling and realistic bad dream. It feels like the way you feel when you realize that everything you know is wrong, and a bloody good thing too, because it was painful and stupid and it really screwed you up.

But, for me, living in a question naturally leads to searching for an answer. I can't simply shrug, throw up my hands, and say, "Damned if I know." I have to explore the unknown frontiers, even if I don't bring back any secret treasure. So even if it's incomplete or provisional, I do want to find some sort of definition of what is and isn't sex.

I know when I'm *feeling* sexual. I'm feeling sexual if my pussy's wet, my nipples are hard, my palms are clammy, my brain is fogged, my skin is tingly and super-sensitive, my butt muscles clench, my heartbeat speeds up, I have an orgasm (that's the real giveaway), and so on. But feeling sexual with someone isn't the same as having sex with them. Good Lord, if I called it sex every time I was attracted to someone who returned the favor I'd be even more bewildered than I am now. Even *being* sexual with someone isn't the same as *having* sex with them. I've danced and flirted with too many people, given and received too many sexy, would-be-seductive backrubs, to believe otherwise.

I have friends who say, if you thought of it as sex when you were doing it, then it was. That's an interesting idea. It's certainly helped me construct a coherent sexual history without being a revisionist swine: redefining my past according to current definitions. But it really just begs the question. It's fine to say that sex is whatever I think it is; but then what do I think it *is*? What if, when I was doing it, I was *wondering* whether it counted?

Perhaps having sex with someone is the conscious, consenting, mutually acknowledged pursuit of shared sexual pleasure. Not a bad definition. If you are turning each other on and you say so and you keep doing it, then it's sex. It's broad enough to encompass a lot of sexual behavior beyond genital contact/orgasm; it's distinct enough *not* to include every instance of sexual awareness or arousal; and it contains the elements I feel are vital—acknowledgment, consent, reciprocity, and the pursuit of pleasure. But what about the situation where one person consents to sex without really enjoying it? Lots of people (myself included) have had sexual interactions that we didn't find satisfying or didn't really want and, unless they were actually forced on us against our will, I think most of us would still classify them as sex.

Maybe if *both* of you (or all of you) think of it as sex, then it's sex whether you're having fun or not. That clears up the problem of sex that's consented to but not wished-for or enjoyed. Unfortunately, it begs the question again, only worse: now you have to mesh different people's vague and inarticulate notions of what is and isn't sex and find the place where they overlap. Too messy.

How about sex as the conscious, consenting, mutually acknowledged pursuit of sexual pleasure of *at least one* of the people involved. That's better. It has all the key components, and it includes the situation where one person is doing it for a reason other than sexual pleasure—status, reassurance, money, the satisfaction and pleasure of someone they love, etc. But what if *neither* of you is enjoying it, if you're both doing it because you think the other one wants to? Ugh.

I'm having trouble here. Even the conventional standby—sex equals intercourse—has a serious flaw: it includes rape, which is something I emphatically refuse to accept. As far as I'm concerned, if there's no consent, it ain't sex. But I feel that's about the only place in this whole quagmire where I have a grip. The longer I think about the subject, the more questions I come up with. At what point in an encounter does it *become* sexual? If an interaction that begins nonsexually turns into sex, was it sex all along? What about sex with someone who's asleep? Can you have a situation where one person is having sex and the other isn't? It seems that no matter what definition I come up with, I can think of some real-life experience that calls it into question.

For instance, a couple of years ago I attended (well, hosted) an all-girl sex party. Out of the twelve other women there, there were only a few with whom I got seriously physically nasty. The rest I kissed or hugged or talked dirty with or just smiled at, or watched while they did seriously physically nasty things with each other. If we'd been alone, I'd probably say that what I'd done with most of the women there didn't count as having sex. But the experience, which was hot and sweet and silly and very, very special, had been created by all of us, and although I only really got down with a few, I felt that I'd been sexual with all of the women there. Now, when I meet one of the women from that party, I always ask myself: Have we had sex?

For instance, when I was first experimenting with sadomasochism, I got together with a really hot woman. We were negotiating about what we were going to do, what would and wouldn't be ok, and she said she wasn't sure she wanted to have sex. Now we'd been explicitly planning all kinds of fun and games—spanking, bondage, obedience—which I strongly identified as sexual activity. In her mind, though, *sex* meant direct genital contact, and she didn't necessarily want to do that with me. Playing with her turned out to be a tremendously erotic experience, arousing and stimulating and almost unbearably satisfying. But we spent the whole evening without even touching each other's genitals. And the fact that our definitions were so different made me wonder: Was it sex?

For instance, I worked for a few months as a nude dancer at a peep show. In case you've never been to a peep show, it works like this: the customer goes into a tiny, dingy black box, kind of like a phone booth, puts in quarters, and a metal plate goes up; the customer looks through a window at a little room/stage where naked women are dancing. One time, a guy came into one of the booths and started watching me and masturbating. I came over and squatted in front of him and started masturbating too, and we grinned at each other and watched each other and masturbated, and we both had a fabulous time. (I couldn't believe I was being paid to masturbate—tough job, but somebody has to do it . . .). After he left I thought to myself: Did we just have sex? I mean, if it had been someone I knew, and if there had been no glass and no quarters, there'd be no question in my mind. Sitting two feet apart from someone, watching each other masturbate? Yup, I'd call that sex all right. But this was different, because it was a stranger, and because of the glass and the quarters. Was it sex?

I still don't have an answer.

Michael Ventura

THE PORN PRINCE OF DECATUR STREET

There were three: Dracula, Jesus Christ and Marilyn Monroe. They were my Trinity. And Elvis was their troubadour. That was the *real* world for me. And then there was this world:

It was early 1957, I was 11, and my brothers, my sister, my mother and I lived in a three-room cold-water railroad flat on Decatur Street in Brooklyn. "Cold-water" because the water heater was beside the stove; you heated your own if you could afford it and washed cold if the gas bill hadn't been paid, which was often—hot water wasn't the landlord's job. "Railroad" because the apartment was designed like a boxcar, one long, narrow room from the windows on the street to the windows on the back alley. Discolored wallpaper. Cracked linoleum. Roaches. Occasional rats.

Many lived as we did. Many more lived worse. At this time, a man named Michael Harrington was writing a book called *The Other America,* which would shock the world by revealing that roughly one-fourth of America during the Fabulous '50s lived like us. We weren't shocked. We took it for granted. But we were tired, even more tired than we knew.

To be born poor is to be born tired. All the coffee we drank (and even small children in our families drank strong coffee) was a transfusion of energy in a diet of cornmeal mush and pasta flavored with the cheapest meats and canned vegetables. God knows our furious energy couldn't have come from the food—a lot of it had to be because we kids were hooked on coffee. To live on energy that has no connection with health, energy that lets you go on through any exhaustion, is one of the arts of the poor. Even the littlest ones on our block had dark bags under their bright, bright eyes.

So it would be time to sleep, and tired as I was, I couldn't sleep. But being unable to sleep allowed me my *real* world: Dracula, Jesus Christ and Marilyn Monroe. And Elvis as their troubadour. But those four characters have changed so much in the 35 years since, their meaning in that time takes some explaining.

Elvis and Marilyn, in 1957, were very much alive and at the peak of their beauty. Marilyn's face and body were everywhere, in movies and on magazine covers, not as nostalgia but as an aroma in the air we breathed. No one, at the time, seemed less tragic, less untouched by reality's grind. And you couldn't listen to a half-hour of radio without hearing at least one Elvis hit, and often more than one. What was considered porn then would be acceptable in a newspaper lingerie ad now; there was nothing like the present environment of sexually driven images and music. In '56 and '57, Marilyn and Elvis, almost alone in mass media, poured forth a sensuousness that intoxicated a culture.

And Dracula: the Bela Lugosi film hadn't been shown in 25 years, and graphic horror films as we know them now were another 20 years away. My vampire was the Dracula of Bram Stoker's novel, read every night, over and over, by flashlight—a Dracula that came out of me, *my* images, without any other references, my own raw response to the words. Thus Dracula moved in me, every night. I fleshed him, he rose from the grave of the book into my mind. My horror, I know now, wasn't at the tale; my horror was at how readily my psyche *joined* with the tale.

And the antidote to that horror was Jesus—a plastic, glow-in-the-dark crucifix nailed to the wall above my pillow. It glowed a sickly, purplish white. Who was Jesus in my eleven-year-old world? Someone my mother spoke of and to, the baby in the crib at Christmas, the risen one at Easter, the tiny figure on the rosary cross, the enormous one in church (tender according to my mother, stern according to the nuns)— a conjunction of dissociated fragments, mysterious not in themselves but because Jesus seemed to be both everywhere and nowhere, mentioned a great deal, especially in curses, obviously important (his image, like Marilyn's, was inescapable), but *why?*

It took Stoker's *Dracula* to explain it to me. Jesus was the only thing that could save you from Dracula. *That* was power. You didn't have to understand him, believe in him or even like him, but if you held up his crucifix, or nailed it above your pillow, Dracula couldn't touch you.

I look back now at those three males who fascinated me, and I see: Jesus, who rose from the dead; Dracula, who also rose from the dead; and Elvis, whose energy was such that popular culture would one day raise him from the dead—and I see the female, Marilyn, whom that same culture would kill but not let die. And I see the sex of them: of Dracula, who would suck men's blood if he had to, but infinitely preferred the blood of beautiful women; of Elvis and Marilyn, two sides of the same coin, the same moment in history, who seemed made of sex. And of Jesus, more naked (as an image) than the other three, with his languid, Michelangelo-inspired nudity that radiated sensuality even in torture (in the *Pietà,* even in death).

It wasn't so much sex and death I was steeping myself in as sex and portents of resurrection. Especially because I discovered Dracula, Jesus and Marilyn (to the soundtrack of Elvis) at the same time as my hands discovered my crotch. For after being horrified and titillated by Dracula's stalking of vulnerable English women—under the pale glowing protection of my plastic Jesus, with the radio just barely audible, listening for Elvis—I would touch myself thinking of Marilyn. And then I could sleep.

For a while, this went on every night. Sex among the Undead and the Gods. Dracula and Jesus were the Undead. Marilyn and Elvis were the Gods. Every erection a resurrection. Every coming a burst of terror, pleasure and awe—that inevitable, and unbreakable, linkage. Jesus could save me from Dracula, but who could save me from myself?

The point is, I could not be saved from myself. And that, precisely, is the saving grace.

For we are saved by the insistence of what is deepest in us, in spite of all intrusion—an insistence that survives for longer than one would think possible, considering the odds (and the odds are always terrible, even in the most privileged life). What I mean is:

Consciously, this was my first sex. It would take another 30 years to remember the sexuality with my mother when I was very little, and with the vile hospital attendant when I had pneumonia at the age of 4, and then the older boys forcing themselves on me in the bathroom in the park . . . I'd buried those memories. I see now that, there in that tenement, I was saving myself; I was, by instinct, making for myself a kind of descent into the Underworld, into Hades, the Dreamtime, surrounded by immortals, who . . . I'm resisting the word, but the word that comes is: who *purified* me. Thus does the psyche concoct its own initiations, far from guides and theories, far from the reach of other people, taking the things at hand and imbuing them with power sufficient for a kind of salvation.

The godlike killer and the godlike savior met in my imagination, and their very struggle prepared the entryway for the most beautiful body in the world, while someone sang as no one ever had before. Through the images of Marilyn, Dracula, Jesus and Elvis, terrific energies coursed through me, not merely from my own depths, but from the depths that *are* depths by virtue of being shared by all; energies both light and dark, which did not heal me (such healing may not be a human possibility), but which *gave me back to myself* so that I could at least begin that part of my life, my sexual life, on terms that *I* had chosen, that had not been forced on me. Just that. And it was everything. The difference between being a victim and being a man, a human being, with a say in his own life.

How many other secret and absolutely private ceremonies, ceremonies not perceived as ceremonies, on how many other streets like Decatur Street and yours? How many people saving or at least salvaging themselves, resurrecting some parts of themselves, in how many ways that society, religion and therapy would be quick to try to control?

There are a lot of theories around. And a lot of sweet words. But the important thing is: we're trying to tell ourselves something. I'm trying to tell myself something. You're trying to tell yourself something. And our very lives depend upon telling it and hearing it. If you prejudge the way this can happen, it won't happen, no matter how pretty the theory; you'll just be telling yourself something somebody else (or some other part of you) is whispering in your ear. I had a little luck on Decatur Street, when I was too young to know better and others were too distracted to notice. I told myself something.

And that telling, that ceremony, provoked a test out in the world.

Next door to our tenement was a warehouse. I forget what was in that warehouse, but trucks would load there every day. Out of curiosity, one day I snuck in and climbed onto the running board of a truck to look into the cab. And I saw, taped to the roof of the cab, a *Life*-magazine-size many-colored photo of an incredible naked woman. I'd never seen anything like her, even in my imagination. Not even Marilyn. Then the warehouse guys shooed me off.

At that age, like many on my street, I was an accomplished thief, defined as: I stole what I wanted and never got caught. I wanted that woman. I can hardly believe now that I did this. I don't know where the boy I was got the courage, but I remember what I did: I snuck into the warehouse whenever that truck was there to look at the picture, and finally one day I very quietly opened the door of the cab, got in and shut the door without an audible click. I crouched under the dashboard for the longest time, hearing the men talking their talk. When their voices seemed to turn away from me, I'd reach up and tug on the tape that fastened the photo to the roof of the cab. It took forever. Finally I pulled it loose. I tucked the photo into my shirt and snuck away.

I had stolen other magazines with dirty pictures, but nothing like this. I took it to my stash: a hole in the wall on the stairway to the roof. If you sat still and listened, you'd hear the rats. I'd knock on the wall to scare the rats off, then reach in. Not only was I never bitten, but for some reason the rats, which would eat almost anything, never ate my pictures. It was a safe hiding place, because *nobody* else in our building, not even my mother, would stick an arm into that hole. And so I put my photo of that incredible naked woman in that rat hole. Those crumbs of paper are probably still there.

I was not supposed to have such beauty, or even a secret rat hole. Much less concourse with the Undead, or with the likes of Marilyn and Elvis. I was a street kid, and, like all street kids, I wasn't supposed to have anything, not a mind, not a future, not a chance. But I did have a rat hole, I did have (though I would not have called it this) a ceremony, and I had captured a beauty. Sure, it was just dirty pictures and jerking off, but it was also the first time I had taken charge of my life, inventing myself and my terms as I went along. I tell you this because this is the moment to watch for. When you look back. When you look around.

Years later, I discovered that Henry Miller had grown up on De-catur Street, too—two blocks south of me and half a century before. Unknowingly, I had passed his old building on my way to an ugly and terrifying place that called itself a school (P.S. 113). This school helped teach me something very important: that the people who ran my society were *not* on my side. They made me go to this place, and they de-termined what went on there, and that was proof enough that their in-tentions toward me weren't honorable. But I had a rat hole. I had a ceremony. I had captured a beauty. *Something* was on my side, em-bedded deep in me—it had invoked Dracula, Jesus Christ, Marilyn

Monroe and the singing of Elvis to bring itself to life. Hadn't Miller written once, "The condemned one reaches at last to his innocence"?

Society would not have called what I found "innocence," and yet it was. I had been badly damaged, and I would always carry that damage, but on Decatur Street I mined down to someplace deeper than the damage. Many do this instinctively, as I did, and this is not spoken of enough. All that is spoken of are attempts that have become institutionalized as therapies or movements or religions. But before all that are these solitary delvings. Some people are shocked or disgusted by the image and actions, the forms, such delvings may entail; but those forms seemed and still seem innocent to me, with the kind of innocence you can't get rid of—it's there, waiting in you, waiting for you, till you die.

Joan Nelson

LIGHTING CANDLES

I'm lighting a candle, not to memorialize a particular individual but to alleviate my own sorrow for the tragic death of something that was very real to me: the spirit of sexual freedom and sexual self-expression. I am a sex therapist. And not by accident. I am a sex therapist because of my own long hard fight for personal sexual well-being. As a sex professional I'm not willing to give up the good fight now. I light a candle to help me move on to help lift the pall that AIDS has hung over sexual self-expression.

Sex (in its biggest meaning) is neither an event nor an act. It has a breadth and depth not always recognized. It is a positive energy force permeating the whole of our being. Sex is the joy of discovery and the beauty of shared pleasure. Sex is part of the life force. The giving and receiving of sexual energy is our birthright.

Sexual pleasure, in its biggest meaning, is a life energy, a healing force. Modern science demonstrates an electro-chemical sexual phenomenon that has the power to heal. Hugging, touching, and other physically nurturing behaviors stimulate the body's production of endorphins, which have something to do with fortifying the immune system.

We have always needed one another. But in this time of epidemic we need each other more than ever. Thinking of healers, we call to mind religious figures, doctors, shamans, and psychic channels. In truth, we are the only ones who can channel healing energy to one another. Jesus had His style, Buddha had his style. I have my style. You have your style.

The life force (whether it is nature, God, or endorphins) heals us through one another. Through words and acts. Through meditations focusing on the healthy part of the self. Through sexual pleasure. Touching and holding one another.

Allen Ginsberg

SONG

The weight of the world
     is love.
Under the burden
     of solitude,
under the burden
     of dissatisfaction

     the weight,
the weight we carry
     is love.

Who can deny?
     In dreams
it touches
     the body,
in thought
     constructs
a miracle,
     in imagination
anguishes
     till born
in human—

looks out of the heart
     burning with purity—
for the burden of life
     is love,

but we carry the weight
        wearily,
and so must rest
in the arms of love
        at last,
must rest in the arms
        of love.

No rest
        without love,
no sleep
        without dreams
of love—
        be mad or chill
obsessed with angels
        or machines,
the final wish
        is love
—cannot be bitter,
        cannot deny,
cannot withhold
        if denied:

the weight is too heavy

        —must give
for no return
        as thought
is given
        in solitude
in all the excellence
        of its excess.

The warm bodies
        shine together
in the darkness
        the hand moves
to the center
        of the flesh,

the skin trembles
      in happiness
and the soul comes
      joyful to the eye—

yes, yes,
      that's what
I wanted,
      I always wanted,
I always wanted,
      to return
to the body
      where I was born.

James Broughton

SERMON

You on your seat there
sit up and sing out
Sing out for Eros
Love is unbelievable
so it must be believed

Believe your own loving
your passion and folly
your incredible hopes
Praise the marvels of
joy tube and love pump

If you must feel tortured
respect your misery
and be happy about it
Only the nonsensical is
at ease with the Absolute

Listen to your angels
ripening your secrets
Come to beautiful terms
with the god in your body
with the body of your god

Share flesh with others
Wake love   Make love
Clasp hearts and exuberate
And don't look back till
you are far out of sight

2

EROTIC
INITIATION AND
PASSAGE

Introduction: Part 2

      Erotic initiation, the almost magical process of moving into erotic territory never before explored, contains unique elements of power and vitality. These are erotic happenings in a class by themselves, often felt and remembered, as Jack Morin has noted, more keenly than any others. Psychologically, erotic initiations are formative experiences that powerfully shape much of our subsequent erotic development. Whatever the ingredients of our individual processes of initiation, whatever the trappings that were present at those times, whatever the circumstances, the dangers, the people, the setting—even details like the time of day, the weather, an article of clothing, a smell, a fragment of music, the color of our partner's hair, the form of his or her body—all of these become eroticized for us, often forever, by the supreme intensity of the moment of erotic emergence.

     When we think of erotic initiation, most of us turn immediately to our first experience of sexual intercourse, since our culture so powerfully defines this as the primary distinction between initiate and novice. But, as Greta Christina has pointed out, even if we narrow *erotic* initiation to *sexual* initiation, there is more to be considered than when we first have intercourse. What about the first time we seriously enter the realm of sexual feeling with a partner, whether or not this involves intercourse? What about the first time we experience sexual feeling in ourselves, whether or not this involves a partner? What about the first time we feel that deep inner sense of liquid movement, the first time we are aware of an erotic quickening, whether or not this has anything to do with sex?

     As we become more experienced and hopefully more developed as sexual and erotic beings, there are other erotic initiations as well: the first time we play with a partner in a new way; the first time we experience orgasm; the first time we experience a new depth or quality of orgasm; the first time we explicitly act out a long-cherished fantasy; the first time we use a new sex toy—or any sex toy at all; the first time we find ourselves, for reasons we may never understand, in a corner of the erotic garden we have never visited before, perhaps never so much as imagined; the first time we drop to a deeper level of surrender and psychic nakedness than ever before; the first time we open ourselves to a new sexual partner; the first time we open to a new community of partners, people we previously considered off the erotic/sexual map— perhaps people of our own gender, perhaps people significantly older or younger than ourselves, perhaps people we previously considered unattractive or undesirable, perhaps people of a different ethnic group.

Erotic initiation need not be a one-time, two-time, or three-time experience; it can be a continuing and recurring aspect of erotic development and discovery. The universe of sexual and erotic possibility is immense. There is no danger of running out of territory to explore, *if* we choose to make ourselves available to the wonder and the uncertainty of engaging the unfamiliar.

In a society such as ours, terrified of the full power of erotic potential, we are encouraged to be as narrowly and unimaginatively erotic as possible. We are exhorted to find a comfortable erotic niche for ourselves, a tiny corner of the vast erotic wonderland, and to be content to spend all of our erotic life within that miniscule clearing. Indeed, we usually feel grateful to have *any* place of erotic expression at all.

No wonder so many couples become bored with their erotic connections after a few years, or even a few months. No wonder so many individuals lose their sexual appetite altogether, wonder vaguely how the youthful fire and wonder evaporated, or surreptitiously seek new partners to rekindle a feeling of erotic adventure and discovery.

The pieces in this section focus largely on adolescent initiation, but they also invoke the more general sense of aliveness that is so much a part of crossing erotic thresholds of all kinds. These are tales of individual discovery to remind us how exciting, awkward, humorous, and complex these circumstances often are. Perhaps these stories of erotic expansion will encourage all of us to keep developing imaginative and innovative expressions of eros in our lives.

Therapist Lonnie Barbach begins with a conceptual framework for many of the pieces that follow, calling on us to acknowledge that sexual existence is very much a part of childhood as well as adult life. Her clear, unsensational explication of childhood sexuality, and her honest discussion of the confusing feelings adults often confront when they acknowledge the sexuality of the children around them, encourage us to deal openly and shamelessly with this highly charged and often misrepresented issue.

Henry Miller speaks with characteristic candor about his developing sexual awareness as a boy. His description of the peculiarities of turn-of-the-century New York boy-culture regarding such basic issues as girls, the mysteries of female anatomy, and the terrible, exciting tenderness of his emerging erotic awareness as an adolescent is as innocent and unprotected as the experiences he recounts. Moving into more specifically sexual realms of young adulthood, he contrasts the cavalier attitude of the "man of the world" with his own more complex and vulnerable desire and infatuation with both women and sex.

Novelist H. M. Ruggieri describes the delicate dance of discovery, wonder, pain, and reconciliation of an adolescent boy and girl's first sexual involvement. Gore Vidal portrays a similarly delicate progression of sexual intimacy between two adolescent boys. Together the two stories speak to both the universal vulnerability of adolescent sexual emergence, regardless of sexual preference, and to the additional issues raised when one's budding sexuality crosses the boundaries of socially defined norms.

Novelist and art critic John Berger presents a third tale of adolescent initiation; a warm, tender encounter between a fifteen-year-old boy and his parents' thirty-six-year-old housekeeper. With almost microscopic precision, Berger describes what is occurring for each of the two partners moment by moment, offering us detailed insights into the process of sexual emergence that are almost philosophically profound.

Writer/performance artist Rachel Kaplan speaks of another form of initiation: coming out publicly about one's sexual orientation. Speaking of her shifting sense of herself from lesbian to bisexual, Kaplan asks us to regard ourselves as constantly changing beings, not only in our sexual feelings, but in our sexual attitudes and orientation as well. Two closing poems by James Joyce and e.e. cummings similarly affirm the sanctity of personal choice and the importance of honoring the essence of what we feel day by day.

Lonnie Barbach

Bringing up Children Sexually

All too frequently, children have been treated as innocent, asexual beings. But children most certainly are not asexual. All the sexual organs capable of providing pleasure are present, and children are sexual creatures, from birth. Theirs is not the same sexuality we know as adults, but it is nonetheless sexuality. The baby playing with your breast is at least sensual if not sexual. The two-year-old who seductively crawls into bed between Mommy and Daddy is sexual, although not with the same explicit sexual intent of an adult. The five-year-old girl, who dresses up and sits on her father's lap kissing him and asking him if he will marry her when she grows up, is sexual. The seven-year-old who is masturbating, possibly even to orgasm, is sexual. The eight-year-old prancing around without any clothes on is sexual. These are children passing through learning stages on the way to becoming adult sexual beings. Some of their behavior represents a mimicking of Mommy or Daddy and some results from natural bodily curiosity but it is all sexual though not necessarily with the adult's awareness of what sexuality means.

A major problem in dealing with sexuality in children has been the adult's own embarrassment and discomfort with sex. There has been a tendency to ignore children's sexual questions and gestures, a tendency to believe that an adult doesn't have to answer sexual questions because the child couldn't possibly know what she is asking. This denies the child's sexuality because of the adult's own uneasiness. The result, of course, is that the child gets the message that she is asking improper questions that her mother doesn't like to hear, so the child's tendency is to stop risking her mother's anger, keep quiet, and wonder silently to herself. Meanwhile, the child feels embarrassment, shame, and remains ignorant about sex, and many reach adulthood to experience excessive sexual inhibitions, the absence of orgasm, or the experience of an unwanted pregnancy. . . .

Physical contact is essential for children. Studies show that children in orphanages who received adequate nourishment but were not held, cuddled, kissed, and caressed would often become ill. But in our culture it is frequently customary to discontinue physical contact as the child grows older, especially with sons. Then after marriage, miraculously, people who have been denied physical contact for years are supposed to be able to respond physically and emotionally without inhibitions—which was natural for them as children, but was trained out of them as they grew older. Many of us grew up in families where touching was prohibited and so we tend to maintain a distance from our children. Other of us may find ourselves sexually turned on by our children, and these impulses may frighten us so much that we maintain physical distance in an effort to avoid the unacceptable sexual feelings and possibly even to protect our children from being the objects of our sexual fantasies.

Sexual feelings for our children begin early. It is important to realize that sexual fantasies about one's children are normal. Many mothers report having some such fantasies at least occasionally. Children are sexual, warm, cuddly human beings—we can feel turned on and have the fantasies but we don't have to act them out. Acting them out can be detrimental to the child, while just having the fantasy is perfectly harmless.

Samantha had sexual fantasies about her five-year-old step-daughter who was going through a very seductive stage. Samantha was afraid she might actually try to seduce the child and as a result picked fights with her to keep them physically apart, hoping this would prevent her from acting out her worst fears. Their relationship was getting worse and worse. . . . It was suggested that Samantha allow herself to have the fantasies, to exaggerate them, and carry them, still in fantasy, to the greatest possible extreme. Samantha returned the next week to say that she had followed our advice and actively fantasized sexual situations which included her step-daughter; she found that not only did she not act on them, but she felt closer to her step-daughter and could allow herself to be more affectionate and caring with the child. To her amazement, she tired of the fantasies and soon replaced them with more interesting ones. She also found that she wasn't jealous of the daughter's seductive behavior toward the child's father any more. . . .

There is no reason to keep children from knowing that sex is an enjoyable, pleasurable activity; that sex is for fun first and for babies second. It makes no sense to hide the physical side of a loving relationship. It is important for children to see their parents embrace, kiss, cuddle, and in general act affectionately toward one another. However, in our culture, this does not mean making love with the children as spectators or participants, though two- to four-year-olds have a fantastic ability to open unlocked doors at precisely the wrong moments. It might be good to let your child know that you and Daddy make love in the privacy of your bedroom; that during that time you don't like to be disturbed and any questions and problems can generally wait until afterward. To treat sex with dignity and love rather than to shroud it in awkward and unspeakable mystery is an excellent way of instilling a child with a healthy attitude toward sex. . . .

Children's sexual exploration is like all other areas of exploration. For the child it is a way of learning about her environment and how to make a place for herself within it. Exploration includes urinating while standing up like a boy, wearing make-up like mother, playing doctor with other boys and girls down the street, and exploring sexual feelings with a girlfriend. Physical and loving relationships between two or more girls or two or more boys is a very common and natural part of the growing-up process. It does not mean that the child is heterosexual, homosexual, or bisexual. Each child will have the chance to choose a sexual orientation later on in life. This experimentation is a part of the development process for many children and not a cause for alarm or worry. One should try not to have the child feel abnormal or ashamed about the expression of budding sexual feelings.

Henry Miller

Discovering the World
of Sex

I was about five or six at the time, and the incident took place in a cellar. . . . It was a hairless world I gazed upon. The very absence of hair, so I now think, served to stimulate the imagination, helped populate the arid region which surrounded the place of mystery. We were concerned less with what lay within than with the future vegetal décor which we imagined would one day beautify this strange waste land. Depending on the time of the year, the age of the players, the place, as well as other more complicated factors, the genitals of certain little creatures seemed as variegated, when I think of it now, as the strange entities which people the imaginative minds of occultists. What presented itself to our impressionable minds was a nameless phantasmagoria swarming with images which were real, tangible, thinkable, yet nameless, for they were unconnected with the world of experience wherein everything has a name, a place and a date. Thus it was that certain little girls were referred to as possessing (hidden beneath their skirts) such queer effects as magnolias, cologne bottles, velvet buttons, rubber mice . . . God only knows what. That every little girl had a crack was of course common knowledge. Now and then rumor had it that such and such a one had no crack at all; of another it might be said that she was a "morphodite." Morphodite was a strange and frightening term which no one could clearly define. Sometimes it implied the notion of double sex, sometimes other things, to wit, that where the crack ought to be there was a cloven hoof or a row of warts. *Better not ask to see it!*—that was the dominant thought.

A curious thing about this period was the conviction which obtained among us that some of our little playmates were definitely bad, i.e. incipient whores or sluts. Some girls already possessed a vile vocabulary pertaining to this mysterious realm. Some would do forbidden things, if given a little gift or a few coppers. There were others, I must add, who were looked upon as angels, nothing less. They were that angelic, in fact, that none of us ever thought of them as owning a crack. These angelic creatures didn't even pee.

I make mention of these early attempts at characterization because later in life, having witnessed the development of some of the "loose ones," I was impressed by the accuracy of our observations. Occasionally one of the angels also fell into the gutter, and remained there. Usually, however, they met a different fate. Some led an unhappy life, either through marrying the wrong man or not marrying at all, some were stricken with mysterious illnesses, others were crucified by their parents. Many whom we had dubbed sluts turned out to be excellent human beings, jolly, flexible, generous, human to the core, though often a bit the worse for wear.

With adolescence another kind of curiosity developed, namely, the desire to find out how "the thing" functioned. Girls of ten or twelve were often induced to adopt the most grotesque poses, in order to demonstrate how they made pipi. The skilled ones were reputed to be able to lie on the floor and piss up to the ceiling. Some were already being accused of using candles—or broomsticks. The conversation, when it got round to this topic, became rather thick and complicated; it was tinged with a flavor strangely reminiscent of the atmosphere which invested the early Greek schools of philosophy. Logic, I mean, played a greater role than empiricism. The desire to explore with the naked eye was subordinated to a greater urge, one which I now realize was none other than the need to talk it out, to discuss the subject *ad nauseum*. The intellect, alas, had already begun to exact its tribute. How "the thing" functioned was smothered by the deeper query—*why?* With the birth of the questioning faculty, sorrow set in. Our world, hitherto so natural, so marvelous, slipped its moorings. Henceforth nothing was absolutely so any more: everything could be proved—and disproved. The hair which now began to sprout on the sacred Mons Venus was repellent. Even the little angels were breaking out in pimples. And there were some who were bleeding between the legs.

Masturbation was far more interesting. In bed, or in the warm bath, one could imagine himself lying with the Queen of Sheba, or with a burlesque queen whose tantalizing body, featured everywhere, infected one's every thought. One wondered what these women pictured with skirts whirling above their heads did when they appeared before the footlights. Some said that they brazenly removed every stitch of their gorgeous costumes and stood holding their boobies invitingly—until the sailors made a stampede for the stage. Often, so it was said, the curtain had to be rung down and the police summoned.

Something was wrong with the girls we used to play with. They weren't the same any more. In fact, everything was changing, and for the worse. As for the boys, they were being farmed out one after another. Schooling was a luxury reserved for the children of the rich. Out there, "in the world," from all reports, it was nothing but a slave market. Yes, the world *was* crumbling about us. *Our* world.

And then there were places known as penitentiaries, reformatories, homes for wayward girls, insane asylums, and so on.

Before things were to go utterly smash, however, a wonderful event might occur. A party, no less. Where someone very precious, someone hardly more than a name, was certain to make an appearance.

To me, these "events" now seem like those fabulous balls which precede a revolution. One looked forward to being violently happy, happier than one had ever been before, yet one also had the presentiment that some untoward thing would happen, something which would affect one's whole life. A deal of sly whispering always surrounded the coming event. It went on among parents, older brothers and sisters, and among the neighbors. Everyone seemed to know more about one's sacred emotional life than was warranted. The whole neighborhood suddenly seemed abnormally interested in one's slightest doings. One was watched, spied upon, talked about behind one's back. Such great emphasis was put on age. The way people said, "He's fifteen now!" entrained the most embarrassing implications. It all seemed like a sinister puppet show which the elders were staging, a spectacle in which we would be the ridiculous performers there to be laughed at, mocked, goaded to say and do unaccountable things.

After weeks of anxiety the day would finally arrive. The girl too, at the last moment. Just when everything augured well, when all it needed—for what?—was a word, a look, a gesture, one discovered to his dismay that he had grown dumb, that his feet were rooted to the spot on which they had been planted ever since entering the place. Maybe once during the whole long evening did the precious one offer the slightest token of recognition. To move close to her, to brush her skirt, inhale the fragrance of her breath, what a difficult, what a monumental feat! The others appeared to move at will, freely. All that he and she seemed capable of was to slowly gravitate about such uninteresting objects as the piano, the umbrella stand, the bookcase. Only by accident did they seem destined now and then to converge upon one another. Even so, even when all the mysterious, supercharged forces in the room seemed to be pushing them toward each other, something always intervened to make them drift apart. To make it worse, the parents behaved in the most unfeeling fashion, pushing and jostling couples about, gesticulating like goats, making rude remarks, asking pointed questions. In short, acting like idiots.

The evening would come to an end with a great hand-shaking all around. Some kissed each other good-bye. The bold ones! These who lacked the courage to behave with such abandon, those who cared, who felt deeply, in other words, were lost in the shuffle. No one noticed their discomfiture. They were non-existent.

Time to go. The streets are empty. He starts walking homeward. Not the slightest trace of fatigue. Elated, though nothing had really happened. Indeed, it had been an utter fiasco, the party. But she had come! And he had feasted his eyes on her the whole evening long. Once he has almost touched her hand. Yes, think of that! *Almost!* Weeks may pass, months perhaps, before their paths cross again. (What if her parents took it into their head to move to another city? Such things happen.) He tries to fix it in his memory—the way she cast her eyes, the way she talked (to others), the way she threw her head back in laughter, the way her dress clung to her slender figure. He goes through it all piece by piece, moment by moment, from the time she entered and nodded to someone behind him, not seeing him, or not recognizing him perhaps. (Or had she been too shy to respond to his eager glance?) The sort of girl who never revealed her true feelings. A mysterious and elusive creature. How little she knew, how little anyone knew, the oceanic depths of emotion which engulfed him!

To be in love. To be utterly alone . . .

Thus it begins . . . the sweetest and the bitterest sorrow that one can know. The hunger, the loneliness that precedes initiation. . . .

It is at this point in one's development that someone comes along who has had more experience, someone "who knows women." This is the realistic dolt, the down-to-earth type, who believes that to sleep with a woman is to know her. By virtue of countless collisions with the other sex something which passes for knowledge has accrued to his make-up. Something like a psychological wig, one might say. Faced with a real woman, a real experience, this type of individual is bound to cut as ridiculous a figure as an old man trying to make himself look young. The wig becomes the focus of attention.

I remember a chap who became my boon companion during this transient period. I remember his grotesque antics with women, and how they affected me. He was always voicing the fear that to fall head over heels in love was to court disaster. Never give yourself wholly to one woman! So he made it his business to take me around. He would show me how to behave naturally, as he put it, with a woman.

The strange thing was that in the course of these adventures it happened again and again that the women he treated so cavalierly fell in love with *me*. It didn't take long to discover that the objects of his fancy weren't at all taken in by his swashbuckling behavior. It was only too apparent, from the way these "victims of prey" humored him and mothered him, that he was only deluding himself into thinking that he "had a way with women." I saw that this "man of the world" was just a child to them, even though in bed he could make them whinny with pleasure, or sob or groan, or cling to him with quiet desperation. He had a way of taking leave abruptly, like a coward beating a hasty re-treat. "A cunt's a cunt," he would say, trying to conceal his panic, and then he'd scratch his head and wonder aloud if there wasn't one, just *one* cunt, who was different.

No matter how attached I became to a "cunt," I was always more interested in the person who owned it. A cunt doesn't live a separate, independent existence. Nothing does. Everything is inter-related. Per-haps a cunt, smelly though it may be, is one of the prime symbols for the connection between all things. To enter life by way of the vagina is as good a way as any. If you enter deep enough, remain long enough, you will find what you seek. But you've got to enter with your heart and soul—and check your belongings outside.

H. M. Ruggieri

THE GIRL NEXT DOOR

He had noticed her one day in the back yard. He had noticed she had breasts.

She had always lived next door, but he had only begun to watch
her when he had noticed her breasts. Before that she had not had
breasts, or he had not noticed them. Now he watched the way they
pushed out against her shirts, her sweaters. She was a woman. That's
why they said it, that one day they were children and the next they were
women. The whole body changed, rounded. Laura was a woman. He
was seventeen and had never done it with a woman. Man and woman,
those simple designations he had known all his life were just now assuming their full importance, their full distinction.

From his bedroom window, he was watching her sunbathe in the
yard. He watched the curve of her cheeks. He could just see the top of
the cleft there, the beginning of a shadowy darkness. He followed it
down in his mind from pictures in books, from descriptions in pulp
magazines. Laura, Laura, Woman.

He remembered noting that both sets of parents were absent. He
remembered that he had casually sauntered over to where she sat on
the porch steps.

"Hi, Sollie," she had said. He'd sat down next to her on the step.
He had rubbed the gooseflesh on her thigh.

"Too much sun," he had said. She shuddered. He left his hand
there. Her skin was hot.

"Your hand feels so cool," she had said.

He lost track of what had been said. He remembered the feel of
her skin, how he had begun to move up her thigh, feeling the texture of
her skin, the smooth skin of the inner thigh, and under her shorts until

he felt the crease where the leg joins the body. She had not stopped him, had turned toward him and was leaning against him, her breasts on his chest, and they had somehow moved back behind the railing into the twilight shadows on the porch and she was under him, kissing him, her body arching up into his. He had opened her shirt and kissed the bare flesh of her breast and felt the nipple harden in his mouth and heard her sigh. Even now the intensity of that moment filled him with awe. That moment when he had touched the door of the unknown and entered in. His mind had slipped away into his body as he had slipped into hers. An entity had overtaken him, a thing other than his will. It pushed against the door and the door had opened for him, opened under him like the petals on a rare flower, opening and enfolding him even as the unknown power subsumed him. Oh Jesus, never a time like the first time, never a girl under him like Laura that time.

Laura under him, holding to him so tightly, her hands on his cheeks. He though she might want him to stop but he couldn't, wouldn't, and went on and on, feeling it growing like a lightning shaft striking out into her, and he heard the surprised oh, oh, oh trailing out of her mouth, wondering and startled. They lay still on each other, wet with sweat, sticky with semen, and she had sat up and looked at him.

"Oh Sollie," she had said, "that was wonderful. Let's do it again."

And they had done it again, all that summer, whenever they could. They had done it in the back seat of her father's car parked in the garage, in the living room while her parents were upstairs sleeping, once in his bedroom when his parents were away. They had done it standing up in the toolshed in the morning, laying on the wet grass in the darkness. As the leaves fell, he raked them into a bed at the end of the yard under the arbor of grapes and they had done it there, the leaves crackling under them. They blazed with the life force, stronger than morals, stronger than disapproval. They were afire.

The pattern was set. Laura would say, "No, Sollie, I just washed my hair, I don't want to get all dirty. I always smell like leaves." She would tease him into a kind of madness until he would grab her, hold her against him, rubbing his hands over her, kissing her, until he felt her relax, sigh into him with such totality that she seemed to become a part of him.

He thought of nothing else. . . . It was not just that he loved her: she was his life. Everything was for Laura.

When winter came, things began to change. Laura told him that they shouldn't appear to be so close or their parents would be suspicious. He agreed. It was logical, it made sense. She would say, "Oh, Sollie, no, it's too cold. I won't." He had argued, she had said no. Winter loomed ahead of him, a denial of life.

She would smile at him in school and pass by, leaving him standing in the crowded corridor with a deep ache in his bowels. Sometimes it hurt so much he couldn't walk. He would lean against the cool terrazzo walls and try to control himself, mumbling mathematical equations, something inane from the last class, until he gained control over his body and over the fearful desire, the primitive stranger, that took him.

He thought about that, about how he was split into two entities, and how only Laura mediated between the two, made them come to agreement. Laura, Laura, the key to transcendence, through the body, out of the body, like a parable, a two-edged Greek prophecy.

On Christmas Eve Laura had tapped softly at the back door. His parents had just left for Midnight Mass. He'd opened the door and she had walked in wearing a long coat and high boots. She had dropped her coat and stood naked, saying "Merry Christmas, Sollie."

"Hurry up," she complained, "we don't have much time."

He'd come as he put in into her. She was angry. She put on her coat going out the door, leaving it open. He followed her outside, calling after her, "Laura, Laura." She'd gone into her house and he'd followed right behind her.

"Please Sollie, go away. Be quiet, my parents are upstairs."

He'd knelt in front of her, in the dark kitchen, opening the coat, licking his own juice. He put his tongue between her lips and she liked it and held his head, dropping her coat, arching her back, spreading her legs. Oh she had like that, and had come for him, and he had gotten hard again and they lay on her coat and he had made her come again and again on the kitchen floor, her boots shuffling on the linoleum. She held him against her with all her strength, and when he came she groaned, "Oh Sollie, don't stop, I could do it forever, I don't want you to go, don't leave me, don't take it out, oh stay, stay, oh, oh, oh, hold it in, oh, ohhh."

In January, Laura started to date Rob. He was popular. He was a good dancer and his crowd was fun. They had their own cars and double-dated and went to the basketball games and the movies and to parties. Rob took her places and all the girls were eating their hearts out because he was captain of the football team and he liked her.

Sollie moved through the corridors like an accusing ghost.

"Don't look at me like that," she had said to him once, "everyone will know."

He hated her, he did, while some other part of him loved her, conjured up her image in the darkness before he fell asleep, while he was asleep, laid him in her body and woke him, coming in his own hand.

Spring came early that year. The air got warm, trees and flowers budded, peepers called over country ponds. Laura and Rob were parked on Cemetery Road. He wanted her to go steady, he offered his class ring. He kissed her. The radio was playing that spring's favorite love song. He was kissing her, telling her he loved her, he wanted her. He had laid over her, across the front seat of the car, and come as the head of his prick got inside her lips. Laura was angry and hurt and silent and Rob had taken it for regret and said he was sorry and he loved her. He had taken her home.

She looked up at the light in Sollie's window and went into her house and closed the door and lingered there until she heard the car drive off. Then she walked barefoot over the dewy grass and called softly, "Sollie, Sollie" under his window. And he was there and she was pulling him or he was pulling her, back into the darkness, and he was putting his prick into her, hard, into the wet of Rob's semen. Sollie was doing her, making her body feel involved and whole, molding her under him, taking her into happily-ever-after, saying her name over and over, pushing her back into the wet grass, sliding in and out, the tender pressure of him inside her. She began, "Ohh, ohh, ohhh."

Sollie knew about Rob, but put it away from him. He had her now, he didn't care. One part of him hated her, recoiling from the still warm juice that oozed over him. This part screamed whore, beat her, left her. But the other was already pumping inside her, lost in the caress of cunt, the rich reward for motion, the growing compulsion each stroke brought, until he was emptying, jerking his own cream into her, transforming her from what he hated into what he loved most.

So the spring too had its way. The date with Rob, the return, the evening's ecstasy. She asked him once, "Do you love me, Sollie?" He had told her he loved her more than his mother, his father, and himself combined, he loved her totally, he would do anything for her. He meant it. She was satisfied.

A Warm Emotion Which He Could Not Name

"Come on," said Bob, "let's start down the cliff."

They crawled over the edge and cautiously they worked their way downward, holding onto bushes, finding toe-holds in the rock.

The sun shone brilliantly. There were no clouds and overhead hawks circled and smaller birds flashed between trees. Insects were noisy and their irregular sounds were never quite lost in the river sound.

Garter snakes and lizards watched them as they went down. The snakes rattling the underbrush and disappearing; the lizards, more impassive, remained on their rocks, hypnotized by the sight of humans.

It was very hot and Jim began to sweat. He looked at Bob and saw that his white shirt was dark in patches and sticking close to his slim body. Then, at last, they stood by the river.

Tall gray and black rocks were all about them, jutting out of brown sand and mud. Jim balanced upon one rock and Bob on another. Then together they jumped from rock to rock: it was possible to go for miles without once touching the ground, stepping only on the boulders: relics of a glacier age.

Shortly after noon they came to the cabin. . . .

To the left of the cabin was a large pond made by a stream which came down the cliff. The pond was parallel to the river and edged with willows and tall trees. Here, in this pond, were catfish and frogs and here they swam.

Jim sat on the moss-covered bank while Bob undressed. They could swim without clothes here. Almost no one ever came to this pond.

Bob threw his clothes over a bush and stood on the bank beside Jim, flexing his long muscles and admiring himself in the green smooth water. Though slim he was strongly built and Jim admired him with a strange, different emotion that had no envy in it. When Bob talked of someone who had a good build he would sound jealous and make remarks, even about Jim who was better-looking. But Jim, when he looked at Bob's strong white body, did not envy; rather he felt a twinship, a similarity, a warm emotion which he could not name. He had always felt this way about Bob. Of course it would be silly to say anything for there were no words in his head to describe what he meant; it was an emotion not understood; to consummate it they played tennis together and talked about the girls Bob liked and, now, they were to swim together. Jim wondered as he watched Bob, the sun on his red hair, if he could tell him some of the strange things he thought, carry out in life his most personal dreams.

Bob cautiously put one long foot in the water. "It's warm," he said, pleased, "it's real warm." He stood then, bent over, his hands on his knees, studying the water and his reflection. Jim undressed, watching Bob as he did, fixing his image in his mind. He did this sometimes with people; he always did it with Bob, always memorized the wide shoulders and the slim legs: as if he would never see him again and this would be his final mental image.

Jim put his clothes beside Bob's and joined him at the water's edge. The warm breeze on his bare skin made him feel free and unencumbered, oddly sensual: this day was good.

Bob glanced at him without much interest. "You haven't got a tan either. Gosh, but I feel white. I guess this is almost the first time I been out in the sun like this all spring. Sally and I went swimming once in the pool in town but that was weeks ago. Anyway I had to have more on then." He looked back at the water. Below the dark green surface Jim could see the slow-moving shape of a catfish. Then, suddenly, he was falling and there was a rush of water in his ears and he was underwater; Bob had pushed him in.

Choking and laughing he came to the surface. The water came up to his chest and he stood on the rocky bottom of the pond. Bob was grinning at him on the shore. Quickly Jim grabbed his leg and pulled him in. Grappling, they turned and twisted in the water, making the pond foam and frightening the catfish.

Somehow the violence released Jim from certain emotions and he wrestled furiously with Bob, made free, for the time, by violence.

Finally, exhausted, they stopped and stood opposite each other in the middle of the pond, the water just below their chins.

Jim breathed quickly, trying to get his wind. He saw Bob was also winded; the thick white cords in his neck were prominent and his hair looked black and slick.

"Let's look for frogs," said Bob at last.

They swam to the bank and studied the green moss: frogs blended with the moss. They stood motionless. Then Jim saw a large frog and made a reach for it. The frog leaped first and swam toward the narrow stream which emptied into the pond. Jim and Bob followed the frog to the stream, and watched it bury its head in the white sand. The frog, not seeing them, felt safe.

Bob grabbed it by the legs. "You like frogs' legs?" he asked, dangling the frog in the air.

"Hell, no," said Jim. "Let it go." Bob threw the frog several feet into the air and they were pleased that it made a loud plop when it hit the water again.

All afternoon they swam in the pond, catching frogs, sunning themselves on the bank and, occasionally, wrestling. They talked very little. Bob never talked much and Jim had no need for talking when he was active, when he was with Bob.

At five they decided to go in. The sun was still warm though its light was broken by trees. They sat beside each other on the bank and waited for the breeze and sun to dry them. . . .

It became night.

The sky was dark and blue and stars were shining brightly, appearing one by one in the sky. Across the river the lights of houses gleamed on the river bank and farther downsteam the sky was light and liquid-looking: a city was there.

The night was warm. No insects bothered them and Jim felt relaxed and peaceful, almost complete. There were times, other times, when he had a feeling of loneliness in his stomach that was painful and depressing. When he was a child he often had this feeling and he always thought of it as the "tar-sickness": in summers the tar roads melted and sometimes the children would chew the tar and get sick: he felt like that when he was lonely. Now it was different; it was as if he had never been alone in his life. He always felt this way when he was with Bob and he hoped Bob felt the same though he doubted if Bob was ever lonely or afraid.

Bob took off his shoes and socks and let the river cool his feet. "Sure is nice," he said.

"Yes," said Jim and he put his own bare feet into the river.

The river was cool and the swirling of water was restful.

"I'll miss all this," said Bob for the dozenth time and he put his arm absently around Jim's shoulders.

They were very still. Jim was suddenly hot and the weight of Bob's arm on his shoulders was almost unbearable: wonderful but unbearable. He didn't dare move, though, for fear Bob would take his arm away. Inside of himself strange things were happening and Jim was afraid and happy both.

Bob, perhaps sensing Jim's uneasiness, stood up abruptly. "Let's go start a fire," he said. "One outside."

Jim was glad to be active. Together they built a fire in front of the cabin: a fire that was bright and yellow and burned upward several feet, transforming the dark clearing into a half-lit place of moving shadows.

Then Bob went into the cabin and brought the blankets out and spread them on the ground near the fire.

"There," he said, looking bemused into the fire, "that's done." He stood daydreaming by the fire and Jim watched him: his large hands held to the fire.

Finally Bob turned around, his dream finished and forgotten. "Come on," he said menacingly, "I'll wrestle you."

They met, fell to the ground and rolled, pushing and pulling, fighting for position: then, soon tired, they stopped. They were on the blanket beside the fire. Both were panting and sweating.

"I'm beat," said Bob. Jim only gulped. Bob took his shirt off and Jim did the same. It was a little cooler. Jim mopped the sweat off his face with his shirt and Bob stretched out on the blanket, his shirt under his head as a pillow. The firelight gleamed on his light skin.

Jim, his face dry, stretched out beside Bob, lay close to him. "I'm hot," he said. "It's too hot a night to be wrestling."

Bob laughed and suddenly grabbed him. They clung together a moment wrestling. Jim was suddenly conscious of Bob's body; he pretended to wrestle and then both stopped moving on the blanket still clinging though to each other. Jim was aware of Bob's body as never before. In the back of his mind half-forgotten dreams began to come alive, began to seek a consummation in reality. Neither moved for a minute, their arms about each other, smooth chests touching, breathing fast and in unison, Bob on his back and Jim across him.

Then Bob moved from under Jim and started to pull away, but he stopped before he was free. Jim looked at him and saw that his eyes were closed, that he was frowning. Jim pulled Bob toward him: he was afraid now of what was happening but he couldn't stop. He knew what he was doing, it was as if he had done this thing many times before: in dream countries where things happened like this, naturally without words or withdrawal.

Their faces met, their cheeks touched and with a shuddering sigh Bob gripped Jim tightly in his arms and the magic was made: both were aware.

They stayed like this, quiet in each other's arms for a long time. Jim had a sense of endless time; minutes and hours and years had ceased: only this immediate state was real. Then, as in a dream, they took their trousers off, not looking at each other, not thinking of the outer world and finally, shuddering, their bodies came together and for Jim it was his first completion, his first discovery of a twin: the half he had been searching for. He did not think if it was the same for Bob. He did not think. He felt.

A world of sensation was found. Innocently they discovered each other with their hands and bodies, their eyes shut and seeing for the first time. Jim's movements were natural and familiar, practiced before in many dreams remembered now. Bob, the object, was also a lover in this moment and he repeated the movements and subtleties that he had learned with girls. Then, at the most heightened moment, they were both released, one against the other, made complete.

Jim felt as if his entire body was exploding, was clashing rocketlike in this release. Lights glittered in circles behind his closed eyelids and his breathing stopped. This was his world and he was alive.

They stopped, exhausted.

They separated and Jim lay full length on the blanket, his breath coming in gasps. He could feel the fire on his feet and under the blanket he was suddenly aware of small stones and sticks. Finally he looked at Bob; he did not want to, he was afraid but he had to see him.

Bob was sitting up and looking into the fire, his face expressionless. He grinned quickly when he saw Jim was watching him. "This is a hell of a mess," he said and the moment was gone.

Jim looked at himself, nodded and said, casually, "It sure is."

Bob stood up, the firelight glittering on his sweating body. "Let's go over to the pond and wash up."

With their clothes over their arms they walked to the pond. It was dark by the pond. Through the trees they could see the light from their fire, yellow and distant. Near them frogs croaked and insects buzzed. The water of the pond was still and black. They put their clothes on the bank and slid together into the water.

Jim shivered and felt disembodied, a part of the water and the night. In the dark he could hear, and vaguely see, Bob splashing himself. Then they climbed out and Jim stretched with pleasure in the warm air. Both decided not to dress yet. They would get dry at the fire.

"You know," said Bob, when they were back at the fire, sitting side by side on the blanket, "that was awful kid stuff we did."

"I guess it was," said Jim. He paused. "I liked it, I guess." He had great courage now that he had performed a dream. "Did you like it?"

Bob frowned at the yellow fire. "I suppose so. It was different from with a girl but it was pretty nice. I don't think it's right."

"I don't see why not."

"Well, guys aren't supposed to do that with each other. It's not natural."

"I suppose so." Jim looked at Bob's fire-colored body, long-lined and muscular. Then Jim, controlled by his new courage, put his arm around Bob's waist. Bob didn't move for a moment and then, excited again, they embraced on the blanket.

John Berger

How Did It Happen?

How did it happen that on 2 May 1902, Beatrice was in her bedroom, her hair loose, wearing only a nightdress and wrap, in the middle of the afternoon?

The previous day, walking through the walled vegetable garden, she had noticed that several boughs of lilac had come out on the tree in the northeast corner. She wanted to pick some to take into the house. But to get to the tree she had to cross a bed of wet earth and rotting brussel sprout plants. She took off her shoes and stockings and left them on the path. Her feet sank into the mud up to her ankles. When she reached the tree, she discovered she was not tall enough. A little way along the wall was a black, rotten ladder. (During her absence in South Africa the house and farm had deteriorated dramatically.) She tested the first three rungs and they seemed strong enough. She moved the ladder to the lilac tree and climbed up. A wasp, caught between her skirts and the wall, stung her on the instep of her foot. She cried out (a small cry like a child's or a gull's), took little notice, cut the lilac and went barefoot into the house to wash her feet. By evening, her foot was inflamed and during the night she slept badly.

The next morning she decided to stay in bed. She knew that it was not the kind of decision she would ever have made before her marriage, before she left the farm. Jocelyn expected her to run the house and keep an eye on the dairy: he was away at a point-to-point in Leicestershire. A surveyor who was coming that afternoon expected her to prepare papers for him. Everybody would expect her to treat a small, already less swollen wasp bite as though it were nothing. Before her marriage she did what was expected of her. Now she did not.

She gave instructions and took a bath. Still wet, she stood looking at herself in the tall, tippable mirror in the bathroom.

She did not pretend that her gaze was that of a man. She drew no sexual conclusions as she stared at herself. She saw her body as a core, left when all its clothes had fallen from it. Around this core she saw the space of the bathroom. Yet between core and room something had changed, which was why all the house and the whole farm seemed changed since her return. She cupped her breasts with her hands and then moved her hands slowly downwards, over her hips, to the front of her thighs. Either the surface of her body or the touch of her hands had changed too.

Before, she lived in her body as though it were a cave, exactly her size. The rock and earth around the cave were the rest of the world. Imagine putting your hand into a glove whose exterior surface is continuous with all other substance.

Now her body was no longer a cave in which she lived. It was solid. And everything around, which was not her, was movable. Now what was given to her stopped at the surfaces of her body.

In nightgown and wrap she returned to bed. She lay back against a bank of pillows and imitated the cackling noise of a turkey. When she noticed the portrait of her father, she stopped. Some women might have considered the possibility that they were going mad. She began to move her head from side to side on the bank of pillows, thus tilting her view of the room from side to side. When she felt giddy, she got out of bed and dropped on to her hands and knees: the carpeted floor was level and still. On the level ground in the free space she was conscious of being happy. . . .

Beatrice laid aside the silver-backed, mermaid-embossed hairbrush and going to the window stopped by the vase of lilac.

When the boy came into the room she said: I cannot ever remember any lilac having a scent like this lot. Then she asked him whether he would please find out whether the second cowman was still sick. After he left the room, she thought: I am more than twice as old as he is. . . .

I see a horse and trap drawn up by the front door of the farmhouse. In it is a man in black with a bowler hat. He is portly and unaccountably comic. The horse is black and so too is the trap except for its white trimming. I am looking down on the horse and trap and the man who is so comically correct and regular, from the window of Beatrice's room.

On the table between the window and the large four-poster bed is the vase of white lilac. The smell of it is the only element that I can reconstruct with certainty.

She must be thirty-six. Her hair, combed up into a chignon, is loose around her shoulders. She wears an embroidered wrap. The embroidered leaves mount to her shoulder. She is standing in bare feet.

The boy enters and informs her that the papers for the man in the trap were the correct ones.

He is fifteen: taller than Beatrice, dark-haired, large-nosed but with delicate hands, scarcely larger than hers. In the relation between his head and shoulders there is something of his father—a kind of lunging assurance.

Beatrice lifts an arm towards him and opens her hand.

Pushing the door shut behind him, he goes toward her and takes her hand.

She, by turning their hands, ensures that they both look out of the window. At the sight of the man in black on the point of leaving they begin to laugh.

When they laugh they swing back the arms of their held hands and this swinging moves them away from the window towards the bed.

They sit on the edge of the bed before they stop laughing.

Slowly they lie back until their heads touch the counterpane. In this movement backwards she slightly anticipates him.

They are aware of a taste of sweetness in their throats. (A sweetness not unlike that to be tasted in a sweet grape.) The sweetness itself is not extreme but the experience of tasting it is. It is comparable with the experience of acute pain. But whereas pain closes anticipation of everything except the return of the past before the pain existed, what is now desired has never existed.

From the moment he entered the room it has been as though the sequence of their actions constituted a single act, a single stroke.

Beatrice puts her hand to the back of his head to move him closer towards her.

Beneath her wrap Beatrice's skin is softer than anything he has previously imagined. He has thought of softness as a quality belonging either to something small and concentrated (like a peach) or else to something extensive but thin (like milk). Her softness belongs to a body which has substance and seems very large. Not large relative to him, but large relative to anything else he now perceives. This magnification of her body is partly the result of proximity and focus but also of the sense of touch superseding that of sight. She is no longer contained within any contour, she is continuous surface.

He bends his head to kiss her breast and take the nipple in his mouth. His awareness of what he is doing certifies the death of his childhood. This awareness is inseperable from a sensation and a taste in his mouth. The sensation is of a morsel, alive, unaccountably half-detached from the roundness of the breast—as though it were on a stalk. The taste is so associated with the texture and substance of the morsel and with its temperature, that it will be hard ever to define it in other terms. It is a little similar to the taste of the whitish juice in the stem of a certain kind of grass. He is aware that henceforth both sensation and taste are acquirable on his own initiative. Her breasts propose his independence. He buries his face between them.

Her difference from him acts like a mirror. Whatever he notices or dwells upon in her increases his consciousness of himself, without his attention shifting from her.

She is the woman whom he used to call Aunt Beatrice. She ran the house and gave orders to the servants. She linked arms with her brother and walked up and down the lawn. She took him when he was a child to church. She asked him questions about what he had learnt in the school room: questions like What are the chief rivers of Africa?

Occasionally during his childhood she surprised him. Once he saw her squatting in the corner of a field and afterwards he wondered whether she was peeing. In the middle of the night he had woken up to hear her laughing so wildly that he thought she was screaming. One afternoon he came into the kitchen and saw her drawing a cow with a piece of chalk on the tiled floor—a childish drawing like he might have done when younger. On each of these occasions his surprise was the result of his discovering that she was different when she was alone or when she believed that he was not there.

This morning when she had asked him to come to her bedroom, she had presented a different self to him, yet he knew this was no longer a matter of chance discovery but of deliberate intention on her part. Her hair was loose around her shoulders. He had never seen or imagined it like that before. Her face seemed smaller, much smaller than his own. The top of her head looked unexpectedly flat and her hair over the flatness was very glossy. The expression of her eyes was serious to the point of gravity. Two small shoes lay on their sides on the carpet. She was barefoot. Her voice too was different, her words much slower.

I cannot remember, she said, any lilac ever having a scent like this lot.

This morning he was not surprised. He accepted the changes. Nevertheless, this morning he still thought of her as the mistress of the house in which he had passed his childhood.

She is a mythical figure whom he has always been assembling part by part, quality by quality. Her softness—but not the extent of its area—is more familiar than he can remember. . . . The whiteness of her body is what has signalled nakedness to him whenever he has glimpsed a white segment through the chance disarray of petticoat or skirt. Her smell is the smell of fields which, in the early morning, smell of fish although many miles from the sea. Her two breasts are what his reason has long since granted her, although their distinctness and degree of independence one from the other astonish him. He has seen drawings on walls asserting how she lacks penis and testicles. (The dark beard-like triangle of hair makes their absence simpler and more natural than he foresaw.) This mythical figure embodies the desirable alternative to all that disgusts or revolts him. It is for her sake that he has ignored his own instinct for self-preservation. . . . She and he together, mysteriously and naked, are his own virtue rewarded.

Mythical familiar and the woman he once called Aunt Beatrice meet in the same person. The encounter utterly destroys both of them. Neither will ever again exist.

He sees the eyes of an unknown woman looking up at him. She looks at him without her eyes fully focussing upon him as though, like nature, he were to be found everywhere.

He hears the voice of an unknown woman speaking to him: Sweet, sweet, sweetest. Let us go to that place.

He unhesitatingly puts his hand on her hair and opens his fingers to let it spring up between them. What he feels in his hand is inexplicably familiar.

She opens her legs. He pushes his finger towards her. Warm mucus encloses his finger as closely as if it were a ninth skin. When he moves his finger, the surface of the enclosing liquid is stretched—sometimes to the breaking point. Where the break occurs he has a sensation of coolness on that side of his finger—before the warm moist skin forms again over the break.

She holds his penis with both hands, as though it were a bottle from which she were about to pour towards herself.

She moves sideways so as to be beneath him

Her cunt begins at her toes; her breasts are inside it, and her eyes too; it has enfolded her.

It enfolds him

The ease.

Previously it was unimaginable, like a birth for that which is born. . . .

Her eyes refocus upon him. Their look is for him something as specific and permanent as a house or a particular door. He will find his way back to it. . . .

Behind such a look is a total confidence that at that moment to express something—without thought, without words, but simply through one's own uncontrollable eyes—is to be instantaneously understood. To be, at that moment, is to be known. Hence all distinctions between the personal and the impersonal disappear.

Do not let us even by a hair's breadth misinterpret the meaning of this look. The look is simultaneously and in absolutely equal terms appealing and grateful. This does not mean that Beatrice is grateful for what has passed and is appealing for what is to come.

Don't stop, my sweet, don't stop, is what she may have said or will do: but not with this look.

Such an interpretation implies that eventually, if all is well, her look will be transformed into one which is purely grateful. An interpretation particularly dear to the male as provider and master. But false.

The look in Beatrice's eyes being in equal measure appealing and grateful is not the result of those two feelings co-existing. There is only one feeling. She has only one thing to say with her uncontrollable eyes. Nothing exists for her beyond this single feeling. She is grateful for what she appeals for; she appeals for what she is already grateful for.

To follow her look, we enter her state of being. There, desire is its satisfaction, or, perhaps, neither desire nor satisfaction can be said to exist since there is no antinomy between them: every experience becomes the experience of freedom there: freedom there precludes all that is not itself.

The look in her eyes is an expression of freedom which he receives as such, but which we, in order to locate it in our world of third persons, must call a look of simultaneous appeal and gratitude.

A little later she strokes his back and whispers: You see. You see.

The world is not as we have subsided into it. Within us there is the keenness, the sharpness to perform surgery. Within, if we have the courage to wield it, is the cutting edge to sever the whole world as it is, the world that pretends to be part of us, the world to which by compromised and flabby usage we are said to belong. Say now to me. Now to me say to me.

She places her hand so that his testicles may rest upon the palm.

From the long tight bud the longer petals loosen: their tips begin to separate so that at the far end of the flower there is an open mouth. Then, freed, the petals slowly revolve like propellers: in eight hours one may turn between forty-five and ninety degrees. As they revolve they retreat till they are pointing backwards from their small round calyx which is now thrust forward.

Thus a cyclamen opening. And thus too, greatly accelerated, the sensation of his penis becoming erect again and the foreskin again withdrawing from the coronal ridge.

The clocks keep another time. . . .

They lie abandoned, side by side. The air from the open window cools their bodies and makes them aware of how damp they are, on the front of their stomachs how wet.

It should go on for ever, she says. It is not a complaint. She grips two fingers of his hand. She knows that the pace of time is reverting to normal. She crossed a threshold beyond which space, distance, time were meaningless. The threshold was warm, damp and quivering: animate to a degree for which the inanimate has no qualitative equivalent—unless it be jurassic mountains: animate to a degree at which it seemed that substance become sound alone.

It should go on for ever.

They lie on their backs. He has the sensation of being extended horizontally. He is conscious of the flatness of the bed, the floor, the earth under the house. Everything that is standing looks incongruous and incomplete to him. He is on the point of laughing. Suddenly he notices the portrait of her father on the wall opposite the bed. It is a provincial clumsy painting so that the image of the man oscillates between being a likeness and a childish stereotype of a ruddy-faced country gentleman at an inn. The face looks as though it has been tinted pink. The eyes are blankly fixed. Looking at this portrait of her father, he waves a hand.

Rachel Kaplan

Another Coming Out Manifesto Disguised as a Letter to My Mother

dear mom,
i am a bisexual.

love, rachel

p.s. tell dad. tell him it's not as bad as he thinks it is. tell him it has nothing to do with him. no, don't do that. it's bad policy to lie when you're coming out, because you're always answerable to the image you make of yourself. tell him, oh, tell him whatever you want. because when i say, "hi, mom, i'm a bisexual," what i mean is: i am trying to be free, mom, i am trying to be free.

this letter is about coming out, about what that used to mean to me, and what it means to me now. when i came out as a lesbian in 1981, after hedging for at least two years, i was terrified. i thought people would hate me or kill me, that there would be places i couldn't go, people i couldn't speak with, etc. my first boyfriend, who turned out to be a fag (a distressing story for another time), said to me: "really, rachel, it's much easier than you think. once you say it and you know it's true, you have the power of all that behind you." of course, i didn't believe him until i came out myself and watching his bravery helped me only slightly in getting past the fear of being hurt for wanting to touch women so much. he was right, though. it was easier to talk about who i thought i was than to lie about who i thought i should be, and there was all that power behind the fear, the fear of coming out.

i came out as a lesbian so long ago i'm not even a lesbian anymore.

that first coming out (which i was subsequently forced to retract) taught me a lot about changing. i thought coming out as a lesbian was hard, but it was harder coming out as someone who isn't a lesbian after being a lesbian for so long. that was harder. now i'm occupied with a coming out that has to do with telling different stories about myself. i know that my sexuality changes a lot, along with other pictures of myself, so coming out has become the process of trying to articulate my reality. i still get scared and wonder about my methods, like writing this piece, or getting up on stage and talking about my dad. i still talk about sexuality, but mostly i want to tell the truth about my past, and my survival mechanisms. hi mom. hi dad. still there?

i tell all these stories about my family and my "problem sexuality" because i'm convinced that if i feel something, someone else does too, and that the act of telling the truth carries with it the very real possibility of communion.

what i really want: communion.

to be honest, i don't care what i call myself to get it. and if i call myself a bisexual in 1990 it's because that's the closest approximation of freedom i can find.

what i really want: freedom.

i've been looking all along for words that spell FREEDOM and i think i have to deal in words/labels because if i don't pick one, someone will pick one for me. language makes boxes and boxes are bad if you're forced into them, but if you're choosing a box where you want to live, it's important to find one that's comfortable. which is why coming out matters. coming out is a process of choosing an identity before it gets chosen for you. it's about finding explanations for yourself and making decisions about who you want to be.

now i have to figure out what i mean by "bisexual." someone with a column in a sex magazine ought to know but the only real truth is in my body and that's a truth beyond the reach of my language. which is why i say bisexuality is an approximation, a process of surrender and survival in a world that seeks to constrict and control my desires. it is my inner child saying NO to a world where gender determines my desire and my behavior; it is my inner child saying: i want to come out and play with you. and you. and you. and it doubles my opportunities for terror and intimacy all at once.

i called myself a lesbian when i did because when i was with women i felt like a lesbian and when i was with men i still felt like a lesbian. i have always been more comfortable on the margins of things. i have a real fear of men. and i thought being a lesbian meant i could do whatever i wanted, but guess what? it means YOU SLEEP WITH WOMEN. i finally quit because everyone i know was too busy reading mary daly to fuck me and i was bored as shit. but it was a politically valiant move in the 80s, just like bisexuality is a politically valiant move in the 90s. don't let anyone tell you different. the problem with all sexual politics is its reliance on language to create reality when the only real truth about sexuality is in the body. and that's not something language addresses because the language of the body is movement and words aren't about movement, they're about stasis. and that's the paradox of this polemic.

what i wanted then, and what i want now, is to somehow escape the strictures on my identity and my desire. i want to be able to do what i want and to feel what i feel. (i can hear you now, mom, dad. something about being spoiled, or difficult . . .) i am bisexual in defiance of an idea of a static sexual identity, and i challenge the idea that identity is constant. there is a constant presence of desire, but no constancy about what that desire is. i don't believe my sexual identity can be determined outside my body.

my great moment of truth in going from being a lesbian to being bisexual was learning that it isn't so much about gender, the problem of being with someone else. the problem is my fear of intimacy, which has to do with a fear of the difference (and similarity) of the other. gender is a sham, a cover for the real fear, the fear of being seen. and the more language i used to cover my fear, the more boxed in i got, and the farther i got from my body and my desire, and all i had were some theories about the (im)possibility of desire and love which are about as much fun to sleep with as mary daly. i got bored as shit. and then i got seduced by a beautiful boy and started believing in the project of being seen and being love. i found a new definition: COMING OUT IS THE PROCESS OF BEING SEEN IN LOVE.

coming out is different now than it was that first time. it's easier in one sense because i have less terror over my emergence every time i do it and find myself alive and loved. but it still has to do with identity formation and that's always hard. now i know that things are true only in their moment of being true, and i try not to hold myself to anything for any longer than it exists. i have a practice around coming out and i call it: returning and letting go.

i learned i wasn't as queer as i thought, and that my version of queerness has its own beauty, so my coming out right now doesn't have to do with being sexually queer so much as it has to do with being my own self. i think the real work, as a performer or a writer or whatever you are, is coming out, every day, as whatever you are, every day, and that it really can change, every day, if you let it. i want to believe i feel what you feel. nao said to me: "i'm alive and so i owe it to the world to talk." that's why i spend my time telling you who i am. i think the circles of attention generated by coming out have the power to transform the world.

i'm committed to this coming out because a revelation of my self is resistance in a culture that radically suppresses our differences. it is only through the acknowledgment of our individuality and difference that i can begin to see someone else. and that's communion, seeing and being seen, and that's what i want: communion.

the more each of us comes out and articulates the truth about our lives the closer we get to understanding the forces that serve to separate and unite us. because it is the act of coming out that is about freedom, not the label you choose. so i guess i should have started like this:

dear mom,

    I am coming out.

                    love, rachel

    p.s. tell dad.

James Joyce

On the Beach at Fontana

Wind whines and whines the shingle,
The crazy pierstakes groan;
A senile sea numbers each single
Slimesilvered stone.

From whining wind and colder
Grey sea I wrap him warm
And touch his trembling fineboned shoulder
And boyish arm.

Around us fear, descending
Darkness of fear above
And in my heart how deep unending
Ache of love !

e. e. cummings

I LIKE MY BODY WHEN
IT IS WITH YOUR

i like my body when it is with your
body. It is so quite new a thing.
Muscles better and nerves more.
i like your body. i like what it does,
i like its hows. i like to feel the spine
of your body and its bones, and the trembling-
firm-smooth ness and which and i will
again and again and again
kiss,   i like kissing this and that of you,
i like, slowly stroking the, shocking fuzz
of your electric fur, and what-is-it comes
over parting flesh . . . . And eyes big love-crumbs,

and possibly i like the thrill

of under me you so quite new

3

THE EROTIC
IMAGINATION

Introduction: Part 3

If erotic behavior is complex, misunderstood, and often feared, the intricacies of the erotic imagination are even more so. We can, after all, fashion reassuring rules for the regulation and control of overt erotic behavior; we can develop social conventions and laws with various rewards for appropriateness and punishments for transgression. But despite the techniques we devise to keep erotic practice within the boundaries of propriety, erotic imagination seems to travel its own course and, to our consternation, often gravitates to the very themes we designate forbidden, bizarre, even perverse. If Eros is a rash, irrepressible, rebellious mischief-maker, he seems most uncontrollable when he inhabits the realm of the imagination.

The sensational, distorted, almost hysterical language that dominates contemporary political and social discussion of the issues of erotic art and pornography reflect our cultural fear and confusion about our erotic natures. We equate the symbolic content of our erotic fantasies, dreams, or works of art with a literal intent to enact what is being portrayed or fantasized. In no other realm of imagination do we fear confusing fantasy with reality.

If a woman wakes from a dream of leaping off a cliff and soaring effortlessly away, she does not imagine that she is in danger of killing herself by leaping off a cliff while awake. But if she dreams of being sexual with a prohibited partner (father, mother, brother, daughter, man next door, woman at work), she may well fear that there is something dangerously wrong with her. If a man daydreams of being on a luxurious estate, surrounded by opulence and the ultimate of creature comforts, he smiles at the creative excesses of his imagination. But if he becomes similarly excited imagining elaborate scenes in which one glamorous woman after another aches to have wild sex with him (as is typical of men who masturbate with pornography), he may well be told (or tell himself) that he is a sex addict, a potential rapist, someone with a hidden desire to dominate or degrade women—someone who should be fundamentally suspicious of his sexual desires.

That we treat sex-related imagination so differently from other forms of mental creativity displays our deep-seated fear that the erotic impulse and its harbinger, erotic imagination, are dangerous forces which must be kept in constant check, lest they destroy the very foundations of our rational, orderly lives.

Sadly, when we impose reasonableness on our erotic desires and dreams, or literal accuracy on erotic photographs and poems, we deny our erotic complexity, and lose a great deal of our erotic power, energy, and spontaneity. We become good boys and nice girls, maintaining the approval of parents, friends, society at large, but at tremendous cost to ourselves. If we cannot tolerate our forbidden erotic thoughts and desires, if we cannot trust ourselves to separate fantasy from reality, thought from action when it comes to erotic and sexual matters, we necessarily cut ourselves off from much of our erotic wellspring.

It is possible, however, to step back from this culturally exaggerated suspicion of eros and to ask real questions about how erotic fantasy and imagination actually function. We can address erotic imagination on its own irrational, symbolic, psychic terms. We then become capable of appreciating not only our own fantasies but also works of erotic art and literature, as we appreciate other creative works—differentiating symbol from fact, art from life. By creating room for fantasy as fantasy, we can begin to understand and enjoy how wonderfully creative our erotic imagination can be, and to take pleasure from the diverse fruits of its inventiveness.

There are two main public forums for sexually explicit imagination. The most widespread is commercial pornography—the traditional medium in our culture for the public exploration of sexual fantasy. Because we have relegated the creation of sexually arousing material to an underground and outlawed subculture, commercial pornography is, for the most part, trivial and formulaic, filled with gender and racial stereotypes, and almost universally male-oriented. (It should be noted, however, that as pornography has become more widespread, with an audience that now includes almost as many women as men, it has also become more joyous and more sex-friendly, drawing its appeal increasingly from direct sexual voyeurism and less from sexual guilt and the thrill of "being bad.")

In recent years, a second arena of public sexual expression has blossomed, quite distinct from commercial pornography in its aesthetics, its content, its general perception of sexuality and gender roles, and also its network of distribution. We have begun to see for the first time some legitimacy conferred on specifically *sexual* art, writing, and photography. These new forms of sexual art go beyond pornographic conventions to offer complex, creative expressions of sexual themes and practices. Although serious artistic respect for sex-related art is still embryonic, increasing numbers of talented artists and writers have begun to address sexual issues in their work, to defend the legitimacy and importance of a wide variety of sexual themes, and to wrestle with the elusive artistic questions raised by the emerging genre.

What is the task of sexual depiction in art, beyond the literal documentation of sexual acts? What aspects of human sexuality can be addressed through literature, photography, film, painting or sculpture? How can something as subtle and complex as sex be portrayed effectively and truthfully? What are the technical, artistic, and emotional issues that must be confronted in, say, photographing or filming sexual activity in an imaginative way? What is it that artists want to convey about sexual feeling and experience, beyond the initial statement that sex should be a legitimate subject for artistic expression? And how do artists who address sexual matters deal with the efforts of so many other artists, gallery managers, publishers, museum curators, funding sources, government agencies, police, and even the courts to discredit, dismiss, defame, or imprison them for their work?

These are some of the issues now being addressed seriously for the first time, issues made all the more acute by the growing political climate of intolerance for sexual depiction of any kind. Despite current political and cultural obstacles, growing numbers of innovative writers and artists *are* developing new genres of unapologetically and unambiguously sexual art. Thus we have fine writers such as Anne Rice (under the pseudonym A. N. Roquelaure), Pat Califia, Marco Vassi, John Preston, Dorothy Allison, Carol Queen, and Dodie Bellamy; poets such as Lenore Kandel, James Broughton, Deborah Abbott, and Danielle Willis; photographers such as Robert Mapplethorpe, Michael Rosen, Mark I. Chester, Ron Raffaelli, Annie Sprinkle, Tom Millea, Trevor Watson, Grace Lau, and Charlie Clark; artists such as Betty Dodson, David Wojnarowicz, Gary Epting, and Harriet Moore;

and film directors such as Candida Royalle, Monika Treut, Debi Sundahl, and Suzanne Myers—whose work involves sexual portrayal that is direct, intelligent, and imaginative.

This section begins with three pieces that explore the inner dynamics of erotic imagination—why erotic fantasy and imagination function as they do. Critic Camille Paglia examines the continuing cultural conflict between Judeo-Christian sexual values and what she sees as the irrepressible legacy of the roving, pagan eye. She sees both Hollywood and pornography as expressions of pagan eye-intensity, which cannot be controlled by pious moralism. Columnist Richard Goldstein examines how both heterosexual and gay pornography express the unreasonable, irrepressible nature of the erotic unconscious. Distinguishing between the waking world and the worlds of fantasy and dream, he emphasizes how each must be understood and evaluated on its own terms.

Turning to some of the issues particular to the creation of erotic art and literature, Barbara Wilson speaks of her concerns as a writer of lesbian erotic fiction, attempting to portray sexuality in the emotional and situational context of her characters, though she knows that readers may objectify her sexual portrayals by lifting them out of the contexts in which she sets them.

The collected statements from a wide variety of erotic writers, artists, poets, and photographers—women and men of various sexual perspectives and persuasions who deliberately pursue erotic and sexual themes in their work—offer an overview of the diverse points of view of these artists, both with regard to the emerging genres of sexual art and with regard to eroticism itself.

Three short literary pieces stand as examples of the new imagery and of the attention to more subtle issues common to new erotic work. Michael Rubin's short novel excerpt describes how a young man discovers new aspects of his emerging sexuality while riding bareback through meadows and streams. "The High Priestess" offers my own brief psychic excursion into a world of dreamlike desire. And poet Lenore Kandel takes us inside the rich imaginings of two lovers as they go deep into their separate worlds of fantasy while experiencing the shared reality of their mutual masturbatory encounter.

Camille Paglia

THE ROVING EROTIC EYE

Western culture has a roving eye. Male sex is hunting and scanning: boys hang yelping from honking cars, acting like jerks over strolling girls; men lunching on girders go through the primitive book of wolf whistles and animal clucks. Everywhere, the beautiful woman is scrutinized and harassed. She is the ultimate symbol of human desire. The feminine is that-which-is-sought; it recedes beyond our grasp. Hence there is always a feminine element in the beautiful young man of male homosexuality. The feminine is the ever-elusive, a silver shimmer on the horizon. We follow this image with longing eyes: maybe this one, maybe this time. The pursuit of sex may conceal a dream of being freed from sex.

Sex, knowledge, and power are deeply tangled; we cannot get one without the others. Islam is wise to drape women in black, for the eye is the avenue of eros. Western culture's hard, defined personalities suffer from inflammation of the eye. They are so numerous that they have never been catalogued, except in our magnificent portrait art. Western sexual personae are nodes of power, but they have made a torment of eroticism. From this torment has come our grand tradition of literature and art. Unfortunately, there is no way to separate the whistling ass on his girder from the rapt visionary at his easel. In accepting the gifts of culture, women may have to take the worm with the apple.

Judeo-Christianity has failed to control the pagan western eye. Our thought processes were formed in Greece and inherited by Rome, whose language remains the official voice of the Catholic church. Intellectual inquiry and logic are pagan. Every inquiry is preceded by a roving eye; and once the eye begins to rove, it cannot be morally controlled. Judaism, due to its fear of the eye, put a taboo on visual

83

representation. Judaism is based on word rather than image. Christianity followed suit, until it drifted into pictorialism to appeal to the pagan masses. Protestantism began as an iconoclasm, a breaking of the images of the corrupt Roman church. The pure Protestant style is a bare white church with plain windows. Italian Catholicism, I am happy to say, retains the most florid pictorialism, the bequest of a pagan past that was never lost.

Paganism is eye-intense. It is based on cultic exhibitionism, in which sex and sadomasochism are joined. The ancient chthonian mysteries have never disappeared from the Italian church. Waxed saints' corpses under glass. Tattered armbones in gold reliquaries. Half-nude St. Sebastian pierced by arrows. St. Lucy holding her eyeballs out on a platter. Blood, torture, ecstasy, and tears. Its lurid sensationalism makes Italian Catholicism the emotionally most complete cosmology in religious history. Italy added pagan sex and violence to the ascetic Palestinian creed.

And so to Hollywood, the modern Rome: it is pagan sex and violence that have flowered so vividly in our mass media. The camera has unbound daemonic western imagination. Cinema is *sexual showing,* a pagan flaunting. Plot and dialogue are obsolete word-baggage. Cinema, the most eye-intense of genres, has restored pagan antiquity's cultic exhibitionism. Spectacle is a pagan cult of the eye. . . .

That popular culture reclaims what high culture shuts out is clear in the case of pornography. Pornography is pure pagan imagism. Just as a poem is ritually limited verbal expression, so is pornography ritually limited visual expression of the daemonism of sex and nature. Every shot, every angle in pornography, no matter how silly, twisted, or pasty, is yet another attempt to *get the whole picture* of the enormity of chthonian nature. Is pornography art? Yes. Art is contemplation and conceptualization, the ritual exhibitionism of primal mysteries. Art makes order of nature's cyclonic brutality. Art is full of crimes. The ugliness and violence in pornography reflect the ugliness and violence in nature.

Pornography's male-born explicitness renders visible what is invisible, woman's chthonian internality. It tries to shed Apollonian light on woman's anxiety-provoking darkness. The vulgar contortionism of pornography is the serpentine tangle of Medusan nature. Pornography is human imagination in tense theatrical action; its violations are a protest against the violations of our freedom by nature. The banning of pornography, rightly sought by Judeo-Christianity, would be a victory over the west's stubborn paganism. But pornography cannot be banned, only driven underground, where its illicit charge will be enhanced. Pornography's amoral pictorialism will live forever as a rebuke to the humanistic cult of the redemptive word. Words cannot save the cruel flux of pagan nature.

The western eye makes *things,* idols of Apollonian objectification. Pornography makes many well-meaning people uncomfortable because it isolates the voyeuristic element present in all art, and especially cinema. All the personae of art are sex objects. The emotional response of spectator or reader is inseparable from erotic response. Our lives as physical beings are a Dionysian continuum of pleasure-pain. At every moment we are steeped in the sensory, even in sleep. Emotional arousal is sensual arousal; sensual arousal is sexual arousal. The idea that emotion can be separated from sex is a Christian illusion, one of the most ingenious but finally unworkable strategies in Christianity's ancient campaign against pagan nature. Agape, spiritual love, belongs to eros but has run away from home.

Richard Goldstein

PORNOGRAPHY AND
ITS DISCONTENTS

If my thoughts/dreams could be seen
They'd probably put my head in a guillotine
But it's all right, ma
It's life and life only.

BOB DYLAN

What light through yonder TV breaks? It is Little Kimmi Johnson, with her blue dress threatening to ascend and her school-girl pumps, aflutter with anticipation as she coos, "I'm ready. I'm ready now."

An English teacher is "tutoring" Little Kimmi. Mother is eager to engage her in incest. Mother's boyfriend (despite a stern warning, delivered in the bland tones of video erotica) teaches her to fellate him—and more. Little Kimmi goes through it all with blithe assurance, taking sex in as if it were a calliope. She never yearns for innocence or regrets her absence from what Nabokov called "the concord" of children's voices.

In reality, Little Kimmi would be a budding schizophrenic. In life, we would pity her and loathe her mentors. As testimony before a congressional subcommittee, her story would be stunning in its depravity. But in the video, Little Kimmi Johnson—played, I should point out, by a woman pushing 30—is hot.

Little Kimmi Johnson is an icon of heterosexual pornography; by which I mean, she turns me on. But how can I admit it? How can I acknowledge that, though this film arouses socially destructive passions, it also arouses me?

The personal is what's missing from critiques of pornography. D. H. Lawrence doesn't say that, by propelling him toward masturbation, smut leaves him drained; instead, he informs us that it leaves the body "a corpse, after the act of self-abuse." Steven Marcus doesn't confess that pornography makes him feel things he identifies as infantile; he merely defines as pornographic "any discourse which presents sexual material, and is inconsistent with a mature adult sexual life."

In my reading, the closest anyone comes to acknowledging a personal response to pornography is Susan Sontag, who earnestly asserts that "works of pornography *can* belong to literature." They say "something worth listening to," she explains, but only in the context of a political critique. (Observers of Sontag's odyssey ought to go back to "The Pornographic Imagination" for the fervor she invests in blaming capitalism for our need to become involved with the stuff.) More typical is Andrea Dworkin, who never admits to being aroused by any of the pornography she so lavishly deconstructs. This mirror image of Norman Mailer would rather mimic the intensity of a film called *Whip Chick* than own up to a response. (". . . He rips her clothes and slaps her. He keeps hitting her. She screams. Then she says, 'Ooh, master. Hurt me. Punish me,'" Dworkin bristles, in a description and analysis that occupies six pages of her book, *Pornography*.) What's missing from Dworkin's posture of rage, and from Lawrence's and Marcus's less threatened stance, is confession: Father, I have lusted. In my hand.

The evasion is understandable. Owning up to arousal by pornography shreds the purdah behind which our imaginations operate. It forces us to confront the implications of our fantasies. For pornography posits a world in which sexual impulse is at the heart of all action, in which the actions that spring from desire are inevitable, in which there is no escape from role except through another role; a world without consequences.

This is the realm of infancy, to which we may not, must not, return. Except symbolically. We don't want to live in a world where children are initiated into sex by their parents and teachers, but we may want to imagine it.

Men of the Midway opens with a Walker Evans landscape. Inside the faded clapboard house, Charley is awakened by his father, who announces between blasts from his cigar, "Things are gonna change around here." Now that "the old lady's not around anymore," Charley has to raise his share of cash by taking to the streets. And pop proceeds to teach Charley the tricks of that trade with a thick rubber dildo. "Talk to Daddy," he says when Charley begins to express his enjoyment, and, as the ordeal reaches its climax, "You're better than your mother."

Sick of the customers he's assigned and tired of having his legs tied to the ends of a broomstick for their convenience, Charley runs away from home and ends up at the carnival, where he's promptly impressed into sexual slavery by Randy. This surrogate turns Charley over to two black men, who greet his arrival with a hearty, "Good, the other one's spent."

Men of the Midway, as dreadful to behold as *Sister Carrie,* is also an anthology of conventions in gay pornography. It features a father/son dichotomy as well as polarities in race and physical prowess—all of them used as signatures of authority. The "old lady's" gone, leaving Charley at the mercy of men and their hierarchies, which must be navigated in a series of painful submissions until one's place in the order is secure. Charley does eventually find love, and reciprocal sex—with his boss!

If we manage to overlook the injustice of this paradigm, we can understand its logic. To dwell in the obvious, gay male films have no female object. They must either abandon sexual polarities altogether (hence, the preponderance of group action as well as solo performances in gay erotica) or reformulate them. From varieties of race, class, age, status and physical appearance, gay men eroticize the differences between them; and gay male porn reflects these castes. It adds the crowning touch of *attitude*—the sense of self we all project onto sex. Attitude hinges on a response to power (though it can involve aggression or submission). Charley begins as a wimp, whining in protest but too weak to resist; he's transformed by attitude into an eager bottom and ultimately, into a clone (Everygayman).

Men of the Midway has more in common with *Little Kimmi Johnson* than most men might like to admit. These erotic *bildungsromans* share an age-old obsession with infantile helplessness and parental power. Charley is literally awakened by his father, while Kimmi is unveiled by the camera in a series of "candid" interviews. If she seems oblivious to sexual trauma—while Charley seems overwhelmed by it—that's because straight sex films, when not trafficking overtly in degradation and cruelty, disguise their intentions with elaborate displays of female ecstasy. From her yummy-yummy look at the sight of a man's penis to her squeals at the moment he plunges, poised in full muscular display, there must be no question about a woman's receptivity to the action on screen. But the men in gay films are often indifferent, if not downright hostile, to the acts they perform.

In place of consent, gay male porn romanticizes coercion. For a man to be brought to submission by another man, and thereby to "suffer" arousal—is that rape or football?

This subterfuge is hardly unique to pornography. You can spot the same response to aggression in most action/adventure films. What makes *Indiana Jones and the Temple of Doom* so shocking to good liberals (and so exhilarating to conservatives) is its unabashed embrace of traditional polarities. Race and sex are thinly disguised manifestations of a hierarchy of power in which the white male hero is the source of all strength and, ultimately, decency. He risks death to recover the stolen sacred object and then, rather than cashing in, turns it over to its rightful owners—people of color unable to recover it for themselves. As a fantasy of male omnipotence, it's right up there with the conversion of rape to love.

Steven Spielberg's secret weapon may not be his pilfering of bygone clichés, but his genius at priming the adrenal pump. Violence is to *The Temple of Doom* what sex is to pornography. It serves no higher purpose than to jolt us into arousal. Surges of shock, predictably paced, send us on a chemical roller coaster ride. We watch, not for meaning but for the impact of imagery. It is the pace of this movie we remember, not the plot.

Even the most ambitious porn films fail the way *Flashdance* does: they're only compelling once the dancing starts. The more sex is treated as a form of choreography, the more precisely it can be set to music; any similarity to rock video is not a coincidence. In *Men of the Midway,* the score sweeps from Prokofiev to Bach; *Romeo and Juliet* accompanies a rape; *The Passion According to St. Matthew* is appropriated for a homosexual love scene. That religious music can serve such a blasphemous master and still retain its core of meaning is incredibly arousing, almost as if the "passion" of submission and suffering were heightened by its association with pornography. The characters, too, are exalted by overcoming degradation. They are transformed by a desire that is ultimately beyond their control: the bottom doesn't want to have sex but comes to enjoy it; the top begins by demanding release but ends up expressing love.

For "good" Freudians—for instance, Robert Stoller—this conversion is always present in neurotic behavior; but it's also endemic to sexual fantasy. It recurs in so many guises in pornography that I've come to regard conversion as the mark of successful erotica, straight or gay. It's the ritual ground of porn, and partly explains its obsession with indignity, inequality, coercion, and rape.

If you're wondering whether Kimmi and Charley turn me on—poor waifs—they do. I am implicated in their transformation. I enact it as arousal and I come, signifying my triumph over trauma.

Even if there were no pornography, there would be pornography. The libido will not be denied its representations; though they may be covert, to the eye of the beholder, their intentions will be clear. Which is why the popular iconography of the 50s, when everything explicit was under-the-counter, seems comically intense to us today. The visual and written rhetoric of that decade is overwrought with pornographic implications we now relegate to "adult" films and magazines. I remember the Marilyn Monroe calendar my father brought home when I was a kid more vividly than any spread-beaver shot—and, I dare say, it had a greater impact on my hormones. The folds of red satin on which she lay are lodged so firmly in my imagination that I am still reminded of them at the sight of a red foulard protruding from the breast pocket of an ordinary business suit. To each his own *madeleine*.

Even if pornography were banned as a clear and present danger, we would still be left with the content of our fantasies, and our fantasies would still be laced with those images of "submission and display" by which anti-porn activists define pornography. The menu of insult and injury in the adult section of any home-video store is—and would remain—the stuff of dreams.

Readers of the *New York Times* were shocked (or perhaps consoled) to learn last year that men and women, straight and gay, frequently fantasize about forced sexual encounters. According to that study, coercion ranks with group sex and anonymity in the basic repertoire of sexual reverie. Among lesbians surveyed, rape was the most frequent sexual fantasy. But such variations are less significant than the similarities between homo- and heterosexuals, at least in the realm of imagination. Dreams of romantic interludes, the meat and potatoes of women's pulp fiction, ranked far behind those of rape and promiscuity.

Porn, a free-market enterprise if there ever was one, reflects this hierarchy with brutal precision. Those who yearn for an erotic literature of full-blown characterization, where men and women exchange intimacies as in life, are at the wrong counter of the psychic emporium. What folks want in a stroke book (or film) is freedom from the trammels of personality. Those who long for realism in pornography—ordinary acts with plausible partners—ought to be condemned to dream that way. What we want, in those moments of escape from tangibility, is excess and extremity.

If there's no great porn film—not even *Last Tango in Paris,* for all its value as dramatic tour de force—that's because there's no unity in people's fantasies; some of us will always think a stick of butter is for bread. The result is that most pornography is an anthology of acts, only some of which arouse a given viewer. We wait out the rest, and sometimes we turn away. One man's ecstasy is another woman's boredom.

It's not only men who eroticize male power. That ought to be evident from a casual stroll through the world of Harlequin Romance. "Your passport to a dream" is how these hundred-million-selling bonbons are advertised; and the men in these books are as monumentally armored as any creation of gay pornography. "No trace of tenderness softened the harsh pressure of his mouth on hers," writes Elizabeth Graham in *Mason's Ridge.* "There was only a savagely punishing intentness of purpose that cut off her breath until her senses reeled and her body sagged against the granite hardness of his."

Though the penises are transmuted into "hard fingers brushing her arm . . . and bringing an urgent flutter of reaction from her pulse," there can be no mistaking the harsh polarities of gender in these books, or the roles men and women are bound to at the risk of offending each other's expectations. They are "permeated by phallic worship," writes critic Ann Snitow. "Cruelty, callousness, coldness, menace, are all equated with maleness and treated as part of the package." There's not a moan or metaphor in the Harlequin oeuvre that can be called sexually explicit, but in form and intention they're pure pornography. "The novels have no plot in the usual sense," Snitow continues. "There is no society, only surroundings." The women who anchor these books exist "in a constant state of potential sexuality." They "have no past, no context. They live only in the eternal present of sexual feelings, the absorbing interest in the erotic sex object."

This is surely what Steven Marcus had in mind when he described pornography as "a relentless circumscription of reality, with its tendency, on the one hand, to exclude from itself everything that is not sexual and, on the other, to include everything into itself by sexualizing all of reality." For Marcus, the neo-Freudian and lately neoconservative, this appropriation poses the terrible threat of regression into infantile sexuality—the bosom of omnipotence we all (reluctantly) leave behind. For Snitow, the radical feminist, the "boundlessness . . . of infant desire and its furious gusto" are something to be cherished; its persistence in fantasy is "a legitimate element in the human lexicon of feelings."

Pornography, Snitow reminds us, is "a memory"—not of events but of feelings: terror, rage, helplessness, and their transcendence through power, devotion, ecstasy. We use it to convert the raw material of degradation and depersonalization into erotic energy. It may be false to the spirit of everything we believe about men and women, love and even lust. But porn is true to fantasy. And fantasy is not fair.

But hold on! If pornography faithfully reflects fantasy, why aren't there homosexual acts in heterosexual films? Though "lesbian" sex is about as common as rape in straight pornography, sex between men virtually never occurs; if two guys so much as touch each other while working over the woman they are sharing, you know you're in for high kink. Indifference does not appear to be the reason for this lapse. The same survey that insists most of us are turned on by thoughts of sexual coercion also reports that homosexual fantasies are common among heterosexuals, and vice versa. Why doesn't pornography pander to that need?

The answer is evident: for straight men, there are grounds to fear arousal from gay pornography, even though, if truth be known, a hard-on does not a homosexual make. If our fantasies are mediated by our fears, so much so that we can't bear to look at how the other half lusts, why *can* we bear to look at the degredation of women? Why is there a market for that?

I've rented a film called *Bittersweet Revenge*. It's as different from *Little Kimmi Johnson* as the Marquis de Sade is from Uncle Remus. Two women—haughty and rejecting—are overpowered and bound, on the pretext that they're part of a drug ring and information must be wrung out of them. The women are whipped between the legs and across the breasts, prodded with clothespins, forced to drink semen from a jar, and left hanging by their hands in the dark. Their tall, dark inquisitioner—equally haughty and cool—never removes an article of *his* clothing, never shows an inkling of passion; he moves in a trance, like the killer in *Halloween*. And though he's finally shot dead by the women, there's no transformation of the victim or reconciliation with the victimizer.

If the other films I've described leave me with the option of insisting I've been watching erotic fairy tales, *Bittersweet Revenge* is all too plausible. Its aura of real destruction leaves me mortified, ashamed of the erection I'd sustained until the situation got to me. "I'll never think of straight sex films as innocent again," I remember telling my video dealer when I returned the tape. "It makes you feel real dirty," he smirked. "It makes you want to take a shower."

This, too, is pornography, available for home viewing by anyone who can muster up the two bucks and the gall. Though it has no explicit sex at all, its prurient intentions are inescapable; though it resembles *The Texas Chainsaw Massacre,* the unrelieved focus on a woman's pain at the hands of a man sets it apart from even the most brutal splatter film. Its mood is neither gothic nor fantastic; you can't laugh at its excess or take refuge in its special effects. *Bittersweet Revenge* is acted, but in a style that's utterly, grimly verité.

To feel the threat a film like this must pose to women, I have to perform a transformation of my own. I have to imagine a film about a slave owner tormenting black women, or a Nazi and Jews. I have to imagine a whole genre of pornography in which straight men torture gay men. ("It makes you feel real dirty," says the dealer, and I run screaming from the store.) Or the whipping of a dog, and what it would mean if I could watch such a film for ninety minutes with an intermittent erection.

Why does the presence of a woman as victim give me permission to last through *Bittersweet Revenge?* The answer reveals the power relationships that inform our desires. In this culture, at this time, men see animals as innocent, blacks as underserving victims, gays as threatened—at least, some of us do; but we see women as powerful, desirable, implicated in their condition, and needing to be punished. Pornography is misogynist because the culture is misogynist, not the other way around. Sexual fantasies reflect—or, more precisely, refract—society. The libido is not a fixed and timeless entity; it is part of the dialectic between the world and our selves.

Anti-porn activists are right to regard pornography as, at best, a joke at their expense, and, at worst, a threat. They correctly read the hostility and contempt in its playfulness, the reality of rape in its rituals. They are right to fear its intentions. But need they fear its consequences?

The question is being thrust upon science with a bizarre urgency these days. Federally funded experiments are under way to measure the levels of androgen in the blood of boys exposed to *Playboy*; researchers are testing the effect of repeated exposure to images of sexual violence on the capacity of men to respond with horror to the real thing. The underlying assumption in these experiments is that pornography functions as an intoxicant, under whose influence men commit violence against women, as well as promiscuous and homosexual acts. Though the ambitions of individual scientists vary, those who are funding the research have been quite precise about what they hope to achieve: a Justice Department memo predicts "an action plan that will evolve from this process [with] the potential of linking theoretical research to clinical research to real world criminal justice intervention techniques on a national scale."

So the aim of those in government who seek to ban pornography is much broader: they want to use the criminal justice system to bolster the nuclear family; regulating fantasy is, for them, a prelude to intruding upon the most fundamental aspects of sexual choice. Many of the women spearheading the current drive against pornography would ultimately find the choices they have made subject to judicial review by their former allies. The revolution, too, will swallow its young.

Thirty years ago, when Alfred Kinsey demonstrated that sexual acts we weren't allowed to watch or read about were going on all around us anyway—that extramarital sex and homosexual experimentation were commonplace—"humanist" critics of that time were aghast. No less a personage than Lionel Trilling railed against Kinsey's "tendency to divorce sex from the other manifestations of life," and warned of a body of sexual knowledge so devastating that it could smother "the mystery and wildness of spirit." The "bland tyranny" Trilling saw coming down the pike is now upon us, although today it's not the liberal imagination or its libertarian fringe that is bent on setting science loose on sex. Trilling saw the authoritarian edge behind this process of materializing desire. "The act of understanding becomes an act of control," he warned. Regulating behavior through the manipulation of symbols and signs is what the New Pornology is all about.

We have been through this before. The Women's Christian Temperance Union was concerned with men leaving their homes, beating their wives and children, squandering their wages on drink. Alcohol was the *cause* of this behavior, Carrie Nation argued; ban the booze, and men would be proper husbands and fathers. The WCTU went so far as to urge a ban on tobacco as well, since men who smoked were likely to drink. They managed to convince Congress, not because their agenda was a kind of deformed feminism, but because it tapped a fundamentalist reaction to the modern era.

The anti-porn agenda is prohibitionism writ lib. It, too, depends for its success on an alliance with fundamentalists whose ultimate interests run counter to those of feminism. It, too, lays the blame for sexual violence on an "intoxicant." And it, too, imagines all men as the servants of their impulses, incapable of conscience or analysis. In the New Pornology, male sexual behavior is reduced to a sequence of responses to stimuli. There is no room for individual responsibility, not to mention environmental conditioning. Our lusts, our yearnings, our ambivalences, are merely the products of a hormonal cocktail. And we can curb desire by putting America on the wagon.

But even if sexually explicit imagery were contraband, popular entertainment would still be permeated with misogyny. Sexism would still be used to entice men into consuming products. Adolescent boys would still react to the sight of a woman in postures of "submission and display" with a rush of androgen. Even if a network of censors (masquerading as commissioners of civil rights) succeeded in scrubbing iconography off all offensive sexuality, the attitudes that make such imagery effective would remain. Those assumptions would continue to express themselves in real behavior. The danger would not pass.

Though it's no longer fashionable to insist, as Susan Sontag did in "The Pornographic Imagination," that "all art is dangerous," let's admit that *some* of it is. Among the works I'd include in that category are *Birth of a Nation* and T. S. Eliot's anti-Semitic poetry (". . . The rats are underneath the piles/The jew is underneath the lot"). These are compelling works of art which arouse socially destructive passions. Our critique of these passions diffuses the danger and makes it palatable as art.

Were racism not an active agent in our culture, we might be able to read *Amos and Andy* as a pornographic charade about black people, and enjoy its conversion of oppression into comic sensuality. Were homophobia not a clear and present danger, we might be able to grant

Eddie Murphy's antigay routines the benefit of moral doubt. Is his comedy an attempt to overcome the trauma of black manhood by creating an inferior class of white males? Does his audience laugh to overcome its own terror of homosexuality?

But if I consider Eddie Murphy a pornographic comedian, how can I take *Bittersweet Revenge* less seriously? The answer is a revelation of my status as a man. I have nothing to fear from erotica; but in racist art (with its resonance of anti-Semitism) and in homophobic art, I feel the hot breath of retribution. As long as I am the object of such pornography, it makes me uneasy, and I look upon those who enjoy it as potential assailants. But when I become the subject, as a consumer of erotica, the threat abruptly melts away. If I lived in a world where straight men typically enjoyed films in which homosexuals are tortured, where magazines featured lavish spreads of gay men splayed across the hoods of cars like big game trophies, I might feel differently. (Indeed, I'd be afraid to walk down the street.) But since I don't live in such a world, I can afford to eroticize violence, even when it's directed against folks like me.

If I insist that pornography is not the cause of violence against women, mustn't I accept the same claim from all those people who line up to buy Eddie Murphy albums? Mustn't I grant those folks the right to engage in a ritual of personal transformation, and admit that it's not the root of my oppression?

I think I understand where the rage of anti-porn activists comes from. I, too, feel the weight of sexism. I, too, struggle against its definitions. I share a vulnerability to violence at the hands of men. And I know how tempting it is to wallow in helplessness before representations of that rage. But trying to destroy dangerous art is like shooting at a rainbow; you can never hit the source. No sooner do you succeed at banning one offensive work than others, more covert, arise. The intention remains intact and all the more dangerous for the illusion that, in attaining power over a text, we have managed to control the condition it describes.

Some day, Little Kimmi Johnson will rescue Charley from the midway, and together they'll ride off into the sunset (of polymorphous perversity?). When a film of that scenario is *hot,* we'll know the world has changed. We won't know that, if such a film cannot be made.

Barbara Wilson

THE EROTIC LIFE OF FICTIONAL CHARACTERS

I've written sex scenes between my characters for a good ten years, written how they feel about their bodies and their lovers. Sometimes I've described them making love, sometimes just fantasizing.

Until recently I've almost always taken those scenes out or modified them before publication. Timidity, uncertainty about the quality of the writing, a desire to remain private, to protect myself, a desire not to limit my audience, internalized homophobia, fear of exposure. All these reasons and one more: a serious question about standards, my own perhaps more than any real or imaginary censor. The old question, *Is literature supposed to have sex in it or not?* is not as relevant as *How can I, as a lesbian writer, write about sex in a way that is meaningful to me?* Is it enough that the sex scenes stand on their own, or should they be used in the pursuit of a larger goal: to further the reader's understanding of the characters' lives and thus the understanding of the reader's own life?

I also ask myself, what is the difference between writing a scene or a story that is meant primarily to arouse and writing a scene or a story about characters who express the erotic side of their nature with each other? Or is there no difference? Why, if I can write a description of two women making love in one of my novels or stories, do I balk at the idea of writing a five- or ten-page piece of erotica that also shows two women making love? As a writer I am interested in learning to write about sex well, interested in new ways of describing very time-worn acts, interested in seeing if I can find words for sensations I might have experienced. Why then not take to writing erotica as a form of practice, as a pleasure, as an end in itself? Readers have found my sex scenes arousing. What is the difference if they remain embedded in a novel or story and if they stand alone?

When I began to write my novel *Cows and Horses,* I knew that the sexuality of the protagonist, Bet Gallagher, would be very important to the story. Why? Because she was a woman in deep unrecognized mourning for the loss of her ten-year relationship with Norah Goldman. I didn't want her to understand her sexuality or to be able to express her grief other than through her sexuality. There was something I wanted to explore, and that is how sex is connected to loss. How, when we feel empty and abandoned, we sometimes turn to something powerful that we think will fill us. In this case Bet became involved with a woman who was a highly inappropriate partner for her, not necessarily sexually unsuitable, but inappropriate in terms of compatibility, expectations, background—all the things couples manuals tell you to watch out for. Possibly their personal incompatibility made the sexual encounters between Bet and her butch lover more highly charged. Bet was always resisting getting involved with Kelly; part of the erotic intensity came from the knowledge that this was "wrong" for her.

When I look back on this novel I see that the sexual scenes between Bet and Kelly drew on certain conventions of erotica. There was first of all the fact that the characters hardly knew each other. Second was the fact that Bet realized almost immediately that Kelly was not the right person for her but was attracted against her will, again a staple of erotic writing. Third were the sex scenes themselves, in which Bet often began by resisting Kelly, if not physically then psychologically, and ended by "giving in" to her. The basic scenario did not really depart significantly from a soft-porn or erotic model in its message that we are often attracted to the wrong people against our will and that "wrongness" and "resistance" can play a major role in heightening erotic attraction.

I'm more aware now than when I wrote the book of some of the conventions I was using; at the time, however, I was gropingly insistent that these sex scenes served another purpose in the novel than just to titillate the reader. Sex was the arena in which Bet was playing out her grief: Bet's sex with Kelly, her memories of sex with Norah, and Bet and Norah's quarrels over their past sex life were all important in trying to describe Bet's feeling of emptiness, her anger at Norah for betraying and leaving her, and her gradual move toward recognition and acceptance of her loss.

In writing the sex scenes themselves I tried hard not to objectify the characters too much (for reasons of feminism and curiosity as to whether it could be done), but to present their sexuality as an integral part of their personalities. Kelly made love the way she did because she was Kelly; Bet responded and made love only as Bet, being Bet, could. One of the methods I chose to keep objectification at a minimum was to describe the lovemaking in terms of metaphor. I wanted to get beyond mechanistic descriptions of what our limbs and organs do during sex to what sex actually feels like. In writing these descriptions I at first relied on trying to conjure up what making love feels like to me, but as I wrote and rewrote them the descriptions became closer to what I imagined sex might feel like to Bet. I knew her quite well by then, knew her childhood, her hopes and fears. Her sexuality was something I had to know about her too.

The second way I tried to minimize voyeurism is that I never, in the course of the entire novel, described Bet physically. I did describe the rest of the characters in great detail, but Bet was physically transparent. I hoped in this way to prevent the reader from looking at her as she made love and from getting an erotic charge from the sight of Bet's body. I wanted to keep the reader's eye focused on the person Bet was making love with, so that the process would be less like watching two women make love and more like making love oneself. In much erotica we already identify with at least one of the participants, but I wanted to increase identification with Bet as much as possible. Not so that the reader would get a greater thrill, though perhaps that was also an effect, but so that the reader would understand what sex meant to Bet. One of the end results of this desire not to objectify Bet was that Kelly became objectified, for she was the character who was *seen*.

There are five explicit sex scenes in *Cows and Horses,* and I worried a great deal about them. I worried about exposing myself as a sexual being (if I could write about lesbian sex I obviously must have experienced it, and now people would know for sure), I worried about the authenticity (does it feel anything like this to anyone else?), and I worried about the critical reaction (if I wrote about sex and wasn't Norman Mailer, could I still be a literary writer?).

The heavens didn't fall after the book was published, even though the review in *Publishers Weekly* warned that "the graphic sex may preclude a wide audience." In fact, ironically (predictably?), the sex scenes were all that some lesbian reviewers liked about the novel. They couldn't understand that I was writing the story of a woman's grief and how she tried to mask it through sex; they said it was a pity the book was so "bewildering" in its focus on a depressed and "boring" person because I did write erotica awfully well.

For every reader who said to me, "My lover died and for two years after that all I did was have sex," or "That was a wonderful description of the grieving process," there were three readers who said, "Great sex scenes!"

I had become an erotic writer. I had become an author in danger of having her pages turned down.

Statements by Erotic Writers,
Photographers, Poets, and Artists

ON EROS AND
EROTIC ART

ADELE ALDRIDGE *(artist):* "For me, making love and making art are about passion, rapture, roots, growth, regeneration, explosions, the cosmos. I often feel sexual energy while drawing, and creative energy while making love."

ANTLER *(poet):* "Eroticism is our nature, in our nature—like rings on a tree, ripples on a lake, branching of antlers, or the zen and cosmicity of bird migration. Nature is the author of eros, more than any single poet or photographer. The erotic is something much bigger than our individual love-ache yearnings."

MARK I. CHESTER *(photographer, writer):* "Somewhere in my karmic past I was forced to write on the metaphysical blackboard of life, one million times, I believe in the beauty and power of sex, sexuality and eroticism. It is a refrain that I just can't get out of my head. It is constant, like the tide washing against the shore. I am suspended in its powerful undertow and I just can't get away. The pain of living is so beastly and so great that it is unbearable. But then the joy of sex, sexuality and eroticism is so beautiful and so powerful that it almost makes life bearable. I can't help it: I believe in hard dicks."

CHARLIE CLARK *(photographer):* "My erotic work is an outgrowth of my dissatisfaction with the too plastic, or too sexually graphic, images of women found in the media. I have been seeking to produce nude images of men and women which are neither overtly sexual nor oppressive, experimenting with forms based on the works of Edward Weston and Ruth Bernhard, using friends, mostly in their 30s and 40s, as models."

Lucien Clergue *(photographer):* "It is up to you, then, to understand the women and men who are posing for you and to allow them to feel natural. You don't know why they have consented to pose for you; in many instances, their bodies are not all that they are exposing. . . . You are responsible to your model first and your art second. Besides, the model *must* participate in your creative exaltations—otherwise you can't hope for any sort of success."

Tee Corinne *(photographer, writer):* "The celebration of sexuality in visual erotica has been central to my work for the last fourteen years. I'm interested in the magic of this kind of imagery: the shield and heraldic forms of labia; the grace with which we touch our own bodies and others'. I love the power of sex in art, the bringing forth of what in Western societies has been both hidden and forbidden. My goal is to produce loving, beautiful, sexy images—pictures that call me back to something essential about the connections women can make between and among ourselves. I also want the images to be a turn-on, to create an adrenaline high, a rush of desire so intense that the act of looking is sexual, the image itself visually consumed, creating a lasting change in each viewer's awareness of self, sexuality, and art."

Morgan Cowin *(photographer):* "Most of my subjects are not classic beauties (I even have a ninety-two-year-old woman friend whom I long to photograph), but I see something worth celebrating in each of them. Recording their loss of inhibition and their growing freedom to express themselves in an intimate fashion is fascinating to me."

Ruth DeMada *(writer):* "Sex to me is the most serious matter in our culture. I like doing sex. I feel exalted when I do sex the way I like. Sometimes I have felt demeaned by doing sex, but that was when I was younger and exploitable and didn't know better. Besides being fun, sex is sacred, so I write about sex as a hilarious sacred act. One of its purposes is to reach an altered consciousness—levels of prophecy and oneness with the universe. When I write about erotic sex, I feel sexy—I get consumingly horny. I want my readers to react the same way."

GARY EPTING *(artist):* "Sex comes in colors, sometimes like a sunset, sometimes like a cheap TV. As AIDS, homophobia, and censorship continue to grow and the darkness deepens, making erotic art is an essential, vitalizing political act."

NINA GLASER *(photographer):* "I want to cut through and see beyond the foundations of our morality, our politics, our lifestyles. Are they held together with the lifeless string, paper, and tape of a merely utilitarian vision, a vision that confronts us in our dreams and in our isolation? My work celebrates beauty in the human body and finds meaning in our struggles. In success and even in failure, there are moments out of time when we transcend the limits. These are the moments I attempt to capture."

KALEIILIAHI HENKELMANN/MULLER *(artist):* "I view sex as holy communion, and erotic art in the same manner. Erotic art is the expression of one fine art form by another."

DONNA IPPOLITO *(writer, dancer):* "Seeking to discover and affirm what was really mine, I went back to the body. Moving deeply into the physical, I searched for my spirit. I was attempting to inhabit myself fully, to open into myself and let the inner woman take flesh. I began to explore my deepest feelings about desire, passion, touching, being touched. When I was lyrical, I accepted it. When I was vulgar, I accepted it. When I was tender, I accepted it. When I was angry, I accepted that too. There was no contradiction between instinct and love when I simply let both flow."

LENORE KANDEL *(poet):* "Poetry is never compromise. It is the manifestation/translation of a vision, an illumination, an experience. If you compromise the vision you become a blind prophet. . . . Euphemisms chosen by fear are a covenant with hypocrisy and will immediately destroy the poem and eventually destroy the poet. Any form of censorship, whether mental, moral, emotional, or physical, whether from the inside out or the outside in, is a barrier against self-awareness. . . . One primary responsibility on the part of the poet [is] that he tell the truth as he sees it. That he tell it as beautifully, as amazingly, as he can; that he ignite his own sense of wonder; that he work alchemy within the language."

DAVID LEBE (photographer): "I make sexual art because it's there to make; part of the whole. I simply refuse to censor it. Sexuality is part of everyone's personal, social, and political lives, even if most people conspire to pretend that it's not. Being a gay man, I'm aware of the pain and the harm this pretending can cause, and something in me refuses to participate in the conspiracy."

M. E. MAX (poet): "I see the erotic as both bright and dark: bright for the beauty and pleasure that spring from it; dark because it touches our deepest, sometimes violent, instincts and convictions. While much modern fiction is saturated with facile sexuality, we need more writers and artists who will explore the eroticism of our time in depth."

DEENA METZGER (poet, novelist): "I've devoted my life, personally and professionally, to the exploration of the relationship between eros and peace, eros and healing. The erotic, in all its dimensions, is the force that binds us to each other, and so it has personal, social, and political consequence. Nature is eros itself, and culture—when it is vital—is grounded in eros. The heart depends on eros. Perhaps it is now our task to eroticize Mind."

DUANE MICHALS (photographer): "What is this want that makes me turn to look at you? I do not know. It is of me as is my breath. Do you tell yourself to breathe? It is my nature, and being nature is not right or wrong or good or bad, but innocent of purpose. It is my body's music and its truth. And I become a queer and peculiar thing, out of harmony, when I silence my song because you find it inappropriate."

TOM MILLEA (photographer): Art is the search for meaning, the experience of meaning made visible. In a work of art, soul meets soul; essence meets essence. I seek contact, intimate contact, with other human beings through my work. Art is selfless love. It is the continuous removal of veils in order to expose the soul—the individual soul, the common soul, the universal soul. Human beings making love is the condensed form of this contact. It allows me to see and photograph the entire range of human emotions: passion, tenderness, intimacy, surrender, anger, and giving. It is the gateway to the most noble aspect of the human soul and the deepest pits of hell."

HENRY MILLER (writer, painter): "I was talking one day to some Japanese girls. They said they were disgusted with 'porno' films. Sheer dirt. I don't agree. I say it's unnatural for anyone to turn his eyes away no matter how lousy the films are. It's a cock and a cunt and they are fucking and it's exciting. Erotic literature and art after all is such an elemental force. Fucking is more than sex. It's just as magical and mysterious as talking about God or the nature of the Universe."

RON RAFFAELLI *(photographer):* "The first time our parents punished us when we were caught in the innocent act of sex-play, a sensual Garden of Eden vanished which it is the responsibility of the erotic artist to recreate and vivify. The laughter, fondling, licking, and kissing are natural human manifestations, but once abandoned they are difficult to rediscover. The role of the erotic artist must be more than simply to entertain: I must strike an innocent, long-silent chord in the viewer's imagination—that part of us which unabashedly plays with our sexuality, experiments, laughs at our awkwardness, and celebrates every sensuous success."

ANNE RICE *(novelist):* "What I find sexy has to have a certain mixture of tenderness, tension, and balance. . . . I regard my writing of pornography to be a real moral cause. And I don't want a bunch of fascist, reactionary feminists kicking in the door of my consciousness with their jackboots and telling me that sadomasochism isn't politically correct. . . . Our artists and writers on all levels should be able to be mad men and mad women. That's the function of Art. We want our mad men and our mad women to be offensive; we need them to be obscene. That's the way culture works. It's only when you have a free artistic marketplace that people have the freedom to create the classics of tomorrow."

MAGI SCHWARTZ *(poet):* "Frankly, making a public commitment to erotica has been a way to thumb my nose at a repressed sexual upbringing. Inside I was always a potboiler; outside, the mores of my family were sitting on the lid. Divorce and parental death freed me to explore my sensuous nature and erotic mind-set. I blossomed from a tight clitoral bud into a wild flower of sensations. Delighted to have reached this state, I share the elixir with whoever cares to sip from the cup."

JEANLOUP SIEFF *(photographer):* "Our eroticism is as unique as our fingerprints. If there's one area in which we are truly alone, it is that of sensual pleasure and fantasy, creating in us, as they do, the vital impulse of original desire. Any representation of the human body, whether photographic or pictorial, is imbued with a privileged moment of voyeurism and a simple need to conserve that moment."

STEPHEN SIEGEL *(photographer):* "I hope to confront the viewer with images of states of feeling, and not with facts alone, however beautiful. The bodies I photograph are alive; they have nerves and brains; they move and speak; they muse and laugh and sing; they are you and me."

ANNIE SPRINKLE *(photographer, performance artist):* "I find that people will do things for a camera that they wouldn't normally do. It's a great excuse to have fun, put on sexy little outfits, be a voyeur, an exhibitionist, to be creative, to break taboos, to get turned on, to have sex, to have orgasms. The pictures are just a souvenir, a document of the experience."

MARCO VASSI *(writer):* "Sex is a key to doorways of knowing. For me it has been a yoga through which new qualities of self evolved. Like the alchemist who works with potions for decades and in the process brings about a transmutation of his essence, I have spent all my conscious life since the age of eight mixing elements in the crucible of sex, sifting enormous amounts of material to produce a few grams of pure substance. After completing the entire route, I find it was all simply a doorway to devotion."

Michael Rubin

Horseman, Pass By

Never in his life had Sidney sat on the back of a horse. But his grandfather, his grandfather had been reared with them back in Rakhov. Not long before the old man died, he had told Sidney in the rasping remains of a voice of the smells of Carpathian summers that used to drive him mad. So mad that he would find himself stripping off all his clothes and, stealing his milky blue mare from the barn without his stern father's permission, he would ride out into the mountains to get drunk with her on those sweet summer smells. Sometimes they would be driven so wild as to plunge into the river together, the steep muddy bank oozing between hooves and toes until the earth gave way beneath them, the mare sinking beneath the waves, then surfacing to swim across the waters while he floated above her, his legs drifting into her seaweed tail, his hands full of the thick wet silk of her mane, until they could mount the far bank and race naked and barebacked through the hot high meadows, his flesh sweating into the flesh of his mount as they pulled together up and down and up and down so that often he came all over her flank and continued to ride and came again, at long last limping home to be led into the barn by the stableman, chiding Sidney's grandfather but full of amused understanding as he washed both the boy and his milky blue mare with hot water until they had melted apart and he could be carried to bed exhausted by bliss.

David Steinberg

THE HIGH PRIESTESS

The high priestess sits at the entrance to the temple, her eyes open and still, her hands folded in her lap. From across the great chessboard plane I approach her. She never looks away, yet never looks at me, never moves, never gives a clue if she notices me or not. I ache to be seen by her, keep moving closer to her, despite her stillness, because of her stillness. As I reach her, she opens her arm to one side, spreading her robe into a curtain, taking me inside, into her temple, the home of wisdom.

Her robe is white and full-flowing, white and rippling with grey shadows. I pass under her arm into the folds, the billowing curtain all around me like wind in high grasses, like smoke in a still room, like Northern lights, like dance. And then there is nothing but the stillness, the stillness and everywhere the magic, which is everything and nothing. All direction is gone: I am snow blind. Even the ground is silken curtain calling, soothing, stroking. I am to be exploded into a million droplets of whatever I have been. I can feel the charge building. I ache to be blown apart, and also I am afraid. Only the texture, and somewhere too a scent, sweet and mysterious—only the texture and the smell of the flowing whiteness keep me from running away.

Lenore Kandel

SEVEN OF VELVET

brocade and tapestry, you lean back
your head against blue velvet
the sun dancing sparks of light across your naked skin
you lie there, your balls nibbled by teen-age succubi
and your hands on their snaky heads
their moonglow fingers twining around your rigid cock
and their little tongues darting and licking
as you stroke their smoky hair

across the room, I lie between the paws of a tiger
almost faint from the scent of his violent fur
he holds me to his belly and his paws bind me
his huge head purring like thunder at my shoulder
his white belly is velvet against me
and I am velvet to him

slowly, subtly, his paws tighten around me
and he enters within my body
I look at you from the embrace of the tiger
and our eyes meet in wonder
little tongues, little hands, move faster
and you cry out as you come
spurting a fountain of flowers
into the tiger's mouth

4

EROTIC DIFFERENCES BETWEEN MEN AND WOMEN

Introduction: Part 4

The erotic impulse could be the basis for a joyous dance of the genders, a lens through which we could better understand each other as men and women, a medium through which we could better understand the masculine and feminine within each of us. Heterosexually speaking, it could be a profound opportunity to experience a little of that which we are not and cannot be, an honoring of otherness, a way of glimpsing the world on the other side of the gender looking glass.

In place of these intriguing possibilities, what we often experience in erotic connection between the genders is more a tug of war—the battle of the sexual marketplace. Men trying to *get sex* from women. Women resenting the sexual *preoccupations* of men. Men angry that women *have* sex and won't *give it* to them. Women angry that men try to take something from them through sex.

We become embroiled in elaborate sexual power games, overt and covert. As Wilhelm Reich pointed out, sex becomes a commodity, whose value is inflated by induced scarcity. As with all commodities, a primary question becomes who gets what from whom and at what cost. Implicitly and explicitly, sex comes to be exchanged for money, financial security, attention, personal favors, the illusion of affection.

Instead of a dance of love and mystery, we too often experience the erotic as an arena of manipulation. And we feel the grand emptiness of it and then the anger, confusion, and tears—all of which we turn against the impulse itself, as if it were to blame.

A great deal of this gender-based sexual confusion and pain derives from the radically different ways that men and women are acculturated with regard to sexuality. The erotic training of boys is so radically different from that of girls that we might as well have been raised in entirely different cultures. Indeed, it can be helpful to think of our situation in just those terms. If we were to come together as, say, Iroquois and Japanese, curious to learn about each other's customs, we might be able to perceive, without judgment, our different perspectives on eros. One person could say, "Among my people, sex is generally a prelude to intimacy, a way of making oneself emotionally vulnerable." Another person could respond, "Really? Among my people it is just the opposite—emotional intimacy is required before a person would feel safe enough to allow the vulnerability of being sexual." No need to make one right, the other wrong. No need to laugh at or resent how different from each other we are.

Almost from birth, adults relate to boys' bodies differently than they do to girls'. Boys are held less, fondled less, allowed to cry longer before being answered with touch. Later, they learn not to be sensual because sensuality is defined as feminine, and there is a masculine identity to be forged in rejecting the dominant figure of the mother. Boys are taught that it is not OK to want to be held and comforted, not OK to want to be softly stroked. What is OK, even required, is to want sex. All the urge for touch, comfort, care, gentleness, and intimacy is condensed into the single outlet of sex.

Meanwhile, girls are taught that sex is their enemy. Sex is a beast, a male beast, and it is the female task to tame this beast. Sex contains the danger of pregnancy, and also the danger of destroying one's status among the society of *good girls*. Sex as pleasure is permitted if it's essentially an expression of love for a partner, but sex for its own sake—lust, desire—is unfeminine.

So the boys, and later the men, try to get all of what they have compressed into sex from the girls and women, who have reduced sexual desire to a romantic nicety. Inevitably, the males feel rejected and angry; the females feel put upon, objectified, and angry. We all bleed. And the original erotic gender dance is lost, along with all its potential for magic, healing, pleasure, intimacy, and fulfillment.

This section provides an opportunity to explore some gender-based perspectives on eroticism, to look at the erotic issues that are particular to being men and women in our culture. How is desire aroused differently in women than in men? What are the consequences of teaching men to pursue sexual experience at all cost, while teaching women to be afraid of sex? How do the primal childhood experiences of boys and girls—for example, the fear of being subsumed into a monumental, ever-present mother, versus the fear of being abandoned by an absent, emotionally distant father—differently affect sexual desire in men and women later in life? What is the effect of changing sex-role expectations on how women and men relate sexually, what we expect from each other, what we expect from ourselves, what we enjoy, what we fear, what leaves us cold? How do we address the difficulties of communicating erotically across the chasm that separates boy-culture from girl-culture?

The section opens with three perspectives on how the erotic impulse affects women. Writer Anaïs Nin takes an archetypal and almost traditional point of view on what women want from erotic experience, emphasizing the importance of relational context, emotional grounding in love, and the primacy of emotional continuity. More radically, she insists categorically that sexual desire in women be accorded every bit as much legitimacy and respect as it is in men.

Writer/editor Susie Bright offers a decidedly more contemporary look at the same issues. Where Nin claimed (in 1974) that "woman has not made the separation between love and sensuality which man has made," Bright wants immediately to "get one thing straight" about women's erotic yearnings: namely, "some women want the stars, some the sleaze. Our sexual minds travel everywhere and embrace every emotion."

Feminist writer Paula Webster amplifies this clearing of erotic territory for women. Extrapolating from her own experience, she looks at how difficult it is for women to allow their erotic desires to move in directions that have been designated taboo or unfeminine, even in these supposedly liberated times. Urging women to respect the emotional difficulties they will face in moving beyond the limited sexual world of *good girls,* she nevertheless encourages them to "break taboos, rebel against prohibitions, and rally around pleasure in fantasy and action" as a means of personal empowerment.

Shifting to erotic issues that are specific to men, Nancy Friday takes a sympathetic look at how men deal with their erotic conflicts. She explores the contradiction men feel between wanting to enter deeply into erotic/sexual feeling and being afraid of becoming overly dependent on women; the conflict between men's almost worshipful attitude toward beauty in women and their rage at being repeatedly rejected by their (self-created) objects of desire; the war between men's need to establish independence from the primal mother figure and their feelings of dependence that arises from the power of their (hetero)sexual desire.

Jungian psychologist Thomas Moore offers a look at the archetypal role of eros in shaping masculinity. Moore distinguishes carefully between the "light and desire" of the true shining phallos and the dangerously exaggerated, caricatured expressions of erotic masculinity we so commonly witness. Photographer Nan Goldin discusses the dilemmas of establishing erotic contact across the gender gulf, describing in starkly realistic terms both the power and danger of sexual attraction, how "the mythology of romance contradicts the reality of coupling," how sex can become "a forum in which struggles in a relationship are defused or intensified."

Finally, two poems by Robert Bly and Carolyn Kleefeld offer decidedly differing male and female perspectives on erotic desire and union, while sharing a profound appreciation for the depth and wonder of human sexuality that transcends all gender.

Anaïs Nin

EROTICISM IN WOMEN

From my personal observation, I would say that woman has not made the separation between love and sensuality which man has made. The two usually are combined in woman; she needs either to love the man she gives herself to or to be loved by him. After lovemaking, she seems to need the assurance that it is love and that the act of sexual possession is part of an exchange which is dictated by love. Men complain that women demand reassurance or expressions of love. The Japanese recognized this need, and in ancient times it was an absolute rule that after a night of lovemaking, the man had to produce a poem and have it delivered to his love before she awakened. What was this but the linking of lovemaking to love?

I believe women still mind a precipitated departure, a lack of acknowledgment of the ritual which has taken place; they still need the words, the telephone call, the letter, the gestures which make the sensual act a particular one, not anonymous and purely sexual.

This may or may not disappear in modern woman, intent on denying all of her past selves, and she may achieve this separation of sex and love which, to my belief, diminishes pleasure and reduces the heightened quality of lovemaking. For lovemaking is enhanced, heightened, intensified by its emotional content. You might compare the difference to a solo player and the vast reaches of an orchestra.

We are all engaged in the task of peeling off the false selves, the programmed selves, the selves created by our families, our culture, our religions. It is an enormous task because the history of women has been as incompletely told as the history of blacks. Facts have been obscured. Some cultures such as the Indian, Cambodian, Chinese, and Japanese have made their sensual life very accessible and familiar through their male artists. But many times, when women have wanted to reveal the facets of their sensuality, they have been suppressed. Not in as obvious a way as the burning of D. H. Lawrence's works, or the banning of Henry Miller or James Joyce, but in one long, continuous disparagement by the critics. Many women resorted to using men's names for their work to bypass prejudice. Only a few years ago, Violette Leduc wrote the most explicit, eloquent, moving descriptions of love between women. She was introduced to her public by Simone de Beauvoir. Yet every review I read was a moral judgment upon her openness; Henry Miller's characters—merely an objection to language. In the case of Violette Leduc it was upon the character herself.

Violette Leduc in *La Bâtarde* is utterly free:

> Isabelle pulled me backwards, she laid me down on the eider-down, she raised me up, she kept me in her arms: she was taking me out of a world where I had never lived so that she could launch me into a world I had not yet reached; the lips opened mine a little, they moistened my teeth. The too fleshy tongue frightened me; but the strange virility didn't force its way in. Absently, calmly, I waited. The lips roved over my lips. My heart was beating too hard and I wanted to prolong the sweetness of the imprint, the new experience brushing at my lips. Isabelle is kissing me, I said to myself. She was tracing a circle around my mouth, she was en-circling the disturbance, she laid a cool kiss in each corner, two staccato notes of music on my lips; then her mouth pressed against mine once more, hibernating there. . . . We were still hugging each other, we both wanted to be swallowed up by the other. . . . As Isabelle lay crushed over my gaping heart I wanted to feel her enter it. She taught me to open into flower. . . . Her tongue, her little flame, softened my muscles, my flesh. . . . A flower opened in every pore of my skin. . . .

We have to shed self-consciousness. Women will have to shed their imitation of Henry Miller. It is all very well to treat sensuality with humor, with caricature, with bawdiness, but that is another way of relegating it to the casual, unimportant areas of experience.

Women have been discouraged from revealing their sensual na-ture. When I wrote *Spy in the House of Love* in 1954, serious critics called Sabina a nymphomaniac. The story of Sabina is that in ten years of married life, she had known two lovers and one platonic friendship with a homosexual. It was the first study of a woman who tries to separate love from sensuality as man does, to seek sensual freedom. It was termed pornographic at the time. One of the "pornographic" passages:

> They fled from the eyes of the world, the singer's prophetic, harsh, ovarian prologues. Down the rusty bars of ladders to the undergrounds of the night propitious to the first man and woman at the beginning of the world, where there were no words by which to possess each other, no music for serenades, no presents to court with, no tournaments to impress and force a yielding, no secondary instruments, no adornments, necklaces, crowns to subdue, but only one ritual, a joyous, joyous, joyous, joyous impaling of woman on man's sensual mast.

Another passage from *Spy,* labeled pornographic by the critics:

> His caresses were so delicate that they were almost like a teasing, an evanescent challenge which she feared to respond to as it might vanish. His fingers teased her, and withdrew when they had aroused her, his mouth teased her and then eluded hers, his face and body came so near, espoused her every limb, and then slid away into the darkness. He would seek every curve and nook he could exert the pressure of his warm slender body against and suddenly lie still, leaving her in suspense. When he took her mouth he moved away from her hands, when she answered the pressure of his thighs, he ceased to exert it. Nowhere would he allow a long enough fusion, but tasing every embrace, every area of her body and then deserting it, as if to ignite only and then elude the final welding. A teasing, warm, trembling, elusive short circuit of the senses as mobile and restless as he had been all day, and here at night, with the street lamp revealing their nudity but not his eyes, she was roused to an almost unbearable expectation of pleasure. He made of her body a bush of roses of Sharon, exfoliating pollen, each prepared for delight.
>
> So long delayed, so long teased that when possession came it avenged the waiting by a long, prolonged, deep thrusting ecstasy.

Women through their confessions reveal a persistent repression. In the diary of George Sand we come upon this incident: Zola courted her and obtained a night of lovemaking. Because she revealed herself as completely unleashed sensually, he placed money on the night table when he left, implying that a passionate woman was a prostitute.

But if you persist in the study of women's sensuality you find what lies at the end of all studies, that there are no generalizations, that there are as many types of women as there are women themselves. One point is established, that the erotic writings of men do not satisfy women, that it is time we write our own, that there is a difference in erotic needs, fantasies, and attitudes. Explicit barracks or clinical language is not exciting to most women. When Henry Miller's first books came out, I predicted women would like them. I thought they would like the honest assertion of desire which was in danger of disappearing in a puritan culture. But they did not respond to the aggressive and brutal language. The *Kama Sutra*, which is an Indian compendium of erotic lore, stresses the need to approach women with sensitivity and romanticism, not to aim directly at physical possession, but to prepare her with romantic courtship. These customs, habits, mores, change from one culture to another and from one country to another. In the first diary by a woman (written in the year 900 A.D.), the *Tales of Gengi,* by Lady Murasaki, the eroticism is extremely subtle, clothed in poetry, and focussed on areas of the body which a Westerner rarely notices: the bare neck showing between the dark hair and the kimono.

There is common agreement about only one thing, that woman's erogenous zones are spread all over her body, that she is more sensitive to caresses, and that her sensuality is rarely as direct, as immediate as man's. There is an atmosphere of vibrations which need to be awakened and have repercussions on the final arousal.

The feminist Kate Millett is unjust to [D. H.] Lawrence. Whatever he asserted ideologically, she was not subtle enough to see that in his work, which is where the true self is revealed, he was very concerned with the response of woman.

My favorite passage is from *Lady Chatterley's Lover:*

Then as he began to move, in the sudden helpless orgasm, there awoke in her new strange thrills rippling inside her. Rippling, rippling, rippling, like a flapping overlapping of soft flames, soft as feathers, running to points of brilliance, exquisite, exquisite and melting her all molten inside. It was like bells rippling up and up to culmination. She lay unconscious of the wild little cries she uttered at the last. . . . she felt the soft bud of him within her stirring, and strange rhythms flushing up into her with a strange rhythmic growing motion, swelling and swelling till it filled all her cleaving consciousness, and then began again the unspeakable motion that was not really motion, but pure deepening whirlpools of sensation swirling deeper and deeper through all her tissue and consciousness, till she was one perfect concentric fluid of feeling, and she lay there crying in unconscious inarticulate cries. The voice out of the uttermost night, the life!

It was a disillusion, in our modern times, to discover that women courting each other did not necessarily adopt more sensuous, more subtle ways of winning desire, but proceeded with the same aggressive, direct attacks as men.

Personally this is what I believe: that brutal language such as Marlon Brando uses in *Last Tango in Paris,* far from affecting woman, repulses her. It disparages, vulgarizes sensuality, it expresses only how the puritan saw it, as low, evil, and dirty. It is a reflection of puritanism. It does not arouse desire. It bestializes sexuality. I find most women object to that as a destruction of eroticism. Among ourselves, we have made the distinction between pornography and eroticism. Pornography treats sexuality grotesquely to bring it back to the animal level. Eroticism arouses sensuality without this need to animalize it. And most of the women I have discussed this with agree they want to develop erotic writing quite distinct from man's. The stance of male writers does not appeal to women: the hunter, the rapist, the one for whom sexuality is a thrust, nothing more.

Linking eroticism to emotion, to love, to a selection of a certain person, personalizing, individualizing, that will be the work of women. There will be more and more women writers who will write out of their own feelings and experiences.

The discovery of woman's erotic capacities and the expression of them will come as soon as women stop listing their griefs against men. If they do not like the hunt, the pursuit, it is up to them to express what they do like and to reveal to men, as they did in oriental tales, the delights of other forms of love games. For the moment their writings are negative. We only hear of what they do not like. They repudiate the role of seduction, of charm, of all the means of bringing about the atmosphere of eroticism they dream about. How can man even become aware of a woman's all-over-the-body sensitivity when it is covered by jeans, which make her body seem like those of his cronies, seemingly with only one aperture of penetration? If it is true that woman's eroticism is spread all over her body, then her way of dressing today is an absolute denial of this factor.

Now, there are women who are restive with the passive role

allotted to them. There are women who dream of taking, invading, possessing as man does. It is the liberating force of our awareness today that we would like to start anew and give each woman her own individual pattern, not a generalized one. I wish there were a sensitive computer which could make for each woman a pattern born of her own unconscious desires. It is the exciting adventure we are engaged in. To question all the histories, statistics, confessions, autobiographies, and biographies, and to create our own individual pattern. For this we are obliged to accept what our culture has so long denied: the need of an individual introspective examination. This alone will bring out the women we are, our reflexes, likes, dislikes, and we will go forth without guilt or hesitations, towards the fullfillment of them. There is a type of man who sees lovemaking as we do; there is at least one for each woman. But first of all, we have to know what we are, what are the habits and fantasies of our bodies, the dictates of our imagination. We not only have to recognize what moves, stirs, arouses us, but how to reach it, attain it. At this point, I would say woman knows very little about herself. And in the end, she has to make her own erotic pattern and fulfillment through a huge amount of half-information and half-revelations.

Puritanism hangs heavily on American literature. It is what makes the male writers write about sexuality as a low, vulgar, animalistic vice. Some women writers have imitated men, not knowing what other model to follow. All they succeeded in doing was in reversing roles: women would behave as men have, make love and leave in the morning without a word of tenderness, or any promise of continuity. Woman became the predator, the aggressor. But nothing was ultimately changed by this. We still need to know how women feel, and they will have to express it in writing.

Young women are getting together to explore their sensuality, to dissipate inhibitions. A young instructor of literature, Tristine Rainer, invited several students at UCLA to discuss erotic writing, to examine why they were so inhibited in describing their feelings. The sense of taboo was strong. As soon as they were able to tell each other their fantasies, their wishes, their actual experiences, the writing, too, was liberated. These young women are seeking new patterns because they are aware that their imitation of men is not leading to freedom. The French were able to produce very beautiful erotic writing because there was no puritan taboo, and the best writers would turn to erotic writing without the feeling that sensuality was something to be ashamed of and treated with contempt.

What we will have to reach, the ideal, is the recognition of woman's sensual nature, the acceptance of its needs, the knowledge of the variety of temperaments, and the joyous attitude towards it as a part of nature, as natural as the growth of a flower, the tides, the movements of planets. Sensuality as nature, with possibilities of ecstasy and joy; in Zen terms, with possibility of *sartori*. We are still under the oppressive puritan rule. The fact that women write about sexuality does not mean liberation. They write about it with the same vulgarization and lower-depths attitude as men. They do not write with pride and joy.

The true liberation of eroticism lies in accepting the fact that there are a million facets to it, a million forms of eroticism, a million objects of it, situations, atmospheres, and variations. We have, first of all, to dispense with guilt concerning its expansion, then remain open to its surprises, varied expressions, and (to add my personal formula for the full enjoyment of it) fuse it with individual love and passion for a particular human being, mingle it with dreams, fantasies, and emotion for it to attain its highest potency. There may have been a time of collective rituals, when sensual release attained its apogee, but we are no longer engaged in collective rituals, and the stronger the passion is for one individual, the more concentrated, intensified, and ecstatic the ritual of one to one can prove to be.

Susie Bright

WHAT TURNS HER ON?

What comes to mind when she shuts her eyes and thinks about sex? What appeals to the female erotic imagination?

Before we can courageously reveal the correct answer to this question, we have to admit it's a tough one. Women's sexual expression has been top secret for as long as we've been wondering. It's such a taboo that women themselves don't share with each other what turns them on. Oh sure, you'll get game show confidences that masquerade as women's desires ("Bachelorette Number One, what color eyes really turn you on?"), but to reveal a woman's lust is to admit a sexual power that not everyone is prepared to bite into.

I began my pursuit of women's erotica looking underneath my girlfriends' beds. Stashed away, but within arm's reach, I discovered back issues of "men's" magazines, Victorian-era ribald short stories, trashy novels with certain pages dog-eared, plain brown wrapper stroke books that seemed to have had a previous owner, classics like *The Story of O* or *Emmanuelle,* and even serious critiques of pornography that were paperclipped to fall open to the *good parts.*

Women build their erotica collections in a dedicated but haphazard manner. One friend raided her brother's bedroom in the early 1960s for pulp novels with lesbian themes. Another holds onto a ragged copy of *Valley of the Dolls* because it was the first risque literature she had ever come across. I can remember when all my junior high girlfriends passed around an excerpt from *The Godfather* (the famous pp. 27–28), describing a woman with a large and insatiable vagina who finally meets her match. One plain brown wrapper in my collection came courtesy of a hitchhiker who left his coat in a friend's car with a copy of *Doris and the Dick* in the front pocket. While many women would never walk into a liquor store to purchase a brand new copy of *Penthouse,* there are always garage sales, wastebaskets and back issues from male friends who never notice that the May 1978 issue has disappeared forever from their stacks.

Feminism opened new opportunities for the female pornographic library. On the blatant side were the feminist erotic pioneers, who proudly issued the first volumes of women's sexual points of view. Nancy Friday's successful fantasy revelations, *My Secret Garden, Forbidden Flowers;* Betty Dodson's call to self-orgasm, *Liberating Masturbation;* Tee Corinne's explicit *Cunt Coloring Book;* and Anaïs Nin's erotic short stories, *Delta of Venus* appeared. Women finally had a handful of literature that could turn us on. Moreover, we could enthusiastically embrace each author as one of our own.

Another side of the feminist movement in publishing revealed a more devious method for women to discover their prurient interest. If it hadn't been for Kate Millett tearing apart Henry Miller's sexist prose in *Sexual Politics,* a lot of us might never have been initiated into one-handed reading. As anti-porn theoreticians made their case, they cited examples as shocking and outrageous as they could find, apparently disregarding that their audience could be just as easily aroused as offended, and probably both.

Since the late 1970s, both mainstream and underground women's erotica have grown in fits and spurts. On the plus side we have an explosion of X-rated home videos, a whopping 60 percent of which are rented by women. Virtually all these movies are made by men, and of moderately-to-extremely poor quality. Women are exasperated but well-practiced in "taking what I can get and making the best of it." This has been the theme song of women's sexual repression. Subverting men's fantasies and using them for our own arousal is the foundation of every woman's under-the-bed bookshelf.

When women have taken a hand in the production of erotica, the results have been underpublicized and thwarted in distribution, but tremendously rewarding. For the first time, we have women producing diverse, contemporary clit's-point-of-view erotica. Note the success of sexual fiction anthologies like *Pleasures, Erotic Interludes* and *Ladies Own Erotica,* of a magazine like the lesbian *On Our Backs,* or women's erotic videos like that of Candida Royalle's Femme Productions and the lesbian video companies Fatale and Tigress.

There's still a lot of confusion about what the label *women's erotica* means. At its worst, it's a commercial term for vapid femininity, a

Harlequin romance with a G-string. The very work *erotic* implies superior value, fine art, an aesthetic which elevates the mind and incidentally stimulates the body. *Women's pornography,* on the other hand, is a contradiction in terms for many people, so convinced are they that pornography represents the darker, gutter side of lust. We are enmeshed in a semantic struggle for which words will describe our sexual creativity. What turns women on? And why have we been silent on the subject for so long? As we begin to reveal, in detail, the complexity and scope of our sexual desires, the appropriate language will evolve.

I recently saw a bumper sticker that said in plain blue letters: *Honor Lustful Women,* and I thought, "Now here's someone who might understand the concept of an earthy woman's erotica or an elegant female pornography."

At least we can get one thing straight before we wander down the path of feminine hedonism: some women want the stars, some the sleaze. Some desire the nostalgia of the ordinary, some the punch of the kinky. And some want all of it. Our sexual minds travel everywhere, and embrace every motion. Our sexual fiction is not so different from men's in terms of physical content. Its uniqueness lies in the detail of our physical description, our vulnerability, and the often confessional quality of our speech in this new territory. Above all, because we have had so little of women's sexual fiction, there is absolutely no formula to follow.

Men's sexual literature has been commercialized and compartmentalized into little catalogs of unvarying formulas. In the same way that women have had to make do with men's porn to satisfy their sexual curiosity, men have had to fit the diversity of their experience into the same pair of tight shoes over and over again. The result is some very stubborn calluses. Men have had the Faustian bargain that if they agree to keep their erotic interests out of their family life, and out of the public eye, they can enjoy the privilege of varied and no-holds-barred voyeurism. But that variety and access only go so far. The embarrassment, shame, and double standard that surround men's license to pornography are stifling, and breed cynicism.

Women's sexual fiction is new, it reflects up our skirts (and jeans) like a patent leather shoe, and it squeaks and pinches, drawing out mysteries and unexpected sighs of pleasure.

How can we tell if it's the real thing? Is there any foundation to women's erotica that will define the new breed?

The most obvious feature of women's erotic writing is the nature of woman's arousal. Her path to orgasm, her anticipation, are front and center in each story. Even if her climax is not part of the scene, it is her sexual banquet that is being served, whether she is the initiator, the recipient, the reciprocator, the voyeur, or the exhibitionist. There are even times when the female reader is drawn to identify with a male character, but it is in the spirit of vicarious interest.

Women's erotica objectifies all the sexual possibilities, which is a more precise way of describing "foreplay." It doesn't matter whether it's describing a lover's body for her own pleasure, or a titillating meal for her consumption. Wake up, class, it's time to redefine *objectification*. We're not talking about being chased around the boardroom or accosted in the street. In sexual literature and art, the process of objectification is a very natural and sensitive one. The reader integrates the words and pictures into her own sexual imagination in order to create heat; this means manipulating images for her own pleasure.

Women have not had the chance to do this before, because men were always exposing themselves to us before we had a chance to give them the once over. They had the permission to look, read, and suit themselves—we were told to wait, refrain, and submit to the inevitable.

Women's contribution to erotic objectification has been to expand the territory of compelling sexual possibilities; not only to romanticize, but to virtually fetishize erotic environments. I used to laugh at traditional women's supermarket novels where every chapter is filled with minute details of what the heroine is going to wear next. Now I realize this was a repressed goody-girl version of sexual objectification. Bad girls, as they say, go everywhere, and costuming is just the tip of the iceberg.

So far, women writing erotica have been ambivalent about the responsibility of sexual portrayal. Danger and physical risks are often a part of sexual fantasy, and each female author seems to have a different take on how much reassurance they should give the reader that this is, after all, fiction. There's a rebellion brewing among female sex writers, because they're desperate to explore sex for sex's sake, not as a health issue. Often they're the same people who have been on the front lines of birth control counseling, or safe-sex education. Women writers have been far more prolific about the consequences of irresponsible or harmful sexual behavior than they have been describing either their erotic identities or the brutal consequnces of sexual repression: on our health, independence and self-esteem as women.

What's hot and what's not for the female audience is going to continue to be controversial and late-breaking news. Those of us who are publishing women's erotic writing are pioneers not only in putting women's sexuality into overt public consciousness, but also in giving respect and diversity to erotic literacy. With any luck, anthologies of women's erotic writing will find their place not only under the bed but on a few coffee tables and in a few libraries as well.

Paula Webster

EROTICISM AND TABOO

A truly radical feature of feminism has been the permission we have given each other to speak. We understood that through speech we could discover who women were and how we had been constructed; talk and the analysis that followed were the first steps toward change. And so we spoke. We shared our doubts and disappointments, rages and fears; we nurtured the strengths we discovered and the insights that had been unappreciated for so long. We talked about our mothers, our fathers, our lovers or the ones we wanted to have. We sought, through the comfort of words, to articulate in a collective effort at clarity what had been vague, confusing, debilitating and painful. We spoke the unspeakable; we broke the taboo on silence.

Looking back at that time now, it remains quite curious that given our commitment to explorations of the mundane and the marvelous, we devoted so little time to open and direct discussion of sexual pleasure. While we spent many meetings talking about our bodies and their particularities, the erotic contours of our imaginations remained buried in layers of propriety and ambivalence. Face to face, when it came to describing our desires, we were strangely mute. Our discussions of sex were barely audible.

In print, however, we were brave. There was the vaunted rediscovery of the clitoris and its many pleasures. With the full force of feminist analysis to support us, we declared with relief and then authority that vaginal orgasms were a myth, that our fears of being inadequate women were groundless. From its lowly position as a second-rate alternative to partner-sex, masturbation rose in our collective esteem and consciousness to a political epiphany. Even if we never went to Betty Dodson's workshops, or answered Shere Hite's questionnaires, most of us felt better knowing that we were like other women and other women were like us. Masturbation became the symbol of autonomous feminist sexuality, a logical reconciliation of our bodies and our lives, and a necessary foundation for knowing what was erotically satisfying.

Reassurance from the printed page enabled women to revise or reinvent a relationship with their own bodies, but when it came to sex with others, an unwritten orthodoxy prevailed. It felt taboo to talk about what we liked and the partner we liked to do it with. As we collectively and individually sought consistency among our beliefs, worldviews and actions, whatever and whomever didn't comfortably fit with our new selves was left out of the discussion. We feared contradicting what we said we wanted, and began to lie or tell only half-truths, keeping secrets that might reveal our deviance to members of our movement, community or preference group. We committed ourselves to correctness and its false but familiar binding, deleting our mistakes, denying desires that had not received group approval. The sexual domain in general had become less taboo, but some wishes, some thoughts, some acts and some partners were as off-limits as before. Feminist orthodoxy, which we created, observed and enforced with righteousness, prevailed.

As we rallied to denounce media depictions of feminine desire and desirability, asserting that women did not want to look like *that* or be treated like *that*, it appeared that we were on the verge of suggesting what in fact we did want. But instead, our list of taboos marked off more and more unacceptable terrain. "Perverse" pleasures, like voyeurism, bondage, s/m, fetishism, pornography, promiscuity, and intergenerational, group, interracial, public or phone sex were presented as incomprehensible. As we disclaimed any identification with, or interest in, these fantasies and activities, that part of the pedestal, supposed to protect our innocence and insure our purity, was rebuilt. Could we admit that we liked to look, when we denigrated those who liked to look at us? What kind of women would we be if we desired to break any of the taboos that domesticated our sexuality, leaving us deprived but safe? Even daring to speak about what we might like seemed dangerous. Could we be thinking unfeminist thoughts?

The idea that sex between women was ideal, equal, perfect and perfectly feminist became a barrier to lesbians who wanted to speak explicitly about their sexual lives. Speaking honestly involves admitting that you have problems, anxiety, ambivalence and conflict, issues that were given little room. Now that the taboo on lesbianism had moved a fraction, for a moment, in this restricted radius of the radical women's movement, lesbians were asked to carry the banner of "good sex" and leave their more complex feelings at the door. After all, we needed Amazons with no problems; we needed some vision of utopian eroticism.

The *ancien regime* was heterosexuality, with its inequality, inefficient and selfish male partners, and millennia of suppression. If heterosexual women could find anything to talk about that was positive, it was suspect. Heterosexual couplings were dismal, and women who could reveal the depth of their dissatisfaction were given some sympathy, but *sleeping with the enemy* was not seen as interesting or liberatory sex. In public, heterosexual desires that were the least bit unconventional were dismissed as heterosexist indoctrination. Fearful of being labeled in this way, straight women grappled privately with the meaning of false consciousness, as did their lesbian friends. For some yet-to-be-discovered reason, we reduced our convoluted relationships with eroticism to issues of preference and purity, alienating ourselves from each other with stereotypes that eliminated contradictions and betrayed our real feelings. Lesbians couldn't have bad sex and heterosexuals couldn't have good sex. Anything that would have proved this untrue was suppressed, in a misdirected effort at unity.

This stereotyping of eroticism led to deep ambivalence among women who had been able to compare and contrast so many other important zones of their experience. Equating preference with the possibilities for pleasure left lesbians and straight women constricted and ashamed to talk of their "deviance." New alliances around desire might have emerged then, but instead respect for old taboos and new feminist taboos was strengthened. Surrounded by silence, we pretended to talk.

The lack of information we had then and have now about our own and other women's sexual lives leaves us anxious to know where we stand in relation to our peers—to women. If we knew how far from or near the average our wishes were, we think we might feel *more* normal, more acceptable and lovable—more *feminine*. But we also fear finding out where we stand because we might feel *less* acceptable, normal, or lovable. When we finally hear about the sexual practices of women who are unlike us, we are never indifferent. First we may wonder what is wrong with them, desiring such "bizarre things," but quickly we turn the question back: what is wrong with me? We weave in and out between contempt and curiosity, wondering who should be placed beyond the pale. We say that we can't believe they like what they like or that they act by choice. Of course, they couldn't be feminists! Or could they? Could it be that these women, who have more sexuality in their lives and have traveled to more exotic places with it, are better than us? Our curiosity is tinged with envy and confusion. Could I do such a thing? Would I want to? Do I want to? How will I know myself when it is done? Am I a nymphomaniac, or am I repressed? Is there a category for me—where do I belong?

Like strangers in a strange land, we ask ourselves these poignant questions when we admit our confusions. The responsibility of creating a sexual life congruent with our often mute desires seems awesome and very likely impossible. How many women do we know (including ourselves) who almost defiantly say they have *no* fantasies, or no *need* to act them out? How many times have we resisted knowing what it is that might give us erotic pleasure? How many women do we know who *just couldn't* have an affair with a married man, enjoy two lovers, buy pornography, flirt with someone she liked, call up someone for a date, use sex toys? Going beyond the erotic territory that is familiar feels forbidden; we stop even our imaginings when confronted with taboo. Our hearts race; the world seems fragmented and threatening; we say *no* over and over again, convincing ourselves that to act or even to dream of new pleasure would be devastating. We meet the taboo head-on, and we are immoblized.

I remember when my reflections on the nature of erotic taboo were made startlingly clear and concrete by a chance conversation with a stranger, Martin, who called one day to ask my thoughts on the future of feminism. He said that he had been very impressed by an article I wrote in the "Sex Issue" of *Heresies,* and wanted to know if I believed that women were getting more powerful, assertive. What an intriguing opener! "Yes," I said proudly, "that is quite true." There was a tense silence. I wondered if he was speaking in code, trying to *tell me something.* Earlier, I had received a call from a man who read an article on matriarchy that I had written, and he wanted to know if women were going to be as *dominant* as they had been in the mother-right past. That time I got frightened and hung up on him. I didn't like the way he sounded; he wanted somebody to dominate him, I was sure. I protected myself with moral indignation because it made me feel very vulnerable to have this complete stranger insinuating that because I wrote about matriarchy I might be looking to dominate men.

Martin, however, did not frighten me; it was he who seemed vulnerable, with his agitated hesitations and unsuccessful subterfuge. I wanted to hear him out. I was curious.

He led up to "it" very slowly, interspersing his questions with compliments to "all feminists," especially those who wrote about sex. He assured me that he was sincere, just a regular guy who worked in an office and carried a briefcase. That is why he had to make this call from a phone booth. And then—"Don't you think that there are feminists who would like to make a man more feminine, more like a woman?" Did he mean smash gender? I doubted it. "Yes," I said. I thought he had a point. There must be. "They could make men act much nicer." That's for sure. "Don't you think that there are some men who would rather be women?" Is that what he wanted to tell me, that he was a transsexual? Would it be cruel to let him go on? Was that nice? There was a subtle change in my understanding of our power dynamic. Suddenly I realized that I could choose to understand what he meant, or I could make him suffer by my incomprehension.

He finally pleaded his case. "Don't you want to give orders to a man? Don't you ever have the fantasy of making a man do exactly what you want, like making him clean your house, wash your clothes, or pick up your laundry?" Was that all? A cleaning service? Of course, he assumed that since I was a woman I might have cleaned many a boyfriend's apartment, and naturally would be interested in altering the division of labor. But I realized that this is not what he was getting at; we were not talking about the radical redistribution of housework, but a sexual scene in which I would run the show.

He assured me that *it* would be easy. I would just have to yell at him when he made mistakes, humiliating him for his incompetence, reducing him to tears and pitiable entreaties for my forgiveness. Curtly, I told him that *I* was a *feminist*, perhaps he hadn't understood, and I believed in equality, not in replicating the oppressive power relations of patriarchy. He apologized and said of course he had understood, but since he was willing to pay for my services, the relationship would be equal. For some perverse reason, I told him to let me think about it. He promised to call again.

In our next conversation I asked what he intended to pay for such an afternoon devoted to his pleasure. Meekly, he said he thought fifty dollars was a reasonable amount. I became indignant, surprising myself. That was too little for such demanding work. He asked me to suggest a just price and without hesitating I demanded two hundred and fifty dollars, considering the time and effort involved. I now realize that this was no abstract calculation, but a poor woman's notion of the value of such tabooed behavior. He said he would think about it and call me again.

In our next conversation I had to withdraw my offer, since I had realized that this whole thing was not a game and more frightening than satisfying. The fantasies I tried to conjure up did not turn me on. I had thought seriously about his offer, tossing it around, trying to see if there was anything there that appealed to me. I must admit that I also thought about the newspaper headlines crying my shame, and the neighbors listening at my door, ready to have me evicted. In truth, what really stopped me was an unnamed and perhaps unnameable fear. I was disappointed that I wouldn't have this experience, this opportunity to see if I could really dominate a man, but I was more relieved. What if I liked it? What if I could get into it?

Each conversation with Martin had become more friendly and inevitably frank, tinged with the intimacy one can have with a stranger. I was struck by his sense of humor, his honesty and the specificity of his desires. I was sympathetic to his commitment to find a woman who was truly interested instead of what he called a "cold professional." I was flattered by his impulse to call a feminist and find out if she shared his desires. Given his limited reading of feminist literature, he thought that feminism was unequivocally in favor of sexual liberation. He was sure that he had come to the right place. "Isn't there one feminist in New York who wants to humiliate a man and get reimbursed for it?" He was amazed and, I think, unconvinced when I told him I didn't know anybody who would take his offer seriously. He was puzzled that my own taboo desires could not be shared. "Do feminists have fantasies?" he inquired. I answered, "Of course."

We said goodbye and wished each other good luck with our respective sexual desires and their eventual fulfillment. Martin would have to find someone, most likely a professional, to let him dress as a woman, to command him as Marta, to allow him to act out his fantasy of being a woman in a sexist society. I would have to. . . .

I thought about my Martin/Marta talks for a long time, marveling at both the urgency and specificity of his desires and the diffuse and lackadaisical quality of mine. Would I have responded differently if he had intuited one of my lazy, unformed wishes; if he could have assured me of total safety and reciprocity; if he had been a friend or lover instead of a stranger? Would I still have found something to stop me from acting out my forbidden wishes for erotic pleasure?

Martin made me think of the limits I put on my sexual longings and my inordinate respect for the conventions of erotic taboo. Our conversations encouraged me to think about what was restricting and denying my research into this area of my life which I had constructed to be free of ambiguity, experimentation and the forbidden.

It is in the nature of taboo that territories are marked off from one another, the known separated from the unknown, the inside/private from the outside/public, the good from the bad, the sacred from the profane, the acceptable from the forbidden. Crossing the boundaries that are supposed to maintain order and predictability is like entering an uncharted space. It feels dangerous. We are not sure how to orient ourselves; we don't know the rules. Embedded in all domains of culture are rules about what behavior is permissible, with whom, when, where, under what conditions and with what accouterments. These rules, internalized and thought to be natural, are reflected in our understanding of what sexuality is and what different desires and acts mean. For each of us the area marked *taboo* is simultaneously personal, cultural, political and social. No matter how wild or conventional we think our sexual thoughts and practices are, contained in what we think is erotically possible for us, as women, are a myriad of zones thought impossible to explore. For example, at a conference workshop on this topic women spoke of what was taboo for them:

"I want to have sex without love."
"I want to buy a strap-on dildo."
"I want to have sex with my student."
"Patriarchal men turn me one."
"I want to be able to say what I want."
"I like sucking cock."
"I want to get married and have children."
"I want to rape a woman."
"I want instant gratification . . . Why don't women have glory holes?"
"I want to sleep with a young girl/boy."
"I want to be watched, but not touched."
"I want more than one lover."
"I want to look sexy on the street."
"I would like to be able to flirt."
"I want to fuck my husband in the ass."
"I want to sexually caress my child."
"I would like to have sex with my brother/sister/father/mother."

"I would like to have sex with my best friend."

"I want to have vaginal orgasms, if there is such a thing."

"I want to go to the limits."

"I want to discover what I want."

"I want to be able to be turned on to my long-term relationship."

"I want to fantasize about being a porn star."

"I want to really like my body."

"I want to be fucked into insensibility, every which way."

"I want to talk dirty in private."

Women's relationship to erotic taboo is complex. For some, playing with the distance from or proximity to the forbidden is a tension-filled turn-on. Without taboo, sex might not feel so delicious. Naughty feels nice, and just "bad" enough to be intensely pleasurable. Taboo thoughts about taboo people, acts, situations and words are often nurtured, honed and elaborated to heighten our fantasies, again and again. Yet, over time, some taboos are assimilated, domesticated and drained of their charge. Others disappear the first time we try something new and are not ashamed. Sexual sophistication, like the sophistication of aesthetic and intellectual tastes, is inevitable, though it is often marked by some vague sense of regret for a past state of innocence (or ignorance). In this way we develop over our lifetime a varied sexual repertoire and, if we are lucky, new sources of erotic pleasure. Personal and historical change reveals the exaggeration of fears and guilt. But how many of us have been able to pursue what fascinates us, or ask for what we want, or take risks with our sexual identities molded by the constraints of femininity? Many of us still stand at the borders of our desires, hesitating, complaining, berating ourselves and/or our lovers for the sexual deprivation we live with and feel helpless to change.

When we imagine traveling into the territory of the forbidden we are obsessed with fears of loss. We have been told, by those who are said to care most about us, that social status drops dangerously low for the woman who seeks pleasure. The very thought of acting on our desires conjures up an unappetizing picture of a creature who is driven and out of control, at odds with how we would like to be seen. We imagine that our fantasies will topple the order of the universe, depriving us of the esteem of parents, friends, lovers, or children. If we threaten the privilege supposedly accorded respectable women, we are convinced we will not survive. Afraid that we will be rejected, humiliated, and expelled from the feminist world, lesbian and heterosexual, we cling tighter and longer to what has always been safe. Consumed by baroque visions of our own voraciousness, we affirm a domino theory of sexual appetite, in which one step will lead to excesses worthy of Boccaccio. The world will have to visit us in the bedroom, or wherever we think our sexual haunts will be; we will stop feeding our children, sending birthday cards to Mom, miss all of our meetings, and pack the typewriter away for good. In this apocalyptic future, our hedonism will take over—we will do anything with anyone. Our good name wil be tarnished, we will be stigmatized, we will destroy our support systems and be isolated. If we don't follow the rules so deeply embedded in our feminine unconscious we fear a terrible retaliation. And so we continue to observe the taboos for our gender, remaining reluctant to even know what could turn us on.

Being interested in sex is a primary taboo for women. Perhaps that is why Women Against Pornography could attract so many women ready to swear that they find none of that sleazy, pornographic sex interesting. Denying their curiosity like the Oedipal daughter, they insist that they could never do anything like that, or want anything like that. They assume that women who like talking dirty, anal sex, voyeurism, or even vibrators are suspect, certainly not feminists. But women are feminism's constituency. How do we understand the differences between ourselves and the women who send their photos to *Hustler,* or write letters to *Penthouse Forum,* or buy sex toys, split-crotch panties, and dream of being dominated, or becoming dominatrixes? We cannot remain indifferent to the sexual tastes and subjects of women's lives if we are to create a feminist discourse on female sexuality that will replace the familiar one of commiseration.

When women discuss eroticism in private, the content of the dialogue is depressingly predictable. Starting with a complaint filled with disappointment, or even rage, it moves to fantasies of a more pleasurable sex life but ends with the imponderable—is it her/him or me? Is it possible to get what I want? Am I asking too much? Is it maybe not really that important to be sexually fulfilled? While the rejection of deprivation in other areas of women's lives has been the agenda of the feminist movement, sexual deprivation has not been theorized to any great degree. Instead, in midnight phone calls, private talks or private walks, women have told each other how sexually unsatisfied they are and how hopeless and helpless they feel about their situation. It feels dangerous to describe the wounds this absence causes and the passivity that overwhelms us, even when we know we want more.

Wrapped in romanticism, we say we will change partners, or wait for the *one* who will do it for us, turn us on, make us feel sexual. Acting in a self-directed way, to know our sexual wishes and to act on them feels selfish, unfeminine, not nice. Like frustrated children who must wait to have their needs attended to by protective adults, the ones who initiate and act, women wait for permission to respond, but we are afraid to insist on pleasure as our right. To get what we want (once we know what it is) is a taboo that needs to be broken.

Our dissatisfaction, however, creates a potential source of action. Accepting our deprivation may be painful at first, but it is a first step toward defining the nature of our sexual appetite. Erotic scarcity has served to debilitate our most constructive efforts to undo the damage of patriarchal repression. There may be more "good sex" available once we know what we like and what we have to do to put it in our lives. We may fear a deluge of sexual feelings that have been denied and suppressed, but in our attempts to be conscious of our choices, the real ambivalence can be exposed and worked through. Breaking some of our own taboos, imposed by patriarchal culture on all women, assented to by feminism and given legitimacy by each of us, could give us a new sense of ourselves and our possibilities.

When shame is replaced by curiosity and fear by self-knowledge gained through experience lived in the world rather than in our heads, dogmatism will no longer be so appealing, and deprivation will not seem "normal." Experimentation, however, is never all or nothing. If we don't see stars the first time, if it isn't perfect, we often conclude that this is bad, or boring, and should never be done again. Actually it may take several tries to learn the social as well as the sexual skills, the techniques and responses necessary to enjoy something. Remember what your mother told you about olives; forget what she said about sex.

Our mothers, to whom we often dedicate our movement, if not our lives, were either bizarrely matter-of-fact when they told us about sex, or bitter and resentful. Either your father wanted too much or too little, and she had to put up with *it*. Needless to say, she never told you *if* she masturbated (or how, when or where) or how she felt about it. Nor did she tell you if she liked rough or gentle sex, being on top or bottom, whether she read pornography, or had fantasies about the milkman, her brother-in-law, her best girlfriend, or her own children. Sexually mute and mysterious, our mothers observed the taboo imposed by motherhood, and presented us with little or no knowledge of what women's sexuality was like or could be. We have no documented erotic heritage, and the exploration is made even more difficult by our mother's sacrifices. We may feel that we betray her when we want more than she had.

We know as little about our feminist foremothers as the women who birthed us; and in both cases it seems an act of deep impropriety to wonder what kind of sex they liked. Yet it feels irresistible to ponder de Beauvoir's demands on Sartre, or the fantasies that fueled Virginia Woolf's longings, or whether Willa Cather was butch in bed. Our contemporaries are as silent as the dead. Sara, Kathy, Nancy and Pat won't talk because it is too personal, and we don't push. If we knew what they were doing, we might feel competitive, jealous, or defeated; we might wonder how their politics were being influenced by their practices. We are ambivalent about knowing; what if we find out something that makes us uncomfortable? Often, with a mixture of relief and disappointment, we change the topic, divert the attention from ourselves, cite taboos on privacy and integrity, and retreat from comparing their lives to our own, their pleasures to ours.

Some conclude from the quiescent sexual state women find themselves in that women's sexuality is like that—calm, passive, romantic, and other-directed. We are seen and come to see ourselves as tame and easily satisfied, more interested in giving than getting pleasure. While feminism has helped us to know ourselves as struggling with complex contradictions on many fronts, it has encouraged us to postpone the exploration of sexual subjectivity by fanning our fears of exclusion from the universal sisterhood we have sought to create. By making sex an ideological battleground where the forces of good and evil fight to the death, complex questions of pleasure, power and feminine desire have been reduced to simple-minded answers.

My desire to encourage women to break taboos, rebel against prohibitions and rally around pleasure in fantasy and action is tempered by a note of caution, not admonition. To break private erotic taboos without being conscious of our unique sexual values would leave us feeling troubled and disoriented. In all new ventures, we need to be aware of our limits, the levels of novelty we can tolerate, the anxiety we can comfortably endure. Women's attachment to magical thinking (for example, men are lustful, women are not; my lover controls my sex life; I have no desires that are not nice; if I am very attractive, I will have good sex) is supported by irrational fears and major denials. Yet these won't wither away or be rooted out by platitudes of support or a new version of toeing the correct line. To name these inhibitions as largely self-imposed, childish, or effective but ultimately destructive defenses against autonomy and pleasure, will not usher any of us into the Golden Age of Gratification. We have had enough experience to prove that naming, while crucial, is never sufficient.

We also need to explore the hesitations women feel when pleasure is realizable and imminently available. When we have come to terms, privately and collectively, with our demons and judges, our sexual shame and guilt, our desire to take and renounce responsibility for our happiness, we may be ready to talk honestly about our erotic particularities, and from there create a politics of sexuality worthy of our best efforts.

We do not need to wait for a feminist or any other type of revolution to explore our sexuality. There are a number of things we can do right now. We can begin to speak of what we were afraid to say in those years of consciousness-raising. We can form new groups in order to have long and intimate conversations with women we know will not be offended, judgmental, or discouraging. We can support each other to learn by doing—starting slow and building on what we learn and what feels good. We could team up with women who have similar questions, or those who have been called perverts by the movement, to get guided tours of places that fascinate us, zones that are definitely off our usual maps: porn shops, sex parties, gay bars. With friends, we might get support to treat ourselves well and take this work seriously. There are books to be read, attitudes to upset, time to be carved out of our busy schedules, skills to learn, and moments to integrate the novelty of being a self-directed sexual actor. If we use our friends merely to mirror our dissatisfaction (she won't fuck me in the ass, he won't go down on me), then we stay stuck, affirming for one another that nothing can be done until *they*, whomever they may be, change and give us what we say we want.

The collective project of creating an erotic culture for women should not be postponed by concluding that the distance from here to there is too far or too difficult to travel. Our friends can alert us to the dangers, both real and imagined, and help us distinguish one from the other. Some fears are appropriate and some merely resistance to change. If we can create a counter-chorus to the vast organization of repression we confront as women, we will be better able to experiment with confidence and a realistic sense of self-preservation. The spaces, rules, protections, information, projects, and productions that will emerge from this collective effort are yet to be imagined. The work is largely ahead of us, but—as we can see—it has begun.

In preparation, we have the task of naming ourselves desiring creatures, with important passions, aversions, and prejudices. We experience a mix of desires for power and powerlessness, love and revenge, submission and control, monogamy and promiscuity, sadism and masochism. Once we are able to acknowledge our own complete relationships to these feelings, we will be less likely to submit to pressures to punish our sisters who have dared to speak, act, and write about the taboos they have broken and the forbidden territories they have explored.

Although the fear is potent and real, we will not perish if we challenge the taboos that domesticate our sexual desires. The more we know about the dimensions of our hungers, their finite limits and requirements, the more entitled we may feel to speak of our own wishes and listen with compassion to our friends. In recognizing our sexual appetites as "normal," we might lose our sense of ourselves as the victims of sex, unable to reject deprivation and erotic underdevelopment by acting in our own interests for pleasure. For many of us, this image of sexual autonomy is as frightening as our fantasies of loss and chaos. We have no models for "good" women who want, and get "bad" sex. And who would we be if we got what we wanted? If we said *yes* instead of *no, I'll try* instead of *I could never,* would we still be women? From those women who have tried, the message is very encouraging— changing the quality of sex immediately improves the quality of the rest of one's life.

There are no guarantees that an expanded sexual style can be slipped on like some chemise from Paris. There will be moments of panic and paralysis. There will be threats from the outside world as well as internal agitation. But we have experienced, withstood, and mastered conflict before, moving closer to ourselves. By recreating feminism in this century, a movement that gave us the very important permission to collectively analyze, challenge, and change our situation, we tapped unpredictable energies that can transform our lives. The women's movement gave us courage. It is time to return that gift and share it with each other.

Nancy Friday

THE MASCULINE CONFLICT

A fantasy is a map of desire, mastery, escape, and obscuration; the navigational path we invent to steer ourselves between the reefs and shoals of anxiety, guilt, and inhibition. It is a work of consciousness, but in reaction to unconscious pressures. What is fascinating is not only how bizarre fantasies are, but how comprehensible; each one gives us a coherent and consistent picture of the personality—the unconscious—of the person who invented it, even though *he* may think it the random whim of the moment.

A man has a reverie of meeting a blond woman in a purple nightgown. He doesn't know why the colors are exciting; his unconscious does, but doesn't bother to explain. The man only knows the blonder, the purple-ier, the more heated he grows. Soon he is inventing scenarios of barebreasted models hired to test new peroxide hair bleaches, supplied by a company that arbitrarily orders all contestants to wear purple underwear. If the plot seems silly, what does it matter? The erotic has its reasons that reason doesn't know.

Like an Einsteinian equation whose logic would take hours to unravel, a fantasy appears in the mind with the speed of light, connecting hitherto seemingly unrelated and mysterious forces in the internal erotic universe, resolving inconsistencies and contradictions that seemed insuperable before. Nothing is included by accident. If the woman is tall or short, if she forgets her birth control pills and so intercourse carries the risk of pregnancy—*if there is a cuckoo clock on the wall*—it is all meaningful to the inventor's heightened sexuality.

In real life, ambivalence abounds. Women want men, men want women; our dreams of one another, fantasies, not only express our most direct desires but also portray the obstacles that must be symbolically overcome to win sexual pleasure. Fantasy is as close as we will ever come again to the omnipotent joys we once knew as infants. In a moment of rage we say, "I'd like to kill you!" This is a fleeting fantasy, a satisfying violent image which expresses the overheated mood of the moment. But how likely are we to pull a gun and do it? It is important to recognize that not all fantasies are frustrated wishes. This is one of the most common misconceptions about fantasy. . . .

All my life I've been haunted by a little girl's voice within that said women needed men—I needed men—more than they needed us. Men could always go off to Singapore or drink alone in bars, but women ceased to exist in their own eyes when men were gone. I watch the ease with which some women today decide to build a life without men (who never lived up to their expectations anyway) in favor of pursuing newly won autonomy. I can understand the sense of freedom born of ridding oneself of the childish—and ultimately false—security that comes from binding oneself to a man; but I do not believe men could ever abandon women so swiftly. I am persuaded that men want women more than the other way around. Toward satisfying their love, need, desire, lust, men will give up more than women will.

Women call themselves the loving sex; we are always waiting for men, always dreaming of them. We need them to put to rest the gnawing anxiety that comes from never being taught a sense of independent worth or self. *Is this love or is it dependency?* When men do offer love, why is it so often felt to be lacking: "Hold me tighter, never let me go," women beg, unable to find in any man's arms that kind of iron security that dependent, passive people need. The point I want to make is this: is it the man she really wants, or is it the relief from anxiety which he symbolizes? . . . .

Men are trained to find their security in themselves. Women are their emotional outlet, their main source of love. If, as women believe, men are so lucky, so self-sufficient, so free, dominant, and irresponsible, living in an option-filled man's world, why do they give it all up for marriage? Men may resist, but in the end most do marry because they want women more than anything else; if responsibilities, mortgages, ulcers, child care, and monogamy are part of the package they must buy to get women, they'll do it.

Men's love of women is filled with rage. Observation shows that in the end love wins out over rage. My research tells me that *men's love of women is often greater than their love of self.* They worship women's beauty to the unhealthy exclusion of their own narcissistic needs.

They discredit the male body as aesthetically displeasing, only to be labelled bestial when they adore women's bodies too openly and too enthusiastically. For women's sake, men give up closeness with their own sex, learn to accept female rules and controls; in marriage they take up the lifelong burden of economic support, often leading to an earlier death; they give their place in the lifeboat to their wives.

Since there is always a question of what love means, let me put it this way: ultimately, men perform the most gallant act of all. At the heart of even the most shocking S&M fantasy, we find that more often than not, men, in a rage at having given up so much, turn their fury not against women but against themselves. Any call girl will tell you that more clients pay to play the victim at a woman's hands than the other way around.

In my books on women's sexual fantasies, the single greatest theme that emerges was that of "weak" women being sexually dominated, "forced" by male strength to do this deliciously awful thing, made to perform that marvelously forbidden act, guiltlessly "raped" again and again.

On the surface, this would seem to be a perfect illustration of the symmetry of desire between the sexes. If women daydream of being overpowered into sex, isn't this desire mirrored in the male fantasy of sexual dominance—the demanding brute who can never get enough women? The answer is no.

Rape or force may be the most popular theme in female fantasy (though I've yet to meet a woman who wouldn't run a mile from a real rapist), but men's fantasies of overpowering women against their will *are the exception.* A closer reading will usually reveal that the woman is a volunteer or has given her consent first. Even in the grimmest S&M fantasy, pain or humiliation of the woman is usually not the goal. They are means toward an end: forcing her to admit to transports of sexual joy she has never known before.

If the cliché were true that men "are only out for one thing," the fact is that masturbation or a homosexual encounter is sex, too; so is sex with an animal or a whore, and this is usually accompanied by no tears, no limits, no oaths of lifelong fidelity—no strings at all. But the majority of men still dream of sex with a loving woman. Men love women at any price, love women even though, beginning in childhood, it is the female sex which makes the male feel guilty about what he desires most from them. One of the reasons men choose the masochistic role is that feeling they are wrong to want sex from women, they accept pain as the symbolic price they must pay. Humiliation is a kind of payment in advance for forbidden pleasures. . . .

Both boys and girls, of course, are told in words, body language, and above all, perhaps, by silence, that sex is bad; mother doesn't approve. The little girl wants to be like mother. *That* is how women are. She tamps down her sexual desires and tries to be a lady. Her sexuality remains in conflict with her introjected mother—her all-important niceness—all her life long.

The little boy doesn't want to be like mother. His body, his anatomy, tells him he is different. He knows mother finds one side of him acceptable: the good boy. The other side is bad, dirty, sexual, willful. This aspect must be hidden—but it is stronger, constantly threatening to overwhelm him.

He wants mother to love him. He swears to himself he will never masturbate again. If mother found out, she would abandon him in a rage. But the difference between the boy and his sister is that while both have taken in mother's antisexual message, the boy wants to accentuate his difference by breaking the rules: he dares to do it anyway. He stands self-convicted: a dirty animal, reveling in his sexuality, angry and forlorn in the knowledge that it is unacceptable to women.

The predicament is agonizing. The boy wants sex but feels he is wrong to want it. Women have placed his body at war with his soul.

Only when he gets out of the house, only when he discovers that other little boys are just like himself, does he get enough reinforcement to bear being *bad:* to experiment with breaking mother's rules, to begin to define himself as separate from her, an individual, a man.

This is how he's going to be, just like the guys, not like silly women and their eternal fussing about don't do this, don't do that. Mother's okay; but after all, she's a woman. What does she know?

In the safety of numbers, and away from mother's censorious eye, boys set out to explore their badness—which has become almost synonymous with masculinity. They talk dirty, spit and laugh and smoke together in vacant lots, play pissing games, and show each other their cocks, ever egging each other on to do everything that would horrify mother. And all in secret. "That's bad," sister says, stumbling on her brother writing a dirty word on the wall. She speaks with the assurance of her fully introjected maternal morality. "I'm going to tell Mom." *The boy is resisting introjecting the same morality.* That's girl stuff. "Get out of here!" he says to sis. In the brave new masculine world of nine and eleven, girls are *out.*

Suddenly, answering the cry of biology, heterosexuality reenters the boy's life in the form of young girls. It's almost as if all the old resentments and dislikes of mother's sex have been forgotten, so pretty are the girls of adolescence—as full of winning smiles and coquettishness as mother herself once had been.

Naively, filled with trepidation and excitement, boys wash their faces, comb their hair, and reach for the phone. Pretty Sally and Jane may be the same sex as Mom, but they are younger, livelier, and the signals they send out seem to say they want what the boys want. Until the boys get too close. Then it becomes, "Yes, I love you, Johnny, but not when you do *that*."

Mother's old lesson has received new and powerful expression. How can a man not be in a rage with members of the sex who make him feel dirty and guilty about the very desires they have gone to such pains to provoke in him? The conflict in the male psyche is reinforced. With characteristic refusal to sentimentalize love in any of its aspects, Freud, in a little-known essay, "The Most Prevalent Form of Degradation in Erotic Life," sadly concludes that men often find supreme sexual excitement in notions of degrading their wives or lovers.

Please don't interpret me too easily, and nod your head, "Oh, I get it, that's the old madonna/whore split that so many men go in for." That is to take a part for the whole. Something more fundamental and inclusive is being discussed here.

Dividing women into the kind you fuck versus the kind you marry is indeed one of the manifestations of male ambivalence—but only one. The masculine conflict is protean: like the Greek god who gave us the word, the ware of love against rage can take many shapes.

Mother used to tenderly tuck you into bed at night, reproving you gently for trying to put your hand on her nightgowned breast. Then she blandly went off to share a bed with dad. Oedipal love, oedipal furies. Women are wonderful, but they drive you nuts, too. The same man who loves women for their maternal sweetness and warmth will invent scenarios in which feminine hypocrisy is sexually degraded down to the man's own bestial level. . . .

It is here that we have reached the heart of fantasy's enchantment: no matter what men may do to/with their imaginary lovers, her reactions are just the opposite of mother's—*she loves him for it.* "Yes!" she shouts, "more!" A fantasy woman does not reproach her man for letting other men peep at her, for wanting to share her with another guy, for dreaming of her having sex with a dildo or a dog. Fantasy gives men the love of women they want, with none of the inhibiting feminine rules they hate. No matter how wild the man's sexual frenzy, the woman does not punish, but rewards. Love conquers rage.

But rage does not go away. It is a commonplace that when children hear their parents making love in the other room, they think they are fighting. "Daddy is killing Mommy." This is usually shrugged off with a smile—the naiveté of children. My own hunch is that the child is intuitively projecting his own infantile sexual rage onto his grown-up parents: This is what he would be feeling if he were in their shoes (or bed). Sex, frustration, and hostility have become associated into one complex of feeling.

Men may love women, but they are in a rage with them, too. I believe it is a triumph of the human psyche that out of this contradiction, a new form of emotion emerges, one so human it is unknown to animals even one step lower in the evolutionary scale: *passion*. It is notorious that a life of quiet affection between two people usually puts their sexual desires for each other to sleep. On the other hand, many warring couples are known to provoke fights and quarrels because, consciously or not, they find it heightens their sexuality afterwards.

There seems to be a need in us not only to recreate—during sex— our earliest memories of physical touch, warmth, and communion, but also to extract revenge for all the pains and frustrations suffered during infancy, too. It may be dismaying, but it is often true that for some people the white-hot pitch of obsessive desire that may be the peak experience sex has to offer is reached when hostility is fused with love.

Thomas Moore

EROS, AGGRESSION,
AND MALE "SHINING"

I am in the hands of the unknown God,
he is breaking me down to his own oblivion
to send me forth on a new morning, a new man.
                                    D. H. LAWRENCE

For the Greeks, Eros is one of the male spirits. Masculinity is erotic by nature. It is male to be erotic, erotic to be male. The rush of desire for another soul is the male spirit doing his job, taking us along, making connections. He mingles and unites. He makes friendships. He hammers out unions. He keeps us within certain orbits. In art, Eros is adolescent, brash, active, uncontrollable. He has wings. He shoots arrows. This is the natural aggression of the male: to bring things together, to join what is joinable.

To be masculine, therefore, is to tolerate the rush of eros, to live by desire. One gets masculine strength from the strength of the desire. It is eros who has power, and the individual becomes powerful in a deep way through participation in that erotic power. William Blake says that desire that can be suppressed is not true desire. Centuries before Christ, Hesiod sang that Eros breaks the strength in the arms and legs of Gods and humans. By all accounts, Eros is a source of immense power.

There is a fundamental difference, however, between the power that eros brings and the manipulative opportunity created by the abuse of eros. A man can enslave another person who is in love (in eros) with him. But he does that only as a defense against the true power of eros that stirs in himself. All false, inhumane loves betray the abuse of eros: addictions, obsessions, fetishes. We are in love with the nuclear bomb because explosive, powerful eros has been blocked. The bomb is our fetish.

But Eros is not only powerful, he is also beautiful, full of life and grace. He is brilliant. His erection is not an emblem of blunt power, it is his showing. The pornographic imagination, repressed wherever Eros is abused, wants to see the display of Eros.

The name *Zeus,* the high god, means "shining." He is known by his brilliant displays of lightning. According to Jung, *phallos* among other things means "light." To be phallic, the great emblem of the male spirit, is to shine. When we don't shine, we swing our fists and butt our chests. People become violent when their male spirit cannot shine forth. When we can't shine, we expect our metallic missiles and our military shoes to shine as fetishes. Shining is the ultimate aggressive act: anything else is symptomatic and therefore deeply unsatisfying. Isn't the satisfaction of boxing in the shining and not the bruising? In the bravura, the exaggeration, the show? Doesn't the ice hockey free-for-all manifest the latent male force that wants to shine?

I don't shine; the male spirit shines through me. My passions burn and glow in my maleness. When the male spirit is vibrant, my character, my daimon, my archon, my angel, shines its halo of spirit in my slightest gesture. There is no need for violence when the spirit radiates. The glint of the steel gun barrel replaces the glow of the angel who is the guardian of light—Lucifer, Light-Bearer.

Lucifer is a dark angel. Sometimes the male spirit shines with an underworld aesthetic, with the beauty of dark mystery. Only a sentimental misunderstanding of religion believes an angel to be superhumanly good. The male spirit has to shine sometimes in his mischief, like the great god Hermes, archetypal thief and liar.

Light and desire are almost indistinguishable, like the penis of sex and the phallos of shining. Desire, the aura of eros, is warm and phosphorescent. It shines. To let desire shine is to heal that man who beats the woman who he thinks has smothered his desire. When desires are not allowed to glow, they turn into addictions and odd loves. There is love within all those things to which we are madly attached: alcohol, sex, money, home, wandering, oneself. These odd loves are the egos of the male spirit. The Greek Orphics said that eros arises from a great egg. We might look for eros in the eggshells that render life brittle and are concealed as phobias, depressions, and dysfunctions. We need not get rid of these eggshell complaints. We have only to look closely into their interior spaces.

We carry our desires around like eggs, going from romance to romance, from orgy to orgy. But eros appears only when the egg is incubated, when it opens and reveals its inside. The heaviness of eros we feel in love and desire is its own maturing nature, its burden, its pregnancy, which is not revealed from the beginning. The true objects of eros sometimes appear only after a long period of engagement with its decoys. Our crazy loves and attachments may be destructive, but they are important as unique embryos of authentic love.

The egg from which Eros appears is often a long-standing obsessive love. It is a truism that in loving another we are in love with love. Love is the object of our love, and the other gives us love that he or she has been holding for us as in a shell. Aphrodite, the great goddess, the awesome and profound mystery of love and sex, was depicted for centuries in the scallop shell.

Part of the mystery of Aphrodite, for a man, is the ironic truth that his sexual fantasy, drive, and emotion are feminine. It is she, the shell, Venus, the sea, Aphrodite, whose name means "foam-Goddess," or perhaps, the scholars say, "the Goddess who shines," who grants the wet and sea-surging tides of sex to a man. Sex itself is a union, then, of male Eros and female Venus. In some ancient stories, she is his mother. But Apuleius, the second-century writer of the *Golden Ass,* shows her giving her son a passionate kiss. The world of Eros is never contained in the rectangular boundaries our morals and customs and expectations build to fence him in. Eros, the Orphics said, is a maker of worlds. We know that he makes relationships, friendships, families, communities, even nations. He also inspires poetry, letters, stories, memories, shrines. In short, erotic sex makes individual and social culture. Or, it makes soul. As James Hillman has said, where eros stirs, soul is to be found. Soul is a sign that eros is truly present. If there is no sign of soul, then the sex is symptomatic, on the path toward eros, but not yet out of its shell.

The mystery of male sexuality, therefore, is not to be found and lived in literal gender or literal sex. The other can only be loved and pleasured when one has discovered the cosmic couple, inside oneself and in the world at large. Only when the male and female have coupled in out-buildings and economies and schools and politics will the god and goddess take their long night together with us, like Zeus and Hera on their three-hundred-year honeymoon, radiating the truth of sex into all our lives. Then the act of sex would be what it is meant to be: a ritual act epitomizing and celebrating the marriage of heaven and earth. Only when the genders of culture enhance their love can two human beings find the fullness of sexuality.

Of course, it works in the other direction, too. Culture is us. Our rediscovery of eros in our own microcosmic lives is the beginning of the cosmic union. When we realize what the Orphics understood, that desire is the fundamental motive force of live and soul, that power is true aggression, its action authentic creativity, then sex can be released from its captivity in literalism. At the moment, our world is frightened by desire, knowing that its limits are not the limits of heroic will and Promethean secularism. But perhps we can risk the pleasures of desire and glimpse the new world it engenders. Then we may discover sex for the first time.

Nan Goldin

THE BALLAD
OF SEXUAL DEPENDENCY

I often fear that men and women are irrevocably strangers to each other, irreconcilably unsuited, almost as if they were from different planets. But there is an intense need for coupling in spite of it all. Even if relationships are destructive, people cling together. It's a biochemical reaction, it stimulates that part of your brain that is only satisfied by love, heroin, or chocolate; love can be an addiction. I have a strong desire to be independent, but at the same time a craving for the intensity that comes from interdependency. The tension this creates seems to be a universal problem: the struggle between autonomy and dependence. . . .

If men and women often seem unsuited to one another, maybe it's because they have different emotional realities and speak a different emotional language. For many years, I found it hard to understand the feeling systems of men; I didn't believe they were vulnerable, and I empowered them in a way that didn't acknowledge their fears and feelings. Men carry their own baggage, a legacy based on a fear of women, a need to categorize them, for instance, as mothers, whores, virgins, or spiderwomen. The construction of gender roles is one of the major problems that individuals bring into a relationship.

As children, we're programmed into the limitations of gender distinction: little boys to be fighters, little girls to be pretty and nice. But as we grow older, there's a self-awareness that sees gender as a decision, as something malleable. You can play with the traditional options—dressing up, cruising in cars, the tough posturing—or play against the roles, by displaying your tenderness or toughness to contradict stereotypes. When I was fifteen, the perfect world seemed a place of total androgyny, where you wouldn't know a person's gender until you were in bed with him or her. I've since realized that gender is much deeper than style. Rather than accept gender distinction, the point is to redefine it. Along with playing out the clichés, there is the decision to live out the alternatives, even to change one's sex, which to me is the ultimate act of autonomy. . . .

What you know emotionally and what you crave sexually can be wildly contradictory. I often feel that I am better suited to be with a woman; my long-term friendships with women are bonds that have the intensity of marriage, or the closeness of sisters. But a part of me is challenged by the opacity of men's emotional makeup and is stimulated by the conflict inherent in relationships between men and women.

Sex itself is only one aspect of sexual dependency. Pleasure becomes the motivation, but the real satisfaction is romantic. Bed becomes a forum in which struggles in a relationship are defused or intensified. Sex isn't about performance; it's about a certain kind of communication founded on trust and exposure and vulnerability that can't be expressed any other way. Intense sexual bonds become consuming and self-perpetuating. You become dependent on the gratification. Sex becomes a microcosm of the relationship, the battleground, an exorcism.

Robert Bly

THE HORSE OF DESIRE

"Yesterday I saw a face
that gave off light."
I wrote that the first time
I saw you; now the lines
written that morning
are twenty years old.
What is it that
we see and don't see?

When a horse swings
his head, how easily
his shoulders follow.
When the right thing happens,
the whole body knows.
The road covered with stones
turns to a soft river
moving among reeds.

I love you in those reeds,
and in the bass
quickening there.
My love is in the demons
gobbling the waters,
my desire in their swollen
foreheads poking
earthward out of the trees.

The bear between my legs
has one eye only,
which he offers
to God to see with.
The two beings below with no
eyes at all love you
with the slow persistent
intensity of the blind.

Carolyn Kleefeld

I Could Die With You

You sweeten my mouths
with the milk of you
My mouths so freshly sweet
with our moistures
part, open—fully open
soften to let all of you be
                    Within me

O fertile generous milk
that you pour into my body
then drink back from my mouths
                    Your milk

This rich milk of you
flows so readily
Its encircling heat—your heat
                    Absorbs me

You, my cradle
rock the womb of me
connecting, covering us
with one velvet skin

From your bowels
your walnut voice
moans of our fusion

My being in surrender
melts into your lips

I could die with you

5

THE
SUPPRESSION
AND DENIAL
OF EROS

INTRODUCTION: PART 5

$\mathbf{W}$e come into the world as highly erotic, sensual beings focused on our senses, at one with our bodies, filled with a life force that we do not suspect, do not fear, are not even separate from enough to conceptualize. In the beginning—before we are taught to divide ourselves and the world into mind and body, order and chaos, good and evil, proper and improper, normal and perverted, male and female—we simply are what we are, and this includes the simple fact of erotic existence. As Lonnie Barbach has pointed out, children of all ages are erotic, sensual, *sexual* beings. We are sexual even in the womb: male fetuses can be seen having erections regularly.

But almost as soon as we are born, our basic erotic feelings come into conflict with the sensibilities of the people who are closest to us. We begin receiving signals, subtle or overt, that being erotic is not as wonderful as it might seem. By the time we have become socialized members of society, much of our original, unequivocal erotic feeling has been thoroughly condemned, judged, castigated, twisted, turned against itself. Because this process begins so early in our lives, we never have the opportunity to discover who we really are as erotic beings, to identify clearly what we want, what we feel in the erotic/sexual realm, let alone to learn how to develop our desires into a rich and satisfying erotic/sexual existence.

Commentator Pat Califia has noted that when it comes to sex, "we live in fear of being known. We know we are ugly before we have even seen ourselves." Before we understand who we are as individual erotic/sexual beings, before our erotic personhood has had a chance to take form, before we have any awareness of self in these matters, we already have a very vivid understanding that there is something fundamentally wrong with us because of how or when or toward whom we feel erotically charged. In other words, we learn that there is something fundamentally wrong with us when we feel sexual without censoring our desire.

Our basic erotic nature is running headlong into our culture's basic fear of the erotic, but we don't understand this. We feel instead that there is something terribly wrong with *us*. We understand that we must choose between much of what we feel in our bodies and what everyone around us is telling us we *should* feel. Gradually or suddenly, we split into two contradictory beings—call it id and superego, call it body and mind, call it primitive and civilized. To gain the approval of those around us, we reject our primal erotic nature and, as we push our erotic sensibilities deeper and deeper into the shadows, we find it increasingly difficult to honor or even be aware of the erotic within us.

These are the dynamics of the suppression and denial of eros. In a culture such as ours, so terribly suspicious of erotic feeling and power, it becomes important to understand how this suppression occurs so that we can begin to reclaim the core erotic vitality that we have lost.

Fortunately, the erotic spirit does not die a quiet death. Indeed, the erotic impulse cannot really be killed at all—it is much too primary a force for that. But it can be stunted, twisted, and contorted so that it becomes limited to expressing itself in ways that are mundane, repetitious, painful, and unsatisfying—even dangerous to ourselves and to others. What most of us struggle with, as we try to develop respectful, loving connections to our erotic natures, is the war between our basic erotic feelings and the various social, psychological, religious, and political forces that attempt to suppress those feelings. We confront what Marco Vassi calls the "great chasm of shame" that stands between our essential eroticism and "a world that despises both its animal and angel natures."

What are these erotosuppressive forces? Where do they come from? How do they operate in the structures of our daily lives, in the underpinnings of our culture, in the psychodynamics of our emotional development, in the sociopolitical workings of law and government?

The essays in this section look at several of the primary forces behind the suppression and distortion of erotic feelings and desire. Sexologist and Catholic priest Robert Francoeur begins by tracing the historical process by which Christianity shifted, in the four hundred years after Christ, from its essentially sex-affirming, Hebraic roots to the virulently anti-erotic crusade that continues to this day. Writer/sex therapist Marty Klein shows how a culturally ingrained fear of the erotic works psychologically—how we are taught that sex is bad, taught to negate and fear our desires, taught to fear others whose erotic and sexual expressions differ from our own.

Psychologist Carol Cassell explains how these forces undermine women in particular, encouraging them to repress sexual feeling in order to become desexualized *good girls*. She takes particular note of the cultural illusion that sexual desire is a uniquely male phenomenon, something that girls and women respond to but do not initiate or even experience on their own.

Feminist anthropologist Carole Vance addresses some contemporary political manifestations of erotic suppression, particularly the ways that fundamentalists and right-wing conservatives tap into our internalized fears about sexual expression, as well as the fears generated by the radical shift in sex and sex-role mores during the 60s and 70s. She analyzes the ongoing attacks on pornography and other sexual depictions as part of a larger campaign to control and suppress all sexual thought and behavior that go beyond heterosexual monogamy and marriage.

Feminist theorist Ellen Willis goes on to discuss the way that some activists within the feminist movement have surprisingly become political forces for the suppression of eros. She argues that many feminist progressives have allowed their own fears and misunderstanding of issues surrounding pornography to make them the unlikely allies of conservative moralists in what is rapidly becoming a great cultural civil war.

In a more optimistic vein, writer Sallie Tisdale discusses her personal interest in pornography as a vehicle for overcoming socially imposed matrices of sexual suppression and denial. From a perspective that is at once fiercely feminist and sex affirming, she sees the limitations of pornography and yet acknowledge its virtue as a source of reassurance, blessing, and permission to explore the intricacies of one's inevitably "incorrect" yet unstillable sexual infatuations.

Finally, two poems offer very different celebrations—the defiant proclamation of "Scarlet Woman," and the quieter, but equally fierce statement by Anne Sexton—of the exhilaration of overcoming the forces of suppression in order to reaffirm the full joy and power of our resilient erotic natures.

Robert T. Francoeur

The Religious Suppression of Eros

Some twenty-five hundred years ago, after the Jews returned home from the Babylonian exile, an unknown, inspired romanic wove together several lovers' songs from their betrothal celebrations. As she swirls around in her lover's arms, the bride sings:

Come! Be swift, my lover!
Be like a gazelle or a wild young stag!
Come! Play on my mountains of myrrh!
The fountain in my garden is a spring of running water, flowing down
from Lebanon.
Arise, north wind!
O south wind, come!
Blow upon my garden, let its alluring perfumes pour forth.
Then will my lover come to his garden and enjoy its choice fruits.

Mesmerized by her dark eyes and sensuous beauty, not at all embarrassed by her provocative and public invitation, the groom responds in kind:

How beautiful you are, my dearest! O how beautiful!
Your eyes are like doves behind your veil.
Your hair is like a flock of goats streaming down Mount Gilead.
Your teeth are like a flock of ewes ready to be shorn, like freshly washed
sheep that are big with twins, none of them thin or barren. . . .

The cheeks behind your veil are like a pomegranate sliced open in two.
Your neck is like King David's tower. . . .
Your breasts like two fawns, young twins of a mother deer. . . .
How beautiful are your breasts, my sister, my bride!. . . . Your
perfumes are more fragrant than any spices!
Your lips drip honey, my bride,
Words drop from your mouth like syrup from the honeycomb.
You flourish like an orchard of rare fruits,
like an orchard of pomegranates.
You are a pleasure ground filled with flowers. . . .
You are an enclosed garden, my sister, my bride,
a garden close-locked, with a secret fountain.

In answer, the bride sings about her passion:

My lover is radiant and ruddy, he stands out among ten thousand.
His head is pure gold; his looks like thick palm leaves, and black as the
raven.
His eyes are like doves beside brooks of water.
His teeth seem bathed in milk, and his smile adorns his face like finely
set jewels.
His cheeks are like beds of spice, treasures of ripe perfumes.
His lips red blossoms, dripping liquid myrrh.
His arms are rods of gold, his hands crystal olive branches.
Hid body is a work of ivory with sapphire veneer.
His legs are pillars of marble supported in sockets of precious gold.
His stature, like the trees of Lebanon, is imposing; his countenance as
noble as cedars.
His mouth is delicious; he is all delight.[1]

The poet titled his collection of sensuous verses *Shir ha-Shirim,* "the loveliest of songs," and dedicated this Song of Songs to King Solomon, the legendary lover of three hundred wives and six hundred concubines. Rabbinic interpretations sometimes gave the song symbolic meanings, relating it to the gift of the Torah and the building of the Temple. But they never replaced the song's literal message of human love and passion with metaphors.[2]

Christians, on the other hand, have long been embarrassed by this love song of hungry passion and desire. Theologians warned it was dangerous, even wicked, to take the song literally. Bizarre metaphors replaced vivid sensuality with an asexual, spiritualized, cerebral love of God in which the Christian soul sucks nourishment from Christ's two breasts, the Old and New Testaments. St. Jerome interpreted it as a poem praising virgins who mortify their flesh. Before he castrated himself to become a eunuch for the kingdom of heaven, Origen warned Christians that "everyone who is not yet rid of the vexations of flesh and blood and has not ceased to feel the passion of his bodily nature should refrain completely from reading this book."[3]

The history of Jewish and Christian responses to the Song of Songs is a microcosm of the evolution of Western culture from a sex-affirming Hebraic perspective to a sex-negative Christian one, ill-at-ease with eroticism, sensuality, passion, and pleasure.

The Hebraic View

Heaven, according to the Talmud, consists of "Sabbath, sunshine and sex." The key to this comfort with sex and passion lies in the way the Hebrews understood humans. In Hebrew culture, the human is a whole person, a psychosomatic unity. The Hebrew *nephesh* refers to "the essential and vital quality of life itself," the *person*—not to a *soul*. Hebrew has no equivalent for the Greek *psyche* or "soul." Nor does Hebrew have a parallel to the Greek dualistic opposition between body and soul. In Hebrew thought, the concept of *flesh* is neither evil nor antithetical to the "higher" parts of man. Instead, *flesh* refers to the whole of our experience, the physical and the mental, to "the situation of man before God," the whole "earthly sphere." New Testament writers reflected this perspective, using the Greek *psyche* only once, and the Hebrew *nephesh* in sixty other places.[4]

The Hebrew tradition consistently celebrates sexuality within marriage. Sexual asceticism, celibacy, and the single life have no religious value. Sexual intercourse establishes a marriage and is a *mitzvah,* a religious duty, a meritorious performance, a charitable and humanitarian act. "In Jewish history coitus has been consistently and unambiguously valued for the sheer joy and pleasure of it, even when procreation was obviously impossible."[5]

In the Epistle of Holiness of Nahmanides, Jews are advised to prefer the Sabbath for sexual intercourse because it is "holy unto the Lord." Herman Wouk, a contemporary Jewish writer, sums up the

Hebraic view when he notes, "What in other cultures has been a deed of shame, or of comedy, or of orgy, or of physical necessity, or of high romance, has been in Judaism one of the main things God wants man to do. If it turns out to be the keenest pleasure in life, that is no surprise to a people eternally sure God is good."

To understand the evolution from the early sex-affirming Hebraic culture to Christianity's persistent discomfort with sex and pleasure, we have to look at three interwoven threads: the dualistic cosmology of Plato, the Stoic philosophy of early Greco-Roman culture, and the Persian Gnostic tradition. Within three centuries after Jesus, these influences combined to seduce Christian thinkers into a rampant rejection of human sexuality and sexual pleasure.

PLATONIC AND NEOPLATONIC DUALISM

Six hundred years before Christ, the earliest images of Eros reveal the Greek god of love as irrational, uncontrollable, mad, and foolish. The Greco-Roman world adopted a dualistic cosmology in which there is a constant conflict, with the soul and mind seeking liberation from the prison of the fleshly body. In this view, the flesh is somehow the source of evil. In *The Laws* for his utopian Republic, Plato claims that the world would benefit enormously if all sexual pleasures were starved. His utopia forbids all nonprocreative sexual relations.

Socrates and Plato viewed all forms of physical sexuality as inferior to abstinence in both essence and quality simply because they involve the body. Although they tolerated homosexual and extramarital heterosexual relations, Socrates and Plato agreed that any sexual activity was harmful to the soul's health. It takes at least a year, Socrates advised Xenophon, "to recover from the scorpion's bite."[6]

Three centuries after Jesus, Plotinus popularized this dualistic view among Christians. Neoplatonism colors much of St. Augustine's views of sex, and through him most of Christian thought down to the present day.

THE STOIC VIEW

Stoicism, the dominant philosophy of the Roman empire at the beginning of the Christian movement, endorsed a form of Platonic dualism. Seneca the Younger, a contemporary of Jesus and tutor to the emperors, was the preeminent Stoic philosopher. His advice: "Do nothing for the sake of pleasure." Sexual desire, he warned, is "friendship gone mad." "It is also shameful to love one's own wife immoderately. In loving his wife the wise man takes reason for his guide, not emotion. He resists passions and does not allow himself to be impetuously swept away by the marital act. Nothing is more depraved than to love one's spouse as if she were an adulteress." Centuries later, St. Jerome repeated this Stoic maxim: "Anyone who has too passionate a love of his wife is an adulterer." On October 8, 1988 in a public audience, Pope John Paul II again endorsed this Stoic point of view, testifying to its hold on Christian sexual values.[7]

The Stoics believed the ecstasy of sex was dangerous, hard to control, and detrimental to men's health. Sex was part of the burden the soul struggles to jettison as it rises to the divine. Many pagan temple rituals required sexual abstinence before and during celebrations. Centuries later, Catholics would wage bloody battles to enforce celibacy on the clergy.[8]

Musonius Rufus, another Stoic contemporary of Jesus highly admired by Christians, maintained that "men who are not wanton or immoral are bound to consider sexual intercourse [morally] justified only when it occurs in marriage and is indulged in for the purpose of begetting children, since that is lawful. [Sexual intercourse is] unjust and unlawful when it is mere pleasure-seeking, even in marriage." The Christian belief that procreation is the natural purpose of sex and that contraception is unnatural comes not from the biblical tradition but from pagan Stoics and Platonic philosophers. (Christian moralists cannot even claim originality for the missionary position. In the second century, it was the Greek Stoic Artemidorus who claimed that the only morally acceptable position for intercourse was male-superior and face-to-face. Oral eroticism was "an awful act."[9]

THE GNOSTIC INFLUENCE

Alongside Platonic and Stoic dualisms, a third influence helped turn Christianity against sex and pleasure. The deeply pessimistic Gnostic cosmology probably originated in Persia shortly before the birth of Jesus. This worldview stressed the worthlessness and baseness of all things. The body was a "corpse with senses, the grave you carry around with you." Demons created this world. The soul is a spark of light from another world captured by demonic powers, banished to this world of darkness, chained to the dark prison of the body. This kind of demonization of the body and all matter was unknown in the Greco-Roman Christian world before the invasion of Gnosticism.[10]

The Gnostics tried to create a harmonious blend of pagan and Christian values. They interpreted Christian faith as a special kind of knowledge, *gnosis,* which the soul/mind can use to transcend this earth and rise to the divine heavenly sphere. The Gnostics, like the Stoics, often wavered between sexual asceticism and libertine behavior, both motivated by their contempt for the body.

In the early fourth century, Emperor Constantine made Christianity the state religion. With pagan religions outlawed, early Christian concern with idolatry was replaced with emphasis on sexual abstinence and celibacy as centerpieces of Christian moral life. Refuting Roman charges that the Jews, Christians, and Gnostics were sexual libertines, Christians increasingly abandoned holistic anthropology in favor of sexual abstinence.[11]

A second wave of Gnostic thought flourished for about a century, roughly betwen 150 and 270 A.D. According to Manichaeus, sexual abstinence was required of true believers. Some churches influenced by Manichaean beliefs baptized only virgins. The triumph of the Manichaean anti-sexual values came about, at least in part, from a political movement that backfired. Jesus had included women among his immediate disciples, women who left home and openly traveled with him.[12] This assault on Jewish customs and patriarchy did not sit well with the church leaders who followed the apostles. Theologian Elizabeth Schussler Fiorenza suggests that as males tried to reassert patriarchal rule in the early church, women may have rebelled with the only weapon they had—withholding sex. This war between the sexes ended, Fiorenza believes, with a victory for the male celibates, who co-opted sexual abstinence as a weapon by picturing women as dangerous seductresses.[13]

TWO MILLENNIA OF CHRISTIAN SEXUAL REPRESSION

Gospel evidence clearly indicates that Jesus said practically nothing about sex, even as he openly opposed the Jewish patriarchal structure. After the death of the apostles, male church leaders quickly moved to reestablish an exclusively patriarchal rule. They found handy and potent weapons in the prevailing Stoic morality, in Platonic/ Neoplatonic dualism, and in Gnosticism. Biblical translations and commentaries, between about 150 and 400 A.D., turned the brothers and sisters of Jesus first into stepbrothers and stepsisters from Joseph's first marriage, and then into cousins. Joseph became as virginal as Mary, who was said to have conceived Jesus by the Holy Spirit and to have given birth in a spontaneous Caesarean section that left her hymen intact and her vagina unsullied. The birth of Jesus was so virginal that there was not even an afterbirth or placenta (*sordes* in Latin). Similarly, succeeding translations of the New Testament promoted celibacy by turning the apostles' wives into sisters and housekeepers.[14]

During the third century, dualism triumphed in the church. At the Council of Elvira (309 A.D.), almost half of the eighty-one canons adopted dealt with sex. These canons reflect an irrational fear of sex as contamination and defilement. Sexual purity was proclaimed the Christian standard. Almost every imaginable form of sex was proscribed or severely limited. By the end of the fourth century, Jerome had twisted the Old Testament story of Tobias into an argument for sexual abstinence in marriage that allowed sex only for procreation. Translating the Bible from Hebrew and Greek into Latin, Jerome forged a statement saying Tobias postponed consummating his marriage with Sarah for three nights, "not out of lust, but out of love of offspring." For Jerome, all sex is impure.[15]

The fourth century also saw debates over the incarnation of Jesus in which the Hebraic perspective of the Christian theologians at Antioch lost out to the Neoplatonic body-soul dualism of the Alexandrian theologians. Augustine, the leading theologian of that era, gave up two mistresses when he moved from the Manichaean camp to the Christian faith. His deeply ambiguous and complex personality reflects this tension in a heady mixture of wisdom and neurosis. Augustine fought the Manichaean/Platonic dualism, but then said original sin was passed from parents to offspring by the passion and desire associated with sexual intercourse. A Christian Platonist until his death, he often quoted Plotinus in his sermons: "Man *but not woman* is made in the image and likeness of God." As Augustine saw it, "nothing so casts down the manly mind from its [rational, spiritual] heights as the fondling of women, and those bodily contacts which belong to the married state."

By 600 A.D., Pope Gregory the Great was able to declare that "sensual pleasure can never be without sin." Anselm of Laon, who died in 1117 and is honored as the Father of Scholasticism, argued that the amount of pleasure in any action determines the extent of its sinfulness. Albert the Great taught that pleasure is an evil punishment, filthy, defiling, ugly, shameful, sick, a degradation of the mind, a humiliation of reason by the flesh, debasing, humiliating, shared with the beasts, brutal, corrupted, and depraved. It infects the offspring with original sin. Aquinas taught that "sexual pleasure completely checks the use of reason," "stifles reason," and "absorbs the mind."[16]

These views of sexual pleasure took on new meaning when marriage was made a sacrament in the early 1100s. The main effect was to extend the clergy's control over sex rather than to bless sexual pleasure. Because it involved sex, marriage was the lowest of the seven sacraments, intended for third-class Christians. Aquinas even argued that the less passion a husband has for his wife, the more children he will have and the healthier they will be.[17]

Early Scholastic theologians invented a new form of marriage, modeled on the purely spiritual bond of the virginal Joseph and Mary, the so-called *Josephite* or *brother-sister* marriage. Only procreation justified marriage and sex. But even if a husband and wife remained frigid and did not experience any passion or emotion in sexual intercourse, the "latent lust" and "habitual pleasure" associated with sex sufficed to transmit the stain of original sin to any offspring. William of Auvergne (d. 1249), the bishop of Paris, advised married couples to "flee all physical pleasure." It was wonderful, he remarked, that "sometimes young men remain cold with their wives, even when they are beautiful."[18]

Abelard, a leading medieval theologian and the famous lover of Heloise, was one of the few to oppose this anti-sexual value system. "No natural pleasure of the flesh may be declared a sin," he declared, "nor may one impute guilt when someone is delighted by pleasure where he must necessarily feel it. . . . From the first day of our creation, when man lived without sin in Paradise, sexual intercourse and good-tasting foods were naturally bound up with pleasure. God himself has established nature in this way." When their scandalous love was discovered, Heloise's guardian sent her to a convent and had servants castrate Abelard in his sleep. Their tragic fate reflected the choice Christians were forced to make between a life of the body and a life of the soul.[19]

THE CONSEQUENCES OF REPRESSING SEXUAL PLEASURE

What is the outcome when a religion does not recognize our basic human need for pleasure and uses its powerful influence as arbiter of social norms to denigrate and repress our God-given need for nurturing sensual and erotic pleasure? What are the consequences of reducing sex to the mechanical interlocking of male and female genitals? What is the result of ignoring the vital sustenance women and men can draw from the sexual rainbow of playful, loving, intimate, responsible, passionate, and transcendent unions and communions?

Numerous studies of child abuse indicate that parents who abuse their children were often deprived of physical affection themselves during childhood, and as adults experience extremely unsatisfying sexual relationships. Studies of animal young deprived of nurturance, comparisons of child-rearing practices in different cultures, and evidence of neurological damage in anti-social animals and humans demonstrate that deprivation of bodily pleasure during infancy and adolescence and the repression of pleasure and eros promote adult violence.[20]

Patriarchal religions that emphasize a high God who actively punishes deviations in human behavior commonly endorse anti-sexual and anti-pleasure value systems. As part of their anti-sexual values, these religions promote negative attitudes about the physical nurturance of infants and children. They also punish adolescents and adults who indulge in illicit erotic pleasures.

"Deprivation of body pleasure throughout life—but particularly during the formative periods of infancy, childhood and adolescence—is very closely related to the amount of warfare and interpersonal violence [in a society]."[21] Conversely, cultures that promote nurturing in child-rearing, that are comfortable with the body and with sexuality and pleasure, produce adults who have little sexual dysfunction, who promote gender and social equality, and a society that does not glorify slavery or war.[22]

In the twelfth century, Hildegard of Bingen, a contemporary of Abelard and Heloise and a great Benedictine abbess, interpreted the myth of Adam's sin as *a failure of eros*. Adam was banished from Eden not because he discovered nudity and sex, but because he did not enjoy deeply enough the delights of the earth.[23]

Recently, Matthew Fox, a Dominican theologian, was silenced by Vatican celibates for his endorsement of Hildegard of Bingen's interpretation of the Eden myth and for his eros-positive creation spirituality. Fox argues that our failure to celebrate the pleasures of the Divine Presence in our loves creates a compulsion to conquer and achieve pleasure elsewhere. He sees a clear causal link between patriarchal religions that deny the nurturance we draw from erotic pleasures, the feminine, and mother earth, and the anti-pleasure, anti-sex value systems of fundamentalism and fascism.

Although Christians talk about "Mother Church," Fox believes that the Christian church is deeply entangled in the lethal embraces of matricidal patriarchy. Religious fundamentalism of any type rests on the literal interpretations of sacred texts by males who determine what rules guide human behavior and spell out punishments for deviation from those rules. Fundamentalism thrives when individuals become terrified by the breakup of comfortable cultural patterns. If, as Fox and others claim, fundamentalism is patriarchy gone berserk, fascism becomes the ultimate expression of father-dominance. Moralizing and condemnation become more important than celebration and play. Self-centeredness and a preoccupation with human-made games and laws substitute for cosmic adventure, pleasure, wonder, and living ritual.

The repression of eros and pleasure makes for strange fundamentalist-fascist bedfellows. One has only to reflect on the early support of Hitler by Christians who agreed with his attacks on contraception, pornography, and sexual permissiveness. More recently, Christians supported neo-fascist attacks on gay bars, sex shops and houses of prostitution in East Germany after the Communists lost control.[24]

Margaret Mead warned twenty-five years ago that we were entering a *pre-figurative* stage. All the myths and symbols that gave meaning and direction to our culture have lost much of their significance, and we are only beginning to create a new cosmology, a culture that respects sex, pleasure and sensuality, icons and myths that provide models for a new consciousness of ourselves and of the earth.

This prospect of cultural revolution frightens, even terrifies, many people around the world. We can expect fundamentalist, law-revering, even fascist, religious sects to join forces across denominational boundaries to oppose the impending changes. Such civil wars are already evident in the ongoing debates about sexual ethics, homosexuality, and alternatives to monogamy among Catholics after the Second Vatican Council and at recent General Assemblies of the Presbyterian, Episcopal, Evangelical Lutheran, Southern Baptist, and United Methodist Churches. Prophetic, sex-affirming documents, such as *Human Sexuality: New Directions in American Catholic Thought* and the Presbyterian *Keeping Body and Soul Together: Sexuality, Spirituality, and Social Justice,* have been firmly rejected by conservative majorities who abide by traditional biblical interpretations and sexual values. But the debate cannot be stopped. The civil war may lead to schism, or even to open violence. Whether one is strongly religious, casually church-affiliated, or not religious at all is irrelevant, as we all live in a culture permeated by Judeo-Christian values and attitudes.

The human race is struggling with a new consciousness, a new sense of morality. Many people still prefer to regulate sexual practice with black-and-white laws. Jean Piaget calls this "heteronomous morality"; Lawrence Kohlberg calls it "conventional morality." In this moral mode, people are concerned about whether genital activity is heterosexual, homosexual, or masturbatory. Is it coital, or noncoital sodomy (oral or anal sex)? Is it procreative, or contraceptive and engaged in solely for pleasure? Is it marital, pre- or post-marital fornication, or extramarital adultery?

Far fewer people appreciate and are comfortable with a morality based on personal responsibility and internalized ethical principles that focus on the qualities of relationships. In this *autonomous* or *post-conventional* moral thinking, one is concerned with the extent to which a relationship expresses the values of Christian humanism by being self-liberating, life-serving, joyful, and offering the potential for transcendence.[25]

We need to understand and appreciate how the Christian traditions lost their original erotic impulse and why religious authorities find it useful to repress sexual pleasure. Personal guilt and the threat of eternal punishment are potent control mechanisms only as long as individuals think in terms of the laws that guide heteronomous conventional morality.

Creating an autonomous, eros-affirming morality will not be easy. Every religion, every philosophical system, and every society we know, past and present, has been built on contradictions when it comes to dealing with sex. All these systems for making sense out of our world are at war within themselves over the nature, the individual and social purposes, and the control of the human experience we call eros. Does eros need ritual binding to control its Dionysian daemonism? Does the repression of eros by religion and society increase its pleasures?[26] If eros is part of the *yin* and *yang* of human existence, can we hope to experience love, pleasure, light, and warmth without the contrasting poles of hate, pain, darkness, and frigid cold?

Because we live in a society that prefers a punitive work ethic over an ethic of love and compassion, it is risky indeed to assert pleasure, especially sexual pleasure, as a legitimate social goal.[27] We are told the *real issues* facing us are economic deprivation, the threat of nuclear holocaust, the destruction of the environment, and on down the grim, familiar list. But we must acknowledge that the issue of human pleasure is neither marginal nor secondary. Indeed, the "real issues" only reflect our vast, collective separation from our bodies, from the earth, and from other life on it. Hopefully, in the decades ahead, the very threats we have created will force us to rethink pleasure as a human goal and to reclaim it as a human project.

NOTES

1. I have compiled the translation provided here from several popular versions of the Song of Songs, with the assistance of Rabbi Rami Shapiro, Temple Beth Or, Miami, Florida.

2. Phipps, W. E., *Recovering Biblical Sensuousness* (Westminster Press, 1975), pp.44–66.

3. Ibid., pp. 50–52; Fox, M., *The Coming of the Cosmic Christ* (Harper and Row, 1988), pp. 163–180.

4. Lawrence, R. J., *The Poisoning of Eros: Sexual Values in Conflict* (Augustine Moore Press, 1989), pp. 6–9, 128.

5. Ibid., p. 17.

6. Ibid., pp. 8–15.

7. Ranke-Heinemann, U., *Eunuchs for the Kingdom of Heaven: Women, Sexuality, and the Catholic Church* (Doubleday, 1990), pp. 11–13, 62.

8. Lawrence, pp. 134–165; Ranke-Heinemann, p. 99.

9. Lawrence, pp. 11–12.

10. Ranke-Heinemann, pp. 48–49.

11. Lawrence, pp. 92–102.

12. Matthew 27:55; Mark 15:40; Luke 8:10.

13. Fiorenza, E. S., *In Memory of Her* (Crossroad, 1984); Lawrence, pp., 104–105; Ranke-Heinemann, p. 184.

14. Ranke-Heinemann, pp. 27–39, 343–344.

15. Lawrence, pp. 109–116; Ranke-Heinemann, pp. 16–17.

16. Fox, p. 31; Ranke-Heinemann, p. 153.

17. Summa Theologiae III q.65a.2ad 1; Ranke-Heinemann, pp. 153–159, 181.

18. Ranke-Heinemann, p. 155.

19. Ethics 3; Lawrence, pp. 150–157; Ranke-Heinemann, p. 169.

20. Prescott, J. W., "Body Pleasure and the Origins of Violence," *Bulletin of the Atomic Scientists,* November 1975; Prescott, J. W., "Affectional Bonding for the Prevention of Violent Behaviors," in L. J. Heryzberg et al., eds., *Violent Behavior, Volume 1: Assessment and Intervention* (PMA Publishing Corp., 1989).

21. Nelson, J. B., *Embodiment: An Approach to Sexuality and Catholic Theology* (Augsburg Publishing House, 1978).

22. Nelson, pp. 261–271; Prescott, p. 14.

23. Fox, p. 26.

24. Fox, pp. 26–27; Ranke-Heinemann, pp. 330–334.

25. Kosnik, A., et al., *Human Sexuality: New Directions in American Catholic Thought* (Paulist Press, 1977); General Assembly Special Committee on Human Sexuality, Presbyterian Church (U.S.A.), *Keeping Body and Soul Together: Sexuality, Spirituality and Social Justice* (Presbyterian Church, U.S.A.), 1991.

26. Paglia, Camille, *Sexual Personae: Art and Decadence from Nefertiti to Emily Dickinson* (Yale University Press, 1990), p. 36.

27. Ehrenreich, B., E. Hess, and G. Jacob, *Remaking Love: The Feminization of Sex* (Doubleday, 1987), pp. 207–208.

Marty Klein

EROTOPHOBIA: THE CRUELEST ABUSE OF ALL

Eroticism is an energy considered outlaw in this culture. Maybe that's because it's a reminder of the goddess, or because it's energy needed for civilization, or because of some obscure reason that made sense thousands of years ago. Three centuries of Puritanism certainly have taken their toll. Whatever the reason, eroticism is taboo energy—and our society spends vast amounts of its precious resources every minute of every year to undermine, co-opt, channel, ridicule, and distort it.

Each of us pays a price for this. We pay it in forfeited pleasure and foregone peace of mind, in the agonies of sexual and relationship dysfunction, and in the rage, guilt, and powerlessness we feel as we torment ourselves and others. Those others—lovers, children, our communities—pay stiff prices as well. Some people even go to jail because of it. We're all erotically crippled in this culture. We're erotophobic: afraid of our sexuality.

Virtually everyone grows up learning that sex is bad. We are taught this in the simplest, most effective ways. Parents do not discuss sexual topics with their children; if they do mention sex, they inevitably say "don't do it." They misname (or refuse to name) our sexual body parts. As children, we are prevented from and punished for masturbating. We are also punished for certain words because they have sexual connotations. We are deliberately told lies about sex.

But as children we also know that we are sexual. We are, for example, titillated by certain smells, curious about bodies (our own, our

175

friends', our parents'), and delighted by genital stimulation. So we inevitably conclude: if sex is bad, *we* are bad. And if we are bad, that means we could be abandoned by our parents, literally or emotionally. We know we could be annihilated simply for experiencing or expressing our natural eroticism.

Since no one tells us why sex is bad, we have no way to test this terrible premise; our life experiences can never prove it wrong. *My sexuality and I are bad* becomes an untestable religious belief.

As we learn that sex is bad, we learn that there is no aspect of eroticism that we can safely reveal to others. We learn that it is *all* impolite, lewd, and dangerous. It must all be hidden. Eroticism is problematic by definition.

We learn to feel sleazy when experiencing our sexuality, and to feel an uncomfortable combination of embarrassment and prurience when we see or hear other people expressing theirs. We soon abandon the truth of our own experience (that sex can be wholesome, playful, and pleasant) in favor of the negative interpretation that is all around us. Eventually we come to believe that this distorted overlay *is* our experience. We are then poised to join the ranks of the erotic oppressors, enforcing this belief on others, continuing the cycle.

The first victims are ourselves. Freud believed that eroticism, active in infancy, lay dormant between early childhood and puberty—the so-called *latency period*. But children's sexuality only *seems* to disappear, as five or six years of constant negative programming teaches them to hide their sexual feelings and experiences from adults.

Our culture strongly believes that exposing children to any expressions of sexuality, such as pictures or words, will harm them, even if the activity being depicted is not itself harmful. Many people believe, for example, that a child will be hurt by seeing a photo of a couple making love, even though the lovemaking itself is in no way hurtful.

There is no other harmless activity that children (or adults) are similarly barred from seeing or hearing about. In no other arena does our society fear that depictions of activities are in themselves harmful. Our society even allows children to see depictions of activities that *are* harmful to those involved. The average American child, for example, sees one hundred murders every month on TV. That's called family entertainment.

One consequence of the social belief that children must be protected from sex is that children are denied accurate sexual information. This systematically-created ignorance is the single biggest influence shaping childhood sexual development. Lack of sexual information makes the normal sexual events of childhood terrifying. These include the onset of menstruation, wet dreams, the desire to masturbate, and unintentionally observing sexual activity.

Withholding sexual knowledge could even be seen as a deliberate engineering of early sexual experiences to make them scary, disgusting, guilt-ridden, and burdensome—that is, anti-erotic. This is, after all, how an anti-erotic culture instills its values in successive generations.

Sexual ignorance is then reinforced by culturally-generated misinformation. Distorted beliefs about masturbation, "nice" girls, fertility, "performance," female orgasm, and homosexuality alienate us from our bodies, from the other gender, and from our own desires.

Society maintains sexual illiteracy in both youth and adults through designated gatekeepers of sexual information. The people who teach about sexuality in our culture are typically anti-sexual, ill-informed, and committed to particular agendas for manipulating sexual thought and behavior. Thus, for example, while people are encouraged to direct sexual questions to their physicians, sexuality is typically excluded from most American medical training.

Most other people with the legitimacy to educate about sex are similarly ignorant and untrained: TV talk show hosts who are uncomfortable with sex and interested primarily in sexual extremes and distortions; clergy who are frightened of sex, often sexually abstinent, and committed to limited sexual choices such as monogamy and reproductive sex; newspaper columnists who are superficial, limited to "family" language, and committed to narrow definitions of sexual normalcy; parents who are often uncomfortable about sex and convinced that good parenting means protecting their children from sexual stimuli; mental health professionals whose training often includes only "abnormal" sexuality, and whose agenda regarding sex is generally to help people adjust and conform to anti-sexual societal norms.

Learning to question our sexual normalcy is a key step in internalizing society's repression of our eroticism. Since real sex is neither honestly discussed nor observed, no one really knows what most other people feel and do. Children grow up in families with sexual secrets, where it is impossible to feel secure with one's sexual thoughts and feelings. Advertisers continuously encourage consumers to doubt their sexuality (always ready to fix the resulting insecurities by selling a product). Further money is to be made from the various institutions set up to define or repair what becomes considered as abnormal sexuality.

Normalcy-anxiety is a form of social control; the power to decide who is sexually normal is the power to validate and invalidate individuals in a powerfully basic way. Fears about not being normal keep us from expressing our eroticism freely and joyfully. Trying to become normal, instead of trying to discover who we are, we act out our anxiety both sexually and nonsexually.

Thus, American culture frightens teenage boys about not being sufficiently masculine. As a result, teenage boys typically project their anxiety by running around deriding each other as *fags*. Of course these boys also then emphatically deny and repress any erotic impulse that could possibly be considered homosexual, such as tenderness, surrender, or any feeling of real emotional warmth toward other males. Boys learn that sexuality is about proving you're a man. How can a boy then be anything but intensely homophobic?

We need to grieve for the loss of our innate sense of gender adequacy, which our culture reduces to a reward tossed us if we perform well, an anchovy thrown to a circus seal. How frightening to have something that should be our birthright culturally transformed into something that must be earned over and over again. With so much at stake psychologically, it's no wonder that sex feels like a matter of life and death. This makes the outcome of sex more important than the process—an ironic tragedy, since sex is in fact one of the premier process-oriented opportunities in life.

Focused on sex's outcome, we become invested in the aspects of sexual expression that are easily measurable, such as erection and orgasm. Aspects of sex that are more diffuse, that are focused on dimensions such as sensuality, powerplay, or intimacy, seem less important and less interesting.

Another way we are taught to distrust our sexuality concerns the fear that our sexual feelings will get out of control. Children of both genders are taught that boys cannot be trusted to control their sexual impulses. We learn that masturbation is bad, and then feel in danger of losing control when our bodies yearn for that forbidden touch. We learn that not only sexual behavior, but sexual thoughts and feelings as well can be bad, and we are painfully aware of the difficulty of continually sanitizing our sexual desires and fantasies.

In a culture that at once fears and magnifies sexuality, we all feel terribly vulnerable to the temptation of the sexually forbidden. This is confirmed by religious attitudes that link eroticism to lust, encouraging us to think of sexual desire as a state which bypasses our usual, responsible decision-making. This attitude is now further confirmed as the Recovery movement asks us to believe that seventeen million Americans are "sex addicts," people who are unable to control their rampant sexual appetites.

We're taught that if our sexuality gets out of control we are likely to damage ourselves, our loved ones, innocent people, even our communities. We will offend God. We will be permanently stained. Since our sexuality is potentially uncontrollable under even the most conventional circumstances, the only way to safely regulate it is to repress it in all its guises, every minute of our lives. This becomes our erotic burden. Sex becomes the most dangerous, most powerful force on earth, *evil* in the classic sense. Controlling such a demonic force requires that we repress not only our own sexuality but the sexuality of others as well. Thus the censor, the crusading rescuer of women and children, is born.

How can we overcome our society's erotophobic heritage and encourage proper respect for both sex and eroticism? While this is a complex question, some directions are clear: we must recognize the existence and validity of childhood sexuality, recognize that pleasure is a need and a right, not a privilege or luxury, and recognize that eroticism can be expressed in many diverse ways without causing problems of any kind. We must also challenge the concept of *normal sex*.

In terms of social consequences, we need to recognize the devastating effects of the suppression of eros, including violence, relationship dysfunction, and poor health; help people understand that feeling anxiety within a sexual context doesn't mean they are inadequate; confront and resolve our core negative feelings about the body; expand the social definition of *sexy* so that everyone is eligible for this confirmation; and see the link between anti-eroticism and consumerism, the belief that the way to enjoy sex is to acquire and consume rather than simply be who you are.

On a policy level, we must take school sex education seriously, as preparation for adulthood and for sexual decision-making; make accurate information about all aspects of sexuality easily available to adults, adolescents, and interested children; and challenge seemingly rational social policies that are actually anti-sexual.

Ultimately, we must change the language of public debate to

recognize the various guises of the suppression of eros, such as *pro-life* (anti-choice) and *anti-smut* (anti-sexual), and we must educate opinion and language leaders on all these issues, including medical students, journalists, clergy, and mental health professionals.

The fear of sexuality has been so strongly bred into us by custom and tradition that we think fear is a necessary part of sex. This is simply not true. Eroticism can, in fact, transform us precisely because it can provide the exquisite experience of fearlessness. Erotophobia is not inevitable. It is the result of cultural, social, and political forces, and is fueled by those who benefit from it.

For centuries, erotic energy has been considered a fundamental problem. The time has come to acknowledge it as a fundamental solution.

Carol Cassell

STILL GOOD GIRLS
AFTER ALL THESE YEARS

> I was brought up to be a Good Girl. I was taught never to cause
> anger, disgust, diappointment or inconvenience. I learned to try
> and please everyone.
>
> ANONYMOUS, AGE FORTY-FIVE

This terse comment in a batch of responses to a questionnaire
gave me an uncomfortable jolt of recognition. In the bare economy of
those lines, I recognized the narrowness and confinement of generations of women's lives, circumscribed by the amorphous and insidious
credo of the Good Girl.

One aspect of who we are is encoded in the messages we receive
about who we *should* be. We learn that certain behavior is rewarded,
other behavior punished. If we learn not to squander our sexual good
on unworthy males, we also know that to be eligible for the attention of
the worthy ones, we must follow certain rules and regulations. We
must be worthy ourselves: Good Girls. The term has endless connotations: chaste, kind, sweet, virtuous, cheerful, coy, and above all, *above
reproach.* We learn this from the way society regulates our behavior, setting up standards of female decorum, using a form of social control
that sociologist Greer Litton Fox identifies as *normative restrictions.*

Normative restrictions work as a social control because the culture as a whole shares the same values, the same norms. Thus the
whole culture is enlisted to preserve the norms: if a member deviates,
he or she becomes a pariah. When the norm is that women's behavior
should conform to the social ideal of a *lady,* her failure to adhere to this

prescription means that it is *her* fault that she is an outcast, not society's fault for having an inflexible or untenable norm. She is thus due any consequences that befall her: ostracism, loss of value as a person, even, in certain societies, public humiliation and death by stoning. It seems an extreme fate for a Bad Girl, doesn't it?

One of the most pervasive norms of our culture is sexual restraint. As Greer Litton Fox notes, "A girl is in a delicate position. She is told to appear and act *sexy* in order to attract as many boys and have as many dates as possible. . . . But at the same time she must hold the line of propriety, because otherwise she risks losing her *good girl* status and, consequently, her prestige." Only if a woman is madly in love, swept off her feet, can she still claim any vestige of her Good Girl status. A woman *in love* is released from the burden of being good so that she can be erotic. She's a nonsexual being who lapsed temporarily into sexuality. She is *overcome* by passion. Sex is something that happens *to* her.

Barbara, twenty-seven, explained how she gave herself permission to be sexual. "I shouldn't admit this, but I can't have sex unless the man I'm with is really persuasive and takes a firm hold of the situation. I'm not talking about rape or anything like that, but he can't just let me beg off too eagerly. He has to sweep me off my feet or I can't enjoy it."

If she initiated a sexual encounter, Barbara feels that she would lose the temporary suspension of the rules of proper behavior that passion allows, leaving her susceptible to condemnation and unworthy of masculine attention. Dr. Karen Cantrell, an anthropologist studying women and power, defines this sexual side-stepping as an aligning action, as the way a woman attempts to resolve the conflict between her personal desire and society's prohibitions. "A woman may account for her sexual behavior by disclaiming responsibility for her actions. She can't be blamed for breaking the rules about sex if *she wasn't in control.* Allowing herself to be overcome by a skillful lover puts the responsibility on the man for her breech." Her need, sexual fulfillment, has been neatly aligned with society's—that she remain nonsexual. She wasn't sexual; the *man* was.

In refusing to acknowledge and deal with her needs, a woman relies on a man's permission, via seduction, to be erotic. The "terrible" power of a woman's sexuality—that eternal power that binds men to women—is constrained when she hands responsibility for it over to a man. A Good Girl, sexual only in male-approved circumstances, is a controlled and dependent woman, relieved of adulthood. Her sexual passivity affects her life as well as her libido. Unable to stand on her own two feet, she must resort to attempting to bind a man to her in the veiled contract. . . .

How do you create a Good Girl? It starts in childhood. Society still doesn't say to girls, "Sex is wonderful. It feels physically pleasurable; it can make you feel emotionally satisfied and good about yourself. There are no rules except (1) Don't get pregnant unless you plan to; (2) Don't get a sexually transmitted disease; and (3) Don't be exploitative." Nowhere is it clearly stated to a young woman that sex is a normal and natural part of life experience.

> I was taught that sex was the most beautiful thing *if two people were in love.* I always convince myself, if only momentarily, that I am in love.
>
> N.N., AGE TWENTY-SEVEN

There are rules, and we learn the lessons well. Sex is meaningful *only* with the right man, *only* in a proper relationship (usually marriage). If the rules aren't spoken aloud, an uncomfortable silence delivers the message.

According to Masters and Johnson, "During her formative years the female dissembles much of her developing sexuality in response to social requirements. . . . Instead of being taught or allowed to value her sexual feelings in anticipation of appropriate and meaningful opportunity for expression, thereby developing a realistic social value system, she must attempt to repress or remove them from their natural context of environmental stimulation." The most pervasive message young women get is *don't* if you want to be loved and respected. As one twenty-two-year-old woman said, "Females have rights in sex and life but it's not necessarily *ladylike* to practice them."

We hear this message at the most unlikely times—pulling the covers back on the bed in anticipation of making love in the middle of the afternoon, glancing in the mirror and seeing yourself taking his shirt off. Voices out of the past, the whispering of the mind combined with the gut feeling that you're doing something just not right, something an authentic Good Girl would never do.

Our society has institutionalized the negative messages that we give our young girls, and still attempts to legislate proper behavior. Senator Jeremiah Denton and like-minded congressional leaders succeeded in getting passed the "Chastity Bill" of 1981. It was purportedly intended to help combat the staggering number of teenage pregnancies—about one million a year. It appropriated money for projects helping teenage *girls* to say no to sexual intercourse. Not one penny was budgeted to providing birth control information: it was a $30 million "Hold the Hymen" campaign, designed to pressure young women to learn to be *good*.

Marjory Mecklenberg, who directed the Adolescent Family Life Program of the Department of Health and Human Services, tried to get legislation passed that would force family planning officials to notify the parents of teens served (read teenager girls here: they are 33 percent of the clientele at family planning clinics). She said she had no illusions about getting teenagers to give up sex, but she felt that counselors should try to dissuade them before they start.

There has been a flurry of sex-education material directed at the "problem." Government posters list dire consequences to teenagers having sex. All the pamphlets advise young *women* to say no under the guise of self-determination. But the answer in the pamphlets, unlike in real life, is never *yes* to sex, nor does the question—to have sex or withhold it—ever seem to be directed at the boy. In a book for teenagers on sex and love, author Ray E. Short listed twenty-five arguments for and *thirty-four* against premarital sex, mostly directed to girls. And a book publisher's recent ad in the *New York Times* trumpeted, "Premarital sex. It's sweeping America because of today's records, movies, magazines and TV. Here are the facts you must know to get your *daughter* safely through dangerous years." (Emphasis added.) The ad is for *Heartbreak U.S.A.,* which promises to "give your *daughter* the knowledge and ability to resist the incredible pressure being placed on her. . . . This book will help any young girl live up to the standards of conduct which were normal and expected, until recently." It's a manual for becoming a Good Girl, a $12.95 solution to the "misery" and "heartbreak" of premarital sex.

Teaching a young girl to be uncomfortable about her sexuality extends to her feelings about her body. Natural functions become occasions for embarrassment; attitudes that seem appropriate to the dark ages are all too apparent today. In a 1981 research report of the Tampax company based on a survey of one thousand people, almost two-thirds (66 percent) felt that menstruation should not be discussed in the office or socially. One-quarter of the respondents felt it was an unacceptable topic for the family at home; one-third felt that even in her own home, a women should conceal the fact that she was having her period. The most startling and dismaying attitude was that 12 percent of male respondents felt that women should make every effort to avoid contact with other people while menstruating, and 5 percent of the women— *very* Good Girls—agreed!

In my own "liberated" household I was brought up short when I asked my seventeen-year-old stepdaughter to buy tampons, a supply for herself, her sister, and me. She blushed and said, "I'll buy yours, but that's all for now. Lisa can get her own, and I'll buy mine when I go to the store again."

I was surprised. "What is this about? Are you feeling embarrassed?"

"I know I shouldn't be, but there are lots of guys from school who work there and I don't want to show up with a basket full of Tampax at the check-out counter."

I remembered the feeling from thirty years ago; I had hoped that I could spare my children, but even if we manage the miracle of raising a daughter who is not ashamed of her normal functions we cannot control the influence of her classmates, friends, and the boys at the check-out counter.

Columnist and moral arbiter Abigail Van Buren is certainly one of the most widely read authorities on proper behavior. Readers write her constantly about their concerns with virginity and premarital sex. Not long ago a reader asked her to repeat the advice to girls that she issued years ago:

> Girls need to *prove their love* through illicit sex relations like a moose needs a hat rack.
>
> Why not prove your love by sticking your head in the oven and turning on the gas, or playing leap-frog out in the traffic? It's about as safe.
>
> Any fellow who asks you to *prove your love* is trying to take you for the biggest, most gullible fool who ever walked. That proving bit is one of the oldest and rottenest lines ever invented!
>
> Does he love you? Someone who loves you wants whatever is best for you. He wants you to:
>
> Commit an immoral act.
>
> Surrender your virtue.
>
> Throw away your self-respect.
>
> Risk the loss of your precious reputation.
>
> And risk getting into trouble.
>
> Does that sound as if he wants what's best for you? He wants what's best for him . . . he wants a thrill he can brag about at your expense.
>
> Love? A boy who loves a girl would sooner cut off his right

arm than hurt her. If you want my opinion, this self-serving so-and-so has already proved that he doesn't love you. The after-maths of *proofs* of this kind always find Don Juan tiring of his sport. That's when he drops you, picks up his line and goes casting elsewhere for bigger, equally silly fish.

Even if unintended by "Dear Abby," untold numbers of young girls may have gotten the idea from this column that premarital sex is dangerous, morally wrong, and liable to punishment. Now, in addition to the other messages, we have the current public schools' education programs on AIDS. Well-intended and urgently needed as these efforts are, the majority are simply warmed-over versions of the "Just say no" (to premarital sex) campaigns focused on girls.

If one million teenaged girls get pregnant every year, that means, as a recent Planned Parenthood public service announcement pointed out, one million teenaged boys were fathers. In an ostrich-like and time-honored fashion, our society virtually ignores male involvement, even to a degree condoning it. We concentrate our prohibitive energy on the female, so that her entry into the sexual world is guilt-laden and fearful. We know, statistically, that almost every young woman in this country will have had sex by the age of nineteen, but because of our societal fear of promiscuity, we choose not to inform our daughters of the real benefits of intercourse—closer relationship, a sense of intimacy, physical release. Even when we are sincerely and justifiably concerned that teens are having sex before they are emotionally and physically ready, and feel that peer pressure needs counterbalancing, we add to the problem if we don't acknowledge that there are positive aspects of sex. Another generation of girls is growing up right now, ashamed and misinformed, and ripe to fall victim to their own ambivalence.

Carole S. Vance

Photography, Pornography, and Sexual Politics

The art world was taken by surprise by the furor over the National Endowment for the Arts (NEA) funding of exhibitions containing photographs by Andres Serrano and Robert Mapplethorpe, which began in the summer of 1989, and by the subsequent indictment of Dennis Barrie, director of the Contemporary Arts Center in Cincinnati, Ohio and the CAC itself in conjunction with the opening of "Robert Mapplethorpe: The Perfect Moment" in April 1990. Observers were startled to find fine-arts photography the target of attack, called pornographic, even "obscene," because of its sexual or erotic content. Some wondered if a time-machine had catapulted them back to the late nineteenth century, when moral crusaders assailed museums and galleries for displaying nude statues and paintings. This new campaign against photography and sexual imagery is far from an anachronism, however. It is the systematic extension of conservative and fundamentalist cultural politics to the world of "high culture," a domain that had previously been exempt from their carefully organized public crusades.

In the past ten years, conservatives and fundamentalists have crafted and deployed techniques of grass-roots and mass mobilization around issues of sexuality, gender and religion. In these campaigns, symbols figure prominently, both as highly condensed statements of moral concern and as powerful spurs to emotion and action. In moral campaigns, fundamentalists select a negative symbol that is highly inflammatory to their own constituency and that is difficult or problematic for their opponents to defend, for example exaggerated and distorted fetal images in anti-abortion propaganda. These groups have orchestrated major actions in the realm of popular culture—the protests against Martin Scorsese's *The Last Temptation of Christ* motivated by the Reverend Donald E. Wildmon, campaigns against rock music led by Tipper Gore and the PMRC (Parents Music Resource Center), and the Meese Commission's war against pornography. Ironically, these growing crusades come at a time when fundamentalist victories in electoral politics are decreasing and perhaps signal the conservatives' recognition that social programs, which could not be attained through conventional politics, could still succeed through more long-term, though admittedly slower, attempts to change the cultural environment.

The attacks on photography designate the first time that such mobilizations have been so overtly directed at "high" culture. The targeting of photography by right-wing religious and political leaders like Wildmon and Jesse Helms is not accidental: it is probably the weakest brick in the fine-arts edifice. A relatively recent historical arrival, photography does not yet have the prestige surrounding painting or sculpture, and photography's institutions, also comparative newcomers, have fewer resources and less authority. In addition, a significant amount of photography circulates through galleries, without the imprimatur of museums. Contemporary photographers and their works remain unprotected, since there has been less time in which to develop a consensus about their value—financial, artistic and cultural.

Photography is also less privileged than other fine arts because of its ubiquity. The proliferation of photographic images in everyday life and mass culture—in advertising and photojournalism—makes it more difficult to shelter photography, even if one wanted to, under the often protective umbrella of seemingly rarified and prestigious high culture. Finally, the realistic quality of photographic representation makes it especially vulnerable to the conservative analysis of representation, which is characterized by extreme literalism. For all these reasons, the choice of photography as the first target in a newly launched conservative movement against the fine arts was shrewd. Indeed, it may have been the only plausible target: imagine, for example, public response to a campaign to remove *The Origin of the World,* 1866, from the Brooklyn Museum's 1988 Courbet retrospective.

Most of the arguments and techniques employed in the recent

campaign against sexual images in photography had been perfected by the Attorney General's Commission on Pornography (the Meese Commission) between 1985 and 1986. Dominated by conservatives and fundamentalists, the commission focused entirely on visual images, usually sensationalized and taken out of context. In their hearings, commissioners experimented with and refined methods of using images to promote sexual anxiety, shame, and agreement with their analysis. The commission favored a literal interpretive frame, in which sexual images directly caused behavior; they disavowed subjectivity and the diverse reactions that arise in response to any sexual image. The commission showed carefully selected images that they imagined would be especially shocking, and provided a coercive narration that informed the viewer what each image meant. Through these manipulative techniques, the panel created a fictional, though apparently almost unanimous public opinion united against sexually explicit images, and used sexual shame to silence opponents. The commission recommended that citizen activism—boycotts, public pressure, and withdrawal of public funds—be directed against sexually explicit materials that could not be removed by using obscenity law. During its hearings, the commission rhetorically observed the distinction between commercial pornography and the fine arts, calling no expert witnesses from the art community and assuring anticensorship witnesses that the panel's draconian recommendations for new restrictions would have no effect on high culture. But those reassurances were soon proved hollow by morality groups' new campaigns against art.

In the Meese Commission's intrusions and subsequent public art controversies, the combination of sexual content and photography makes for a particularly explosive mix, and not just for members of fundamentalist groups. The reasons for their disapproval are clear: images that depict sexuality outside of marriage and procreation encourage immorality (or so we are to believe), and thereby subvert the traditional social arrangements conservatives would like to reinstate. But for the average citizen, sexual imagery can be difficult and disturbing too. Heirs to a Victorian cultural tradition that regarded sexual pleasure with profound suspicion, we greet explicit images of sexuality with anxiety and an underdeveloped history of looking. Distinctions that viewers are accustomed to making—between fantasy and behavior, image and reality—become curiously evanescent when it comes to sex. Our unease often increases if the sexual acts depicted are unfamiliar or unconventional or stigmatized, as the moment of viewing becomes tinged with judgment, and erotophobic and homophobic prejudice. Female viewers may scan the image for signs of sexism and danger, contrasting the seemingly conventional, even ubiquitous female nude with her less frequently seen male counterpart. And although we admire the power of photographic images to arouse feeling and emotion, we remain uneasy, sometimes ashamed, when those feelings are sexual.

This volatile mix is easily exploited by conservatives in their public crusades, as they claim virtually all sexual imagery is "pornographic." The widely shared cultural anxiety about sex and sexual imagery makes everyone fair game. Unlike the term "obscenity," which has a specific and fairly narrow legal meaning established through successive court decisions, most recently in *Miller v. California* in 1973, pornography is a highly subjective and unbounded term, referring to a potentially wide range of material with sexual content, though in a clearly pejorative way. The question, "What is pornography?" is the site of public and political struggles. Does it include commercially produced men's magazines? Sex-therapy films? AIDS safe-sex education brochures? Mapplethorpe's photos? David Wojnarowicz's work? A performance by Karen Finley? Conservatives want to cast the net as widely as possible, and they intuit that the epithet "pornography" effectively invokes sexual anxiety in the general public and the art world alike, putting everyone on the defensive and making an effective and vigorous argument in support of sexual and erotic material often difficult to articulate.

The attack on photography and sexual imagery is a logical outgrowth of the right-wing political efforts to shape the cultural and social climate in which political decisions are made. Sexually explicit images are under attack because they stand in for sexual behaviors and attitudes that conservative groups would like to control, or even eliminate. And this right-wing commitment to controlling images and reducing diversity is enduring, not ephemeral. For this reason, attacks on photography featuring sexual and other "objectionable" imagery are likely to continue, and an effective and vigorous response by the arts community and the mainstream public is crucial. In recent battles about cultural representation, particularly involving the Meese Commission, writers and writers' groups such as the Writers Guild and the National Writers Union have been the most organized and have made the best arguments against censorship and for diversity, in part because of their long history with censorship directed at texts. The arts community and its supporters have begun to emulate that organization and energy, adding their own badly needed insights about visual imagery and representation to the public debate. Interpretation of images cannot be allowed to remain the exclusive province of fundamentalist leaders and their aroused followers. Although we reject the crude literalism of conservative interpretive maneuvers, which reduce an image to a singular meaning and perceive it only in the most narrow political terms, it has become clear that a more generous and expansive view of both images and sexuality will be guaranteed only through vigorous political action by the arts community.

Ellen Willis

FEMINISM, MORALISM, AND PORNOGRAPHY

When I first heard there was a group called Women Against Pornography, I twitched. Could I define myself as Against Pornography? Not really. In itself, pornography—which, my dictionary and I agree, means any image or description intended or used to arouse sexual desire—does not strike me as the proper object of a political crusade. As the most cursory observation suggests, there are many varieties of porn, some pernicious, some more or less benign. About the only generalization one can make is that pornography is the return of the repressed, of feelings and fantasies driven underground by a culture that atomizes sexuality, defining love as a noble affair of the heart and mind, lust as a base animal urge centered in unmentionable organs. Prurience—the state of mind I associate with pornography—implies a sense of sex as forbidden, secretive pleasure, isolated from any emotional or social context. I imagine that in utopia, porn would wither away along with the state, heroin, and Coca-Cola.

At present, however, the sexual impulses that pornography appeals to are part of virtually everyone's psychology. For obvious political and cultural reasons nearly all porn is sexist in that it is the product of a male imagination and aimed at a male market; women are less likely to be consciously interested in pornography, or to indulge that interest, or to find porn that turns them on. But anyone who thinks women are simply indifferent to pornography has never watched a bunch of adolescent girls pass around a trashy novel.

Over the years I've enjoyed various pieces of pornography—some of them of the sleazy Forty-second Street sort—and so have most women I know. Fantasy, after all, is more flexible than reality, and women have learned, as a matter of survival, to be adept at shaping male fantasies to their own purposes. If feminists define pornography, per se, as the enemy, the result will be to make many women ashamed of their sexual feelings and afraid to be honest about them. And the last thing women need is more sexual shame, guilt, and hypocrisy—this time served up as feminism.

So why ignore qualitative distinctions and in effect condemn all pornography as equally bad? WAP organizers answer—or finesse—this question by redefining pornography. They maintain that pornography is not really about sex but about violence against women. Or, in a more colorful formulation, "Pornography is the theory, rape is the practice."

Part of the argument is that pornography causes violence; much is made of the fact that Charles Manson and David Berkowitz had porn collections. This is the sort of inverted logic that presumes marijuana to be dangerous because most heroin addicts started with it. It is men's hostility toward women—combined with their power to express that hostility and for the most part get away with it—that causes sexual violence. Pornography that gives sadistic fantasies concrete shape—and, in today's atmosphere, social legitimacy—may well encourage suggestible men to act them out. But if *Hustler* were to vanish from the shelves tomorrow, I doubt that rape or wife-beating statistics would decline.

Even more problematic is the idea that pornography depicts violence rather than sex. Since porn is by definition overtly sexual, while most of it is not overtly violent, this equation requires some fancy explaining. The conference WAP held in September 1979 was in part devoted to this task. Robin Morgan and Gloria Steinem addressed it by attempting to distinguish pornography from erotica. According to this argument, erotica (whose etymological root is "eros," or sexual love) expresses an integrated sexuality based on mutual affection and desire between equals; pornography (which comes from another Greek root—"porne," meaning prostitute) reflects a dehumanized sexuality based on male domination and exploitation of women.

The distinction sounds promising, but it doesn't hold up. The accepted meaning of erotica is literature or pictures with sexual themes; it may or may not serve the essentially utilitarian function of pornography. Because it is less specific, less suggestive of actual sexual activity, *erotica* is regularly used as a euphemism for *classy porn*. Pornography expressed in literary language or expensive photography and consumed by the upper middle class is *erotica*; the cheap stuff, which can't pretend to any purpose but getting people off, is smut.

The erotica-versus-porn approach evades the (embarrassing?) question of how porn is *used*. It endorses the portrayal of sex as we might like it to be and condemns the portrayal of sex as it too often is, whether in action or only in fantasy. But if pornography is to arouse, it must appeal to the feelings we have, not those that by some utopian standard we ought to have. Sex in this culture has been so deeply politicized that it is impossible to make clear-cut distinctions between *authentic* sexual impulses and those conditioned by patriarchy. Between, say, *Ulysses* at one end and *Snuff* at the other, erotica/pornography conveys all sorts of mixed messages that elicit complicated and private responses. In practice, attempts to sort out good erotica from bad porn inevitably come down to "What turns me on is erotic; what turns you on is pornographic."

It would be clearer and more logical simply to acknowledge that some sexual images are offensive and some are not. But logic and clarity are irrelevant—or rather, inimical—to the underlying aim of the antiporners, which is to vent the emotions traditionally associated with the word *pornography*.

There is a social and psychic link between pornography and rape. In terms of patriarchal morality both are expressions of male lust, which is presumed to be innately vicious, and offenses to the putative sexual innocence of "good" women. But feminists supposedly begin with different assumptions—that men's confusion of sexual desire with predatory aggression reflects a sexist system, not male biology; that there are no good (chaste) or bad (lustful) women, just women who are, like men, sexual beings.

From this standpoint, to lump pornography with rape is dangerously simplistic. Rape is a violent physical assault. Pornography can be a psychic assault, both in its content and in its public intrusions on our attention, but for women as for men it can also be a source of erotic pleasure. A woman who is raped is a victim; a woman who enjoys pornography (even if that means enjoying a rape fantasy) is in a sense a rebel, insisting on an aspect of her sexuality that has been defined as a male preserve. Insofar as pornography glorifies male supremacy and sexual alienation, it is deeply reactionary. But in rejecting sexual repression and hypocrisy—which have inflicted even more damage on women than on men—it expresses a radical impulse.

That this impulse still needs defending, even among feminists, is evident from the sexual attitudes that have surfaced in the antiporn movement. In the movement's rhetoric pornography is a code word for vicious male lust. To the objection that some women get off on porn, the standard reply is that this only shows how thoroughly women have been brainwashed by male values—though a WAP leaflet goes so far as to suggest that women who claim to like pornography are lying to avoid male opprobrium. (Note the good-girl-versus-bad-girl theme, reappearing as healthy-versus-sick, or honest-versus-devious; for *brainwashed* read *seduced*.)

And the view of sex that most often emerges from talk about erotica is as sentimental and euphemistic as the word itself: lovemaking should be beautiful, romantic, soft, nice, and devoid of messiness, vulgarity, impulses to power, or indeed aggression of any sort. Above all, the emphasis should be on *relationships,* not (yuck) *organs.* This goody-goody concept of eroticism is not feminist but feminine. It is precisely sex as an aggressive, unladylike activity, an expression of violent and unpretty emotion, an exercise of erotic power, and a specifically genital experience that has been taboo for women. Nor are we supposed to admit that we, too, have sadistic impulses, that our sexual fantasies may reflect forbidden urges to turn the tables and get revenge on men. (When a woman is aroused by a rape fantasy, is she perhaps identifying with the rapist as well as the victim?)

At the WAP conference lesbian separatists argued that pornography reflects patriarchal sexual relations; patriarchal sexual relations are based on male power backed by force; ergo, pornography is violent. This dubious syllogism, which could as easily be applied to romantic novels, reduces the whole issue to hopeless mush. If all manifestations of patriarchal sexuality are violent, then opposition to violence cannot explain why pornography (rather than romantic novels) should be singled out as a target. Besides, such reductionism allows women no basis for distinguishing between consensual heterosexuality and rape. But this is precisely its point; as a number of women at the conference put it, "In a patriarchy, all sex with men is pornographic." Of course, to attack pornography, and at the same time equate it with heterosexual sex, is implicitly to condemn not only women who like pornography, but women who sleep with men.

This is familiar ground. The argument that straight women collaborate with the enemy has often been, among other things, a relatively polite way of saying that they consort with the beast. At the conference I couldn't help feeling that proponents of the separatist line were talking like the modern equivalents of women who, in an era when straightforward prudery was socially acceptable, joined convents to escape men's rude sexual demands. It seemed to me that their revulsion against heterosexuality was serving as the thinnest of covers for disgust with sex itself. In any case, sanitized feminine sexuality, whether straight or gay, is as limited as the predatory masculine kind and as central to women's oppression; a major function of misogynist pornography is to scare us into embracing it. As a further incentive, the good cops stand ready to assure us that we are indeed morally superior to men, that in our sweetness and nonviolence (read passivity and powerlessness) is our strength.

Women are understandably tempted to believe this comforting myth. Self-righteousness has always been a feminine weapon, a permissible way to make men feel bad. Ironically, it is socially acceptable for women to display fierce aggression in their crusades against male vice, which serve as an outlet for female anger without threatening male power. The temperance movement, which made alcohol the symbol of male violence, did not improve the position of women; substituting porn for demon rum won't work either. One reason it won't is that it bolsters the good girl-bad girl split. Overtly or by implication it isolates women who like porn or "pornographic" sex or who work in the sex industry. WAP has refused to take a position on prostitution, yet its activities—particularly its support for cleaning up Times Square—will affect prostitutes' lives. Prostitution raises its own set of complicated questions. But it is clearly not in women's interest to pit "good" feminists against "bad" whores (or topless dancers, or models for skin magazines).

So far, the issue that has dominated public debate on the antiporn campaign is its potential threat to free speech. Here too the movement's arguments have been full of contradictions. Susan Brownmiller and other WAP organizers claim not to advocate censorship and dismiss the civil liberties issue as a red herring dragged in by men who don't want to face the fact that pornography oppresses women. Yet at the same time, WAP endorses the Supreme Court's contention that obscenity is not protected speech, a doctrine I—and most civil libertarians—regard as a clear infringement of First Amendment rights. Brownmiller insists that the First Amendment was designed to protect political dissent, not expressions of woman-hating violence. But to make such a distinction is to defeat the amendment's purpose, since it implicitly cedes to the government the right to define *political*. (Has there ever been a government willing to admit that its opponents are anything more than antisocial troublemakers?)

Anyway, it makes no sense to oppose pornography on the grounds that it's sexist propaganda, then turn around and argue that it's not political. Nor will libertarians be reassured by WAP's statement that "We want to change the definition of obscenity so that it focuses on violence, not sex." Whatever their focus, obscenity laws deny the right of free expression to those who transgress official standards of propriety—and personally, I don't find WAP's standards significantly less oppressive than the Supreme Court's. Not that it matters, since WAP's fantasies about influencing the definition of obscenity are appallingly naive. The basic purpose of obscenity laws is and always has been to reinforce cultural taboos on sexuality and suppress feminism, homosexuality, and other forms of sexual dissidence. No pornographer has ever been punished for being a woman hater, but not too long ago information about female sexuality, contraception, and abortion was assumed to be obscene. In a male supremacist society the only obscenity law that will not be used against women is no law at all.

As an alternative to an outright ban on pornography, Brownmiller and others have advocated restricting its display. There is a plausible case to be made for the idea that antiwoman images displayed so prominently that they are impossible to avoid are coercive, a form of active harassment that oversteps the bounds of free speech. But aside from the evasion involved in simply equating pornography with misogyny or sexual sadism, there are no legal or logical grounds for treating sexist material any differently from (for example) racist or anti-Semitic propaganda; an equitable law would have to prohibit any kind of public defamation. And the very thought of such a sweeping law has to make anyone with an imagination nervous. Could Catholics claim they were being harrassed by nasty depictions of the pope? Could Russian refugees argue that the display of Communist literature was a form of psychological torture? Would pro-abortion material be taken off the shelves on the grounds that it defamed the unborn? I'd rather not find out.

I find myself more and more disturbed by the tenor of antipornography actions and the sort of consciousness they promote; increasingly their focus has shifted from rational feminist criticism of specific targets to generalized, demagogic moral outrage. Picketing an anti-woman movie, defacing an exploitative billboard, or boycotting a record company to protest its misogynistic album covers conveys one kind of message, mass marches Against Pornography quite another. Similarly, there is a difference between telling the neighborhood news dealer why it pisses us off to have *Penthouse* shoved in our faces and choosing as a prime target every right-thinking politician's symbol of big-city sin, Times Square.

In contrast to the abortion rights movement, which is struggling against a tidal wave of energy from the other direction, the antiporn campaign is respectable. It gets approving press and cooperation from the city [New York], which has its own stake (promoting tourism, making the Clinton area safe for gentrification) in cleaning up Times Square. It has begun to attract women whose perspective on other matters is in no way feminist ("I'm anti-abortion," a participant in WAP's march on Times Square told a reporter, "but this is something I can get into"). Despite the insistence of WAP organizers that they support sexual freedom, their line appeals to the antisexual emotions that feed the backlash. Whether they know it or not, they are doing the good cops' dirty work.

Sallie Tisdale

TALK DIRTY TO ME

Once or twice a month I visit my neighborhood adult store, to rent a movie or buy a magazine. I am often the only woman there, and I never see another woman alone. Some days there may be only a single clerk and a few customers; at other times I see a dozen men or more: heavyset working men, young men, businessmen. In their midst I often feel a little strange, and sometimes scared. To enter I have to pass the flashing lights, the neon sign, the silvered windows, and go through the blank, reflecting door.

It takes a certain pluck simply to enter. I can't visit on days when I am frail or timid. I open the door feeling eyes on me, hearing voices, and the eyes are my mother's eyes, and, worse, my father's. The voices are the voices of my priest, my lover, my friends. They watch the little girl and chide her, a naïf no more.

I don't make eye contact. Neither do the men. I drift from one section of the store to the other, going about my business. I like this particular store because it is large and well-lit; there are no dark corners in which to hide or be surprised. The men give me sidelong glances as I pass by, and then drop their eyes back to the box in their hands. Pornography, at its roots, is about watching; but no one here openly watches. This is a place of librarian silences. As I move from shelf to shelf, male customers gather at the fringes of where I stand. I think they would like to know which movies I will choose.

In the large front room with the clerks are glass counters filled with vibrators, promising unguents, candy bowls filled with condoms. On the wall behind the counter where you ask for help are giant dildos, rubber vaginas, rubber faces with slit eyes, all mouth. Here are the more mainstream films, with high production values and name stars.

Near the door are the straight movies, the standard hard core you can find these days in most urban video-rental stores. Here is the large and growing amateur section: suburban porn. Here is a small section of straight Japanese movies, a section of gay male films, and the so-called lesbian films, directed toward the male viewer: *Dildo Party* and *Pussy Licker.*

The first time I came here alone I dressed in baggy jeans and a pullover sweater, and tied my long hair up in a bun. After a while I was approached by a fat man with a pale, damp face and thinning hair.

"Excuse me," he said. "I'm not trying to come on to you or any-thing, but I can't help noticing you're, you know, female."

I could only nod.

"And I wonder," he continued, almost breathless, "if you like this stuff"—and he pointed at a nearby picture of a blonde woman in red lingerie. "You see, my girlfriend, she broke up with me, and I'd bought her all this stuff—you know, sex clothes—and she didn't like it." He paused. "I mean, it's out in the back of my truck right now. If you just want to come outside you can have it."

I turned my back in polite refusal, and left before it could grow completely dark outside. He didn't follow; I've never been approached there again.

Another day, when I asked for my movies by number, I didn't want the clerk to glance at the titles, and I tried to distract him with a question. I asked if any women still work here. He was young, effemi-nate, with a wispy mustache and loose, shoulder-length hair, and apologized when he said no.

"Even though we're all guys now, we try to be real sensitive," he said, pulling my requests off the shelf without a glance. "If anyone gives you a hard time, let us know. You let us know right away, and we'll take care of it." He handed me my choices in a white plastic bag.

"Have a nice day."

Later. I am home, with my movies. I drink a glass of wine, my lover eats from a silver bowl of popcorn he put beside us on the couch. We are watching a stylish film with expensive sets and a pulsing soundtrack. The beautiful actresses wear sunglasses in every scene, and the wordless scenes shift every few minutes. Now there are two women together; now two women and an adoring man, a tool of the spike-heeled women. A few scenes later there is only one woman, blonde, with a luxuriant body. She reaches one hand slowly down be-tween her legs and pulls a diamond necklace from between her vaginal lips, jewel by jewel. She slides it up her abdomen, across her breast, to her throat, and into her mouth.

Some of my women friends have never seen or read pornography—by which I mean expressions of explicit sex. That I don't find strange; it's a world of women which sometimes seems not to be about women at all. What is odd to me is that I know women who say they never think about it, that they are indifferent, that such scenes and stories seem meant for other people altogether. They find my interest rather curious, I suppose. And a little awkward.

The images of pornography are many and varied; some are fragmented and idealized. Some are crude and unflattering. I like the dreamy, psychedelic quality of certain scenes; I like the surprises in others, and I like the arousal, the heat which can be born in my body without warning, in an instant. I have all the curiosity of the anthropologist and the frank hope of the voyeur. Pornography's texture is shamelessness; it maps the limits of my shame.

At times I find it harder to talk about pornography than my own sexual experience; what I like about pornography is as much a part of my sexuality as what I do, but it is more deeply psychological. What I *do* is the product of many factors, not all of them sexually motivated. But what I *imagine* doing is pure—pure in the sense that the images come wholly from within, from the soil of the subconscious. The land of fantasy is the land of the not-done and the wished-for. There are private lessons there, things for me to learn, all alone, about myself.

I feel bashful watching; that's one small surprise. I am self-conscious, prickly with the feeling of being caught in the act. I can feel that way with friends, with my lover of many years, and I can feel that way alone. Suddenly I need to shift position, avert my eyes. Another surprise, and a more important one: These images comfort me. Pornography reflects the obsessions of the age, which is my age. Sex awakens my unconscious; pornography gives it a face.

When I was ten or eleven my brother shared his stolen *Playboys* with me. The pneumatic figurines seemed magnificent and unreal. Certainly they seemed to have nothing at all to do with me or my future. I was a prodigious reader, and at an early age found scenes of sex and lasciviousness in many books: *The French Lieutenant's Woman,* which granted sex such power, and William Kotzwinkle's *Nightbook,* blunt and unpredictable.

I was not *taught,* specifically, much of anything about sex. I knew, but I knew nothing that counted. I felt arousal as any child will, as a biological state. And then came adolescence: real kisses, and dark, rough fumblings, a rut when all the rules disappeared. Heat so that I couldn't speak to say yes, or no, and a boy's triumphant fingers inside my panties was a glorious relief, and an awful guilt.

I entered sex the way a smart, post-Sixties teenager should, with forethought and contraception and care. My poor partner: "Is that all?" I said out loud when it was over. Is that really what all the fuss was about? But the books and magazines seemed a little more complicated to me after that. I learned—but really just information. I had little enough understanding of sex, and very little wisdom.

At the age of twenty, when I was, happily, several months' pregnant, the social work office where I was employed held a seminar on sexuality. We were determinedly liberal about the whole thing; I believe the point was to support clients in a variety of sexual choices. We were given a homework assignment on the first day, to make a collage that expressed our own sexuality. I returned the next morning and saw that my colleagues, male and female both, had all made romantic visions of candlelight and sunsets. I was the youngest by several years, heavy-bellied, and I had brought a wild vision of masked men and women, naked torsos, skin everywhere, darkness, heat.

I knew I was struggling, distantly and through ignorance, with a deep shame. It was undirected, confusing; for years I had been most ashamed of the shame itself. Wasn't sex supposed to be free, easy? What was wrong with me, that I resisted? Why did I feel so afraid of the surrender, the sexual depths? And yet I was ashamed of what I desired: men and women both. I wanted vaguely to try . . . *things,* which no one spoke about; but surely people, somewhere, did. I was ashamed of all my urges, the small details within the larger act, the sudden sounds I made. I could hear that little voice: *Bad girl. Mustn't touch.*

I was a natural feminist; I knew the dialectic, the lingo. And all my secrets seemed to wiggle free no matter what, expand into my unfeminist consciousness. I didn't even know the words for some of what I imagined, but I was sure of this: Liberated women didn't even *think* about what I wanted to do. My shame was more than a preoccupation with sex—everyone I knew was preoccupied with sex. It was more than being confused by the messy etiquette of the 1970s, more than wondering just how much shifting of partners I should do. It was shame for my own unasked-for appetites, which would not be still.

I was propelled toward the overt—toward pornography. I needed information not about sex but about sexual parameters, the bounds of the normal. I needed reassurance, and blessing. I needed permission.

Several years ago, now in my late twenties, I began to watch what I at first called "dirty movies" and to read what were undoubtedly dirty books: *The Story of O* and *My Secret Life.* I went with the man I was living with, my arm in his and my eyes down, to a theater on a back street. It was very cold and dark inside the movie house, so that the other patrons were only dim shadows, rustling nearby. The movie was grainy, half-blurred, the sound muddy, the acting awful. At the same time I felt as though I'd crossed a line: There was a world of sexual material to see, and I was very curious to see it. Its sheer mass and variety reassured me. I couldn't imagine entering this world alone, though, not even for a quick foray into the screened-off section of the local video store, behind the sign reading OVER 18 ONLY. There were always men back there, and only men.

Watching, for the first time, a man penetrate another woman was like leaving my body all at once. I was outside my body, watching, because she on the screen above me *was* me; and then I was back in my body very much indeed. My lust was aroused as surely and uncontrollably by the sight of sex as hunger can be roused by the smell of food. I know how naïve this sounds now, but I had never quite believed, until I saw it, that the sex in such films was *real*, that people fucked in front of cameras, eyes open. I found it a great shock: to see how different sex could be, how many different things it could mean.

Not all I felt was arousal. There are other reasons for a hurried blush. A woman going down on a man, sucking his cock as though starving for it, the man pulling away and shooting come across her face, the woman licking the come off her lips. I felt a heady mix of disgust and excitement, and confusion at that mix. Layers peeled off one after the other, because sometimes I disliked my own response. I resist it still, when something dark and forbidden emerges, when my body is provoked by what my mind reproves.

Inevitably, I came across something awful, something I really hated. The world of pornography is indiscriminate; boundaries get mixed up. Some stores are violent, reptilian, and for all their sexual content aren't about sex. I was reminded of a story I had found by accident, a long time ago, in a copy of my father's *True* magazine. I was forbidden to read *True,* for reasons unexplained. Before I was caught at it and the magazine taken away, I had found an illustration of a bloodsplattered, nearly naked woman tied to a post in a dim basement, and had read up to the place in the text where the slow flaying of her legs had begun. It was gothic and horrible, and haunted me for years. (Of course, I make my own definitions, everyone does; and to me that sort of thing has nothing to do with pornography. It *is* obscene, though, a word quite often applied to things that have nothing to do with sex.) Pornography is sex, and sex is consensual, period. Without consent, the motions of sex become violence, and that alone defines it for me.

I realize this is not the opinion of conservative feminists such as the lawyer Catharine MacKinnon, who believes that violence, even murder, is the end point of all pornography. Certainly a lot of violent material has sexual overtones; the mistake is assuming that anything with sex in it is primarily about sex. The tendency to assume so says something about the person making the assumption. One important point about this distinction is that the one kind of material is so much more readily available than the other: *True* and slasher films and tabloids are part of the common culture. My father bought *True* at the corner tobacco store. Scenes of nothing but mutual pleasure are the illicit ones.

I fall on a line of American women about midway between the actresses whose films I rent and the housewife in Des Moines who has never seen such a film at all. My female friends fall near me, to either side, but most of them a little closer to Des Moines. The store I frequent for my books and films reflects the same continuum: For all its blunt variety, that store is clean, well-lit, friendly, and its variety of materials reflects a variety of hoped-for customers. There are many places I will not go, storefronts and movie houses that seem to me furtive and corrupt. Every society has its etiquette, its rules; so does the world of pornography.

I am deep into thinking about these rules; my cheeks are bright and my palms damp, and the telephone rings. Without thinking I plunge my caller into such thoughts. I chatter a few minutes into a heavy, shifting silence, and then suddenly realize how ill-bred I must seem. Out here, in the ordinary world, such things are not talked about at all. It's one definition of pornography: whatever we will not talk about.

I know I break a rule when I enter the adult store, whether my entrance is simply startling or genuinely unwelcome. The sweaty-lipped man with lingerie wouldn't, couldn't approach me in a grocery store or even a bar. Not like that, and perhaps not at all. Pornography degrades the male vision of women in this way. When I stand among the shelves there I am standing in a maze of female images, shelf after shelf of them, hundreds of naked women smiling or with their eyes closed and mouths open or gasping. I am just one more image in a broken mirror, with its multiple reflections of women, none of them whole.

I am still afraid. These days I am most aware of that fear as a fear of where I will and will not go, what I think of as *possible* for me. But, oh—I'm curious. I can be so curious. A while ago I recruited two friends, one man and one woman, and the three of us went to a peep show together like a flying wedge, parting the crowds of nervy young men, them jostling each other with elbows in the ribs, daring each other, *g'wan.* We changed bills for quarters, leaned together in the dim hallways, elbowed each other in the ribs—*g'wan.* There were endless film loops in booths for singles, various movie channels from which to choose in booths for two people, tissues provided, and a live show. One minute for twenty-five cents, and the signs above each booth flashing on and off, on and off again in the dark, from a green VACANT to a red IN USE and back again.

I pulled a door shut and disappeared into the musky dark; I could hear muffled shouts from the young men in booths on either side. The panel slid up on my first quarter to a brightly lit, mirrored room with three women, all simulating masturbation. The one in the center was right in front of me, and she caught my eye and grinned at me, in black leather just like her. I think she sees few women in the booths, and many men.

Men—always the Man who is the standard-bearer for what is obscene and forbidden. That Man, the one I fear whether I mean to or not, in elevators and parking lots and on the street, is the man who will be inflamed by what he sees. I fear he will be *persuaded* by it, come to believe it, learn my fantasy and think I want him to make it come true. When I haven't the temerity to go through one of these veiled doors, it's because I am afraid of the men inside: afraid in a generic, unspoken way, afraid of Them.

Susan Sontag, exhaustively trying to prove that certain works of pornography qualify as "literature"—a proof almost laughably pointless, I think—notes its "singleness of intention" as a point against its inclusion. I am interested in literature, pornographic and otherwise, by my responses to any given piece; and my responses to pornography are layered and complex and multiple.

Some pieces bore me: They are cheesy or slow, badly written or mechanical. Others disturb me by the unhappiness I sense, as though the actors and actresses wished only to be somewhere else. There are days when I am saturated and feel weary of the whole idea. Sometimes I experience a kind of ennui, a *nausea* from all that grunting labor, the rankness of the flesh. I get depressed, for simple enough reasons. I rented a movie recently that opened with a scene of two naked women stroking each other. One of the women had enormous breasts, hard balloons filled with silicone riding high on her ribs and straining the skin. She looked mutilated, and the rest of the movie held no interest for me at all.

I wish for more craft, a more artful packaging. I tire of browsing stacks of boxes titled *Fucking Brunettes* and *Black Cocks and Black Cunts* and *Monumental Knockers.* The mainstream films, with their happy, athletic actors, can leave me a little cold. That's how I felt watching a comfortable film called *The Last Resort.* The plot, naturally, is simple: A woman with a broken heart accompanies her friends, a couple, to a resort. Over the next twenty-four hours she has vigorous sex with a waiter, a cook (he in nothing but a chef's hat and apron), a waitress, a waitress and a maintenance man together. The other guests cavort cheerfully, too. I found it all so earnest and wholesome. A friend and fellow connoisseur deplores these films where everyone has a "penis-deflatingly good time squirting sperm about with as much passion as a suburban gardener doing his lawn." These movies are too hygienic. They're not dirty enough.

And now women are making films for women viewers. The new films by and for lesbians can be nasty and hot. But the heterosexual films, heavy on relationships and light on the standard icons of hard core, seem ever so soft to me. (They're reminiscent of those social worker collages.) They're tasteful and discreet. I'm glad women have, so to speak, seized the means of production. I'm glad women are making pornographic films, writing pornographic books, starting pornographic magazines; I'm happier still when the boundaries in which women create expand. I don't believe there are limits to what women can imagine or enjoy. I don't want limits, imposed from within or without, on what women can see, or watch, or do.

Any amateur psychologist could have a field day explaining why I prefer low-brow, hard-core porn to feminine erotica. I've spent enough time trying to explain things to myself: why I prefer *this* to *that.* There are examples of pornography, films and stories both, that genuinely scare me. They are no more bizarre or extreme than books or movies that may simply excite or interest me, but the details affect me in certain specific ways. The content touches me, just there, and I'm scared, for no reason I can explain, or excited by a scene that repels me. It may be nothing more than sound, a snap or thwack or murmur. And I want to keep watching those films, reading those books; when I engage in my own fears, I learn about them. I may someday master a few. When I happen upon such scenes, I try to look directly. Seeing what I don't like can be as therapeutic as seeing what I do.

Feminists against pornography (as distinct from other anti-pornography camps) hold that our entire culture is pornographic. In a pornographic world all our sexual constructions are obscene; sexual materials are necessarily oppressive, limited by the constraints of the culture. Even the act of viewing becomes a male act—an act of subordinating the person viewed. Under this construct, I'm a damaged woman, a heretic.

I take this personally, the effort to repress material I enjoy—to tell me how wrong it is for me to enjoy it. Anti-pornography legislation is directed at me: as a user, as a writer. Catharine MacKinnon and Andrea Dworkin—a feminist who has developed a new sexual orthodoxy in which the male erection is itself oppressive—are the new censors. They are themselves prurient, scurrying after sex in every corner. They look down on me and shake a finger: *Bad girl. Mustn't touch.*

That branch of feminism tells me my very thoughts are bad. Pornography tells me the opposite: that *none* of my thoughts are bad, that anything goes. Both are extremes, of course, but the difference is profound. The message of pornography, by its every existence, is that our sexual selves are real.

Always, the censors are concerned with how men *act* and how women are portrayed. Women cannot make free sexual choices in that world; they are too oppressed to know that only oppression could lead them to sell sex. And I, watching, am either too oppressed to know the harm that my watching has done to my sisters, or—or else I have become the Man. And it is the Man in me who watches and is aroused. (Shame.) What a misogynistic worldview this is, this claim that women who make such choices cannot be making free choices at all—are not free to make a choice. Feminists against pornography have done a sad and awful thing: *They* have made women into objects.

I move from the front of the adult store I frequent to the back. Here is the leather underwear, dildos of all sizes, inflatable female dolls, shrink-wrapped fetish magazines. Here are movies with taboo themes—older movies with incest plots, newer ones featuring interracial sex, and grainy loops of nothing more than spanking, spanking, spanking. Here are the films of giant breasts, or all-anal sex, food fights, obese actresses, and much masturbation. This is niche marketing at its best.

In the far back, near the arcade booths, are the restraints, the gags and bridles, the whips and handcuffs, and blindfolds. Here are dildos of truly heroic proportions. The films here are largely European, and quite popular. A rapid desensitization takes me over back here, a kind of numbing sensory overload. Back here I can't help but look at the other customers; I find myself curious about which movies each of *them* will rent.

Women who have seen little pornography seem to assume that the images in most films are primarily, obsessively, ones of rape. I find the opposite theme in American films: that of an adolescent rut, both male and female. Its obsession is virility, endurance, lust. Women in modern films are often the initiators of sex; men in such films seem perfectly content for that to be so.

Power fantasies, on the other hand, are rather common for men and women both. I use the term "power" to describe a huge continuum of images: physical and psychological overpowering of many kinds, seduction and bondage and punishment, the extremes of physical control practiced by S&M enthusiasts. The word *rape* for such scenes is inappropriate; the fact of rape has nothing to do with sex, or pornography. Power takes a lot of forms, subtle, overt. Out of curiosity I rented a German film called *Discipline in Leather,* a film, I discovered, without sex, without nudity. Two men are variously bound, chained, laced, gagged, spanked, and ridden like horses by a Nordic woman. "Nein!" she shouts. "Nicht so schnell!" The men lick her boots, accept the bridle in cringing obeisance. I found it laughably solemn, a Nazi farce, and then I caught myself laughing. This is one of many similar films, and I never want to laugh at the desires of another. A lot of people take what I consider trifling or silly to be terribly important. I want never to forget the bell curve of human desire, or that few of us have much say about where on the curve we land. I've learned this from watching porn: By letting go of judgments I hold against myself and my desires, I let go of judgments about the desires and the acts of others.

I recently saw a movie recommended by one of the clerks at the adult store, a send-up called *Wild Goose Chase*. In the midst of mild arousal, I found a scene played for laughs, about the loneliness taken for granted in the pornographic world. The actor is Joey Silvera, a good-looking man with blond hair and startling dark eyes. In this film he plays a detective; the detective has a torrid scene with his secretary, who then walks out on him. He holds his head in his hands. "I don't need her," he mumbles. "I got women. I got my *own* women!" He stands and crosses to a file cabinet. "I got plenty of women!" He pulls out a drawer and dumps it upside down, spilling porn magazines in a pile on the floor. He crawls over them, stroking the paper cunts, the breasts, the pictured thighs, moaning, kissing the immobile faces.

The fantasies of power are shame-driven, I think: When I envision my own binding, my submission, I am seeing myself free. Free of guilt, free of responsibility. So many women I've known have harbored these fantasies, and grown more guilty for having them. And so many of those women have been strong, powerful, self-assured. Perhaps, as one school of feminist thought says, we've simply "eroticized our oppression." I know I berated myself a long while for that very thing, and tried to make the fantasies go away. But doing so denies the fact of my experience, which includes oppression and dominance, fear and guilt, and a hunger for surrender. This is the real text of power fantasies: They are about release from all those things. A friend who admits such dreams herself gave me Pat Califia's collection of dominance stories, *Macho Sluts*. I opened at random and was rooted where I stood: The stories are completely nasty, well written, and they are smart. "I no longer thought about the future," one character says, spread-eagle and bound in front of mirrors during sex. "I did not exist, except as a response to her touch. There was nothing else, no other reality, and whim of my own will moved me." Such dreams transcend mere sex and enter, unexpectedly, the world of relationship. I could not read such stories, watch such films, with anyone but a lover. I couldn't act them out except with the person whom I trusted most of all.

It was only last year when I stopped making my lover go with me to the adult store. I make myself go alone now, or not at all; if I believe this should be mine for the choosing, then I want to get it myself. Only alone will that act of choosing be a powerful act. So I went yesterday, on a Wednesday in the middle of the morning, and found a crowd of men. There was even a couple, the young woman with permed hair and a startled look, like a deer caught in headlights. She kept her hands jammed in the pockets of her raincoat, and wouldn't return my smile. There was an old man on crutches huddled over a counter, and a herd of clerks, playing bad, loud rock music. I was looking for a few specific titles, and a clerk directed me to the customers' computer, on a table in the amateur section. It's like the ones at the library, divided by title, category (fat girl, Oriental, spanking, hetero, and so on), or a particular star.

The big-bellied jovial clerk came over after a few minutes.

"That working for you?" he sang out. "I tell you, I don't know how the hell that works."

I tell him I'm looking for a movie popular several years ago, called *Talk Dirty to Me.*

"Hey, Jack," he yells. "We got *Talk Dirty to Me?*" In a few minutes four clerks huddle around me and the computer, watching me type in the title, offering little suggestions. From across the store I can still hear the helpful clerk. "Hey, Al," he's shouting. "Lady over there wants *Talk Dirty to Me.* We got that?"

I still blush; I stammer to say these things out loud. Sex has eternal charm that way—a perpetual, organic hold on my body. I am aroused right now, writing this. Are you, dear reader? Do you dream, too?

A friend called this story my "accommodation," as though I'd made peace with the material. I have never had to do that. I have always just been trying to make peace with my abyssal self, my underworld. Pornography helps; that's simple. I became sexual in a generation that has explored sex more thoroughly and perhaps less well than any before. I live with myself day to day in a sex-drenched culture, and that means living with my own sex. After exposing myself truly to myself, it's surprisingly easy to expose myself to another.

I want not to accommodate to pornography but to claim it. I want to be the agent of sex. I want to *own* sex, as though I had a right to these depictions, these ideas, as though they belonged to us all. The biggest surprise is this one: When I am watching—never mind what. I am suddenly restless, shifting, crossing my legs. And my perceptive lover smiles at me and says, "You like that, don't you? See—*everyone* does that."

Scarlet Woman

RADICAL FEMME

I stand five-foot-ten in my six-inch heels,
My new red hair is blazing in the sun.
Oh my sisters,
        Spare me your judgments.

Let me tell you:
We are violated by those
Who would contain our greatest spirits and
Confine our largest passions
Into the small image of chastity.
We are raped by those who
Would have us believe that
Nice girls don't like sex.
They harm us more, and harm more of us, than
                All the violence
        of meat shot on split beaver.

Have you given the Goddess your orgasm today?

I love all that is sexy of woman:
Lean Atalanta with streamlined hips and
        vulnerable earlobes, poised for flight;
Earthmother, abundant with flesh—
        tits and belly and ass—
        tremendous thighs and
        a clear brown eye stunning me with candor.
A decorated Beauty with mascara on her cheek
        arches her back and clenches her fists,

Eyes gleaming in the candle watching mine eager:
Her muscles bulge as she wails her pleasure,
    Magnificent her passion.
Have you give the Goddess your orgasm today?

In six-inch spiky too-high heels
I went to a party with too many men.
I was five-foot-ten and none of them
    tripped over me:
I don't need to run when I can look them in
    the eye.
When my new red hair blazes in the sun,
    I am not trivial.

I will wear my Self large and shiny,
Loud and passionate like the idols of my youth:
    Mae and Bessie and Tallulah—
Outraging women,
    Not to be ignored.

Yes, I stand five-foot-ten in my six-inch heels,
My new red hair is blazing in the sun—
Oh my sisters,
    Spare your judgments.
Give the Goddess your orgasm today.

Anne Sexton

Us

I was wrapped in black
fur and white fur and
you undid me and then
you placed me in gold light
and then you crowned me,
while snow fell outside
the door in diagonal darts.
While a ten-inch snow
came down like stars
in small calcium fragments,
we were in our own bodies
(that room that will bury us)
and you were in my body
(that room that will outlive us)
and at first I rubbed your
feet dry with a towel
because I was your slave
and then you called me princess.
Princess!

Oh then
I stood up in my gold skin
and I beat down the psalms
and I beat down the clothes
and you undid the bridle
and you undid the reins
and I undid the buttons,
the bones, the confusions,

the New England postcards,
the January ten o'clock night,
and we rose up like wheat,
acre after acre of gold,
and we harvested,
we harvested.

6

EROTIC
FRONTIERS

INTRODUCTION: PART 6

We know that at the edge of our village, at the edge of where we peacefully and safely live, at the edge of our known universe, there is a deep dark forest. We are told that the forest is full of dark, dangerous creatures and forces. We are told that we must never go into the forest, that if we go there we will, like Hansel and Gretel, fall prey to all sorts of witches, devils, and hobgoblins, that we will be captured, tortured, possessed, devoured, destroyed.

Because no one is allowed to go into the forbidden forest, no one knows what it is really like. Because no one is able to go into the forest without being overwhelmed by fear, no one knows what it is like to inhabit the forest world unafraid. Of course, people do go into the forest, but because no one is allowed to talk about their experience, everyone carries their forest lives in secret, or alludes to them so obliquely as to make them incomprehensible to others. Because it is so deeply forbidden to carry even the spirit of the forest within us, we hide this side of our nature even from ourselves.

We hide from ourselves. We condemn ourselves. We ridicule ourselves. We fear ourselves. We hate ourselves. We exile ourselves from ourselves. And we attack with particular passion anything around us that threatens to expose the hidden reality of who we are, and what we want, how we dream, what we desire.

Good/evil; proper/improper; normal/perverted; rational/emotional; light/dark; order/chaos; madonna/whore; heterosexual/homosexual; self/other; mind/body; sane/sick. We are taught to think of all things, and certainly all sexual things, as one or the other. We are taught that we must choose the approved pole over its supposed opposite, now and forever. If we do so, we are praised, accepted, and admired. If we stray to the pole of the underworld, we are condemned, ridiculed, and exiled.

This section includes five reports from the forest world, five writings that offer honest and unapologetic glimpses of what it is like to explore what is currently considered the erotic frontier. As is often the case with forbidden worlds, the truth of what they are like is quite different from what we villagers have been led to believe, so when we hear first-hand reports our initial experience is often severe cognitive dissonance. To preserve our belief systems, we are tempted to dismiss the new information as simply dishonest, misguided, or distorted.

However we react to erotic perspectives that are different from our own, it is important that we hear directly from those on the frontiers, and that we hear from them in their own terms. It is only when these stories are told accurately that we can separate the complex realities of erotic exploration from simplified sound bites and media clichés that only reinforce our fear of the unknown. It is only when these stories are told clearly that each of us can have informed, conscious perceptions of the erotic worlds around us, and can make informed choices as to how we want to construct our erotic lives.

Artist and sex educator Betty Dodson begins by talking about breaking two different erotic taboos—first, celebrating her sexuality in public by exhibiting her powerfully sexual paintings and drawings; and second, becoming a public advocate for a stigmatized form of erotic expression—masturbation.

Writer and sex-educator Carol Queen goes beyond buzzwords and distortive media stereotypes by speaking honestly and personally about the realities of sadomasochism and the s/m subculture. Her account, both anecdotal and analytical, deconstructs many common misunderstandings of this emerging and controversial sexual world by explaining some of the sexual, psychological, and relational issues addressed by s/m—issues such as power, trust, vulnerability, intimacy, and the nature of sensation—and how these can be important paths to personal growth and increased self-awareness.

Writer/photographer Tee Corinne tells a dreamlike tale that is at once the courtship between two separate women, and the dialectic that goes on within any one woman—the interplay between Love and Desire. John Preston deals directly with issues of transgressive sexual thought and practice, focusing on pornography as the medium through which prohibited forms of sexual expression can be made known, and what this says about the responsibility and possibility for gay pornography in this time of AIDS.

The poems by James Broughton and Ron Koertge give two light-hearted, transcendent glimpses of living out one's erotic bliss despite the taboos, in these cases the joys of sex between two men and of solitary sex.

Betty Dodson

GOING PUBLIC

I have always painted the nude, but I originally thought of the nude as sensual, not really sexual. I was always on the periphery of sex. The first year after my divorce, I felt so incredibly good about myself and life and I was so sex-affirmative again that it was the most natural thing in the world to say, "Of course! I'm going to put my nudes together on canvas. I will do huge, magnificent drawings and paintings of humans celebrating physical love."

Today I realize the importance of that decision. The development of my erotic art relates directly to my sexual development. I have always struggled against society's restrictions and censorship. But the worst kind of censorship has been the kind I've been conditioned to apply to myself. Now I understand that once I am able to put it down on paper, whatever it is I fear, I've won. That, in essence, is what I mean when I talk about *going public.*

My discoveries in bed got transferred to canvas, and my first one-woman exhibition was held in New York City in 1968. The whole concept of displaying my interest in sex publicly, naturally, was frightening. I envisioned irate citizens throwing rocks and me getting busted for pornography, but I needn't have. The exhibition dealt with fashionable heterosexuality. Life-size, heroic figures fucking behind huge bright-colored sheets of plexiglass hanging in a gallery right next to the Whitney Museum was quite a sensation. It was beautiful and enormously successful.

Eight thousand people attended that show in a two-week period, even though advertising was largely word-of-mouth. There were many incidents—embarrassing, funny, exciting, and sad. But all profoundly educational. One thing was starkly apparent. *Everyone* was intensely interested, though some tried to disguise or moderate their interest. My being a woman upset the basic social expectations. Why should a woman want to show her interest in sex publicly? She obviously would not just *want to get laid* (like a man) so there must be some *social significance* involved. It became painfully clear that virtually everyone was crippled by socially imposed sex-negative attitudes. Women were more willing to exchange sex information—a most important discovery for me. They admitted their hang-ups, asked questions, and listened. The men were not so open. I realized the tragedy of men who were locked into absurd behavior patterns because of having to constantly bolster (or get women to bolster) their precarious "masculine images." I concluded that women could just have to lead the way.

I decided to devote my second show to the celebration of masturbation. By that time, I had read extensively in the field of human sexuality, and heard many personal sex histories. I had become more convinced than ever that sexual liberation was crucial to women's liberation, and that masturbation was crucial to sexual liberation and the destruction of paralyzing sex roles.

Getting models to masturbate for me turned out to be very difficult, much more so than having models engage in sexual intercourse—a very illuminating commentary in itself. Finally, with a little help from my friends, I was able to get it down on paper: four magnificent, larger-than-life classical nudes jerking off.

I had visions of the redemption of masturbation in a fashionable Madison Avenue gallery. Everyone said I was nuts because the drawings would never sell (absolutely true). But it was an invaluable experience in sexual consciousness-raising.

When the drawings arrived at the gallery the day of the opening, all hell broke loose. The director refused to hang the four masturbation drawings as planned, so I threatened to pull out the entire show of thirty pictures. Finally, two of the masturbation drawings were hung. Opening night the main wall of the front room of this elegant establishment held the six-foot drawing of my girlfriend—legs apart, clitoris erect, approaching orgasm with her vibrator. Actually, she prefers penetration along with her vibrator and uses a peeled cucumber plus her hair dryer covering her ears. I simplified her technique for artistic purposes.

The response to the show was fascinating and informative. I learned that a lot of women did not masturbate, and a lot of men did not know any women masturbated (why should they?), and that the vibrator made a lot of men very hostile and competitive. Several men said emphatically, "If that was my woman, she wouldn't have to use that thing." I was fielding hundreds of questions. Yes, I do it myself and love it. No, you don't get warts. Yes, the girl with the vibrator in the picture has a boyfriend—he's standing right over there. No, despite what society tells us, intercourse isn't necessarily better—it's different. I like to do both.

Many women I talked to said they were reluctant to use the vibrator because they were afraid they'd *get hooked*. While I'm not hooked on mine, I am emotionally involved with it. I am also emotionally involved with my friends, with regular fucking, with oral sex. So far, my observation has been that women who like vibrators either like sex or are starting to like sex for the first time.

If I had any doubts about it before I started, the two weeks I spent in the gallery made it very clear that repression relates directly to masturbation. It follows then that masturbation can be important in reversing the process and achieving liberation.

Seeking sexual satisfaction is a basic drive, and masturbation, of course, is our first natural sexual activity. It's the way we discover our eroticism, the way we learn to respond sexually, the way we learn to love ourselves and build self-esteem. Sexual skill and the ability to respond are not *natural* in our society. Doing what *comes naturally* for us is to be sexually inhibited. Sex is like any other skill—it has to be learned and practiced. When a woman masturbates, she learns to like her own genitals, to enjoy sex and orgasm, and furthermore, to become proficient and independent about it. Our society is made uncomfortable by sexually proficient and independent women.

Which gets us to the sexual double standard—the concept that men have the social approval to be aggressive-independent and sexually polygamous—but that women should be non-aggressive-dependent and sexually monogamous. We became fixed in nonsexuality and a supportive role that induces us to seek security rather than independence, new experiences and sexual gratification.

The way we are made to accept and conform to this double standard is through deprivation of sexual self-knowledge—especially masturbation. In other words, deprive us of our own bodies and a way of discovering and developing orgasmic response patterns. Start early. Instill the notion that female genitals are deficient and inferior and that women's main social value lies in producing babies. Avoid any information about the clitoris and life-affirming orgasm.

Prohibit touching of the genitals through the suggestion of supernatural punishment. Socially ostracize nonconforming women. Maintain the two sexual views of women, the virginal, sexless mother or The Fallen Woman, the prostitute or tramp. Sexual repression is a vital aspect of keeping us in our "proper" role.

The net result is we became crippled human beings. Our pelvises are severely locked. Our shoulders are frozen forward. Our genitals are made repulsive to us and a source of constant discomfort. Our bodies lack muscle tone and often are armored with fat. The insidious thing about this system is that we end up accepting the self-serving male definitions of "normal" female sexuality. We vehemently or sullenly put down masturbation and overt displays of healthy female sexuality. At this point we embellish our own pedestals and become the keepers of Social Morality, the classical image of Mother.

I felt the full brunt of the damage that had been done to women. I was overwhelmed with the realization of how very effectively the church and our whole culture had turned us into sexless mothers and house-slaves. I was furious. I called every woman I knew and asked if she was masturbating. If she wasn't, I suggested she start immediately.

One of those calls was long distance to Kansas—to my mother. She was sixty-eight, living alone, a widow of several years. I started right off with, "Mother, are you masturbating to orgasm?" There was a sputtering pause and then she came right back with, "Why, Betty Ann, of course not. I'm too old for that sort of thing."

I immediately launched into my whole rap about the connection between good health and orgasm. If nothing else, she should do it just as a physical exercise to keep the lining of the vaginal wall lubricating, the hormones secreting, and the uterus contracting. Besides it was a great way to relax and unwind, and it might reduce some of her lower back pains. She could also do it just for fun. Her response was, "Well, honey, I don't know. What you say does make sense. You have always had such different ideas from most people, but I think you're probably right."

Our next conversation—some two weeks later—was beautiful. Yes! she had successfully and very easily masturbated to orgasm, and it was extremely pleasant. She felt she had slept more soundly afterwards, too.

Over the past years, we have exchanged information about masturbation, our different uses of fantasy, and we have even shared our masturbation histories. One surprise for me: she remembered when I first started masturbating (at the age of five in the back seat of the car), something I had no idea she knew. I asked her why she didn't stop me. She answered, ". . . because that was such a long trip and we were so short of money and you kids weren't having that much fun . . . so I didn't want to bother you."

Wow! She associated masturbation with pleasure! One time I asked my mother if she had ever talked about masturbation with any of her friends. She said yes, a friend of hers was complaining about a terrible vaginal itch which the doctor had been unable to cure. Mother suggested that masturbation might help. When I asked what happened, she said her friend had stopped calling her. That, I replied, was the price of being a sexual revolutionary.

Carol A. Queen

EROTIC POWER AND TRUST

I stepped into the world of sadomasochism quite alone, a bright and well-read teenager, stumbling upon books that gripped me with a strange lust. Don't be hasty and assume that I had found a cache of pornography, or that I was dipping into de Sade. Porn was not of too much interest to me in those days; I was still a little afraid of it. De Sade I had yet to discover. I was reading not smut but psychology texts, classic ones that examined (with some distaste) the nether side of human experience. It was in *Patterns of Psychosexual Infantalism,* an old book by Wilhelm Stekel, that I found the material that set me off in search of sadists, masochists, and fetishists—people like me.

Perhaps every child knows the thrill of fear just before being discovered at hide and seek, or has definite preferences as to whether she will be the cowboy or the Indian, the chaser or the chased, the one who ties up or the one who is tied. Perhaps—this is just speculation—every child brings a touch of those preferences into puberty, incorporates them into fantasy and excitement as the hormones hit. As an adolescing girl my relationship to dominance and submission was complex. I swooned at romantic material in which the woman was swept off her feet by a powerful lover. I chafed at the expectations my father had of my behavior and grew angry at his control. I identified with oppressed peoples and underclasses and romanticized (almost as much as I romanticized Cathy and Heathcliff) the overthrow of those in power.

I was a nascent feminist and learned to resent men and boys for the power differential I was told existed between them and me. I fell in love with a man twice my age and at the same time began to eroticize my relationships with my girlfriends. I told myself I wanted equitable love, the kind my peers could provide me, but I soon started developing unrequited crushes that allowed me to wallow (secretly) in my sense of the girls' power over me, power that I generated out of my desire for them.

That was where Stekel came in. His case histories enflamed me. Something about those Victorian deviates spoke to the unconscious wellsprings of my eroticism. Perhaps it was their distance from my life, or the pure way their obsessions for devotional surrender and ritualized power, or their wild fetish-lust in the presence of a piece of fur or a lace handkerchief, mirrored my muddy, inarticulate desires. Amazed and a little ashamed at the pulsing arousal that filled me, I would read as long as I could before touching myself. It was the best sex I had ever had, and my mind was full of images that so shocked me that I could barely believe it was me thinking those thoughts of capture and bondage, bare bottoms and canes and kissing the toes of high leather shoes, schoolboys whipped and humiliated, red-faced and red-assed. I never looked at a romance novel again.

These were the years of political correctness, the mid-70s. In my community old-fashioned sexual propriety, always enforced through ignorance and sex-role expectations, had supposedly given way to a revolutionary new set of sex-role mores—but not the free love of the 60s. It was becoming less acceptable all the time, in my circle of politically-correct feminists, for women to desire men at all, much less to want to be swept away by or fuck as many of them as we could. We were to be the vanguard of a new kind of relationship, absolutely equitable. And we who loved this way would begin to bring the world along with us as we changed. The old ways and the new were like mythical dragons; the new dragon had arrived to slay the old.

Of course, the new dragon didn't kill the old one. Instead the two became twin guards at the gate of my subconscious, keeping politically incorrect dreams—of men tongue-polishing spike-heeled shoes, of imperious and insatiable schoolmistresses, of being a bound and ravished captive—at bay. The dreams only emerged when I masturbated, or when I was being made love to and was straining to come. Afterwards I would be ashamed—more at my politics gone awry than at the sex.

I vaguely knew that people closer to my life than Stekel's lunatic patients lived out those dreams, and I was terrified of becoming like them. I supposed they must be entirely out of control, bereft of morals. I was, as I said, quite alone when I entered the world of sadomasochism, and for some years I titillated and tortured myself with fears of what would become of me if anyone ever guessed my secret desires.

Every kind of rigid morality, political or otherwise, tries to keep bright little girls like me from falling down that rabbit hole, into the fiercely burning center of the earth, where, I would later learn, things are not what they seem. The most effective lie told to guard against our exploring those lands of fetish and passion is that people who venture there are without control. The other lie used consistently, whether the sexual dictatorship is progressive lesbianism or repressive Catholicism, is that sadomasochists and fetishists are very unlike you and me. I suppose we should expect nothing different in a culture that runs shrieking from the responsibility of giving its citizens, particularly its children, even the most basic sex information, that is quick to label deviance and quick to look for someone to blame for it. The part of my sexuality that was exposed to the sun blossomed into lesbianism. The dark root tapped into something more primal than feminist equitability, more blood-quickening than sisterhood. Much as I feared it, it was emerging into my consciousness, chthonic and compelling.

I dealt with it first via a gender split. I began fantasizing myself as a submissive man. In this way I made my desire for submission less threatening; I made an end run around both my sexual preference and my feminist politics. Since women were not being subordinate, the fantasies were easier to accept.

Next, I ventured into the riskier territory of female/female dominant/submissive fantasies, where I had to own my desires as stories I told myself *about myself.* Even if she was clothed in dreamy Victoriana (and she often was; I still have a fetish for lacy white cotton), the maid kissing her mistress's ankle was me, the weeping schoolgirl pulling down her panties for a caning was me. Much as I tried to distance myself, the fantasies were moving inexorably in the direction of honesty.

I believe that, in the absence of terrible repression and in the presence of psychic room to grow, our fantasies will do that—move in the direction of greatest authenticity. Lack of permission and information often thwarts us from coming into our potential, and nothing about our cultural framework encourages us to make a priority of exploring our erotic limits. That any of us do so at all is a kind of miracle, a testament to a stunted but stubborn spirituality that exists in the body before it is ever mythologized in the mind. The first erotic miracle of my life was on the verge of occurring: I had fallen in love with a woman who was willing to explore my fantasies with me.

Discovering a partner who is willing to acknowledge and play with our sexual fantasies is profound, sometimes radicalizing. What would our lives be like if each of us could count on learning at some point that we are not alone in those deep, private places? Suddenly, I was in the company of a real live woman, not Stekel's ghostly patients—and she was my true love, my mate, not some anonymous pervert who had guessed my secret. I trusted her and felt safe with her. She wanted to help me flesh out my dreams (not so much, I think now, because she shared them, but because she loved me and they were my deep desire). We invented stories and began to play.

I always wanted to be submissive. I wanted to be the ravished one, the helpless one. I liked being held down or tied down. I found I liked being spanked, even until I cried, and could then come back to myself securely curled up in her arms. Spiced with these fantasies, our sex was passionate, and our intimacy grew as we ventured into places of emotional vulnerability, where I could start out feeling thrillingly afraid and end up feeling safe and loved. I was lucky to have found a woman whose natural assertiveness lent itself to playing the dominant in these games, for I was really only interested in exploring my desires for submission.

Gradually, though, our differing levels of interest in these games caused conflict. The nonsexual power differential in our relationship began to make the erotic power play emotionally risky. I found it confusing to want her dominance in bed and then try to assert myself in other matters.

I also began to wonder who else might be playing this way. I wanted to meet them, the ones I had thought of as anonymous "perverts" and formerly feared. I wanted to connect with other women in our community, rumored to be exploring sadomasochism, and talk about the intense experiences I was having. My sweetheart, fiercely secretive about our experiments, would have none of it. The conflicts felt threatening and frightening to me. Gradually we stopped playing our games; we had hit a wall and didn't know how to break through.

Attempts to introduce this sex play to my next lover foundered because I didn't know how to talk about the kinds of experiences I was looking for; I didn't have a language for it. All around me were women who could scarcely talk about the kind of clitoral touch they liked, and I was no exception. How was I supposed to break the news to my lover that I yearned for her sexual power? I was back to vivid, unspoken dreams of being taken whenever she happened to lay her full weight upon me. I was again, in my sadomasochistic desires, quite alone.

But I knew that there might be others like me. If I had only known that they comprised a community, a subculture in fact, with a language for their desires and rules to ensure emotional and physical safety, I could have begun looking for them. Some years later, I did just that.

We call it *playing* because it accesses our inner, childlike, adventuresome spirits; because, like many kinds of participatory games, it follows certain rules; and because it is often inspired improvisation, a theatre of roles and emotions. We call it *sadomasochistic* for lack of a better term, and in fact some members of what most call the s/m community won't use that word at all; they call it *erotic power exchange, dominance and submission, sensuality and mutuality, radical sex, fetish and fantasy, sexual magic, power and trust.* Any term is probably as good as the next, for s/m is a catchall phrase for all kinds of erotic activities that involve role-playing and altered physical and emotional sensation. *Sadomasochism* is a term left over from men like Stekel and his forebears—heavy-handed theorists of the elusive psyche who gave names to behaviors, thereby codifying them into something different from the norm, something to study, dissect and cure. The word has a shameful history, invoking the shadows of those so unsuccessful at concealing their difference that they were herded into psychiatrists' offices and asylums. When I use it today it is to acknowledge those turn-of-the-century libertines who so fascinated the doctors, whose case histories made my young heart pound with a new kind of sexual excitement.

What, exactly, do we do? We do so many different sorts of things that it's difficult to delineate—and not all of us do the same things. I find it most useful to talk about dominance and submission separately from sadism and masochism, and to conceptualize each sort of play on a continuum, rather like Kinsey saw heterosexuality and homosexuality blur into each other via bisexuality. There are, however, certain elements common to dominance/submission and s/m. Both are usually ritualized in a *scene,* which can be delimited by costume, by the assumption of fantasy personae and, most importantly, by the agreement of the participants. They will usually assume roles, commonly called *top* and *bottom,* which correspond to master and servant, dominant and submissive, sadist and masochist, respectively. Most s/m scenes will have at least one of each. The bottom allows the top to take control of the scene, but power is rarely conceded unconditionally. Usually the participants have agreed upon a scenario and established basic limits. During the scene the bottom is responsible for alerting the top if his/her limits are reached. Most s/m practitioners use a *safeword,* a verbal signal that activity should slow or stop. *Yellow* and *red* are commonly-used safewords, but any word or phrase that wouldn't ordinarily come up in the course of a scene will do. (*No* and *stop* are poor choices, as a bottom in the throes of delicious agonies may want to shout such things to her heart's content without stopping the scene.) The top, needless to say, is responsible for honoring the bottom's need to slow or end the scene. It is a far cry from my old lurid fantasies of perverts out of control.

Eroticizing dominance and submission brought me into s/m, and I am hardly alone. Whether as hormone-driven animals, children at the mercy of all-powerful parents, or lovers acting out their passion in rituals of possession, most of us have experienced some form of this erotic play. For me it is highly romantic; I have no real interest in dominance and submission games with people I don't feel romantically attached to. Others use it as a stage-set for humiliation and catharsis, or even an earthly access to feelings of spiritual reverence. For me, the thrill of submission is about being desired to the extreme of being possessed. For many, the charge has to do with the feeling of letting go of responsibility (hence the true-to-life stereotype of the successful executive who unwinds at the hands of a dominatrix).

Fantasy and reality do not always reflect each other, nor do we want them to. Erotic fantasy is like dreamtime, in which the subconscious works its strange magic on images that we only think we understand. A fantasy is not a literal desire, even if it is acted out in the protected ritual space of an s/m encounter. A rape fantasy is not a desire for rape, and a scripted rape consensually played out with an s/m partner is neither a real rape nor an expression of a wish for it. It is likely an eroticization of a fear, allowing the dreamer to let go of terror in a controlled way, or a fantasy about being overwhelmingly desirable (or overwhelmingly overcome by desire). Playing out a fantasy of sex with a parent has more to do with reaching for a babyish state of love and protection than desire for a real incestuous connection—though that connection also might be a hot element of the fantasy. The most important thing about s/m play is that practitioners enter into these and other fantasies *consensually*: if it's not consensual, it's not s/m. S/m, by definition, is eroticized power *exchange,* and implicit in the notion of exchange is trade, balance, some form of equitability. Power is so often forcibly or covertly taken in this society that we forget it can function in any other way.

The power exchange in dominance and submission play is mostly emotional, or based on roles and status. The other main branch of s/m uses power in a much more physical way as well. In sadism and masochism, the eroticization of giving and receiving pain, the emphasis on role-playing sometimes disappears altogether, leaving only the physical sensations (and the accompanying emotional ones) created by one for the other. To call intense physical sensation *pain* is itself misleading. Most of us identify pain as something unpleasant and undesirable, something over which we have no control. The extremes of sensation sought by sadomasochists bear no resemblance to the feelings produced by menstrual cramps or a finger slammed in a door. Many masochists don't experience the sensations of a scene as painful, as long as they occur in a controlled and consensual context. Even if they do, they like the sensation, or seek it for its cathartic or consciousness-altering value. For some, lovemaking simply isn't as satisfying without the infliction of bites and scratches. Others find spanking erotic. Still others seek the endorphin high that prolonged, intense stimulation produces.

S/m behaviors and rituals invariably make the outsider wide-eyed and uncomprehending, like a kid's stolen vision of Mom and Dad making The Beast With Two Backs. It is at once a richly symbolic world and a powerfully confronting one. Nonplayers seldom truly understand the range of emotions evoked by sensation, costume, role-playing, and dominance games. Consequently, public commentary on s/m images (the only s/m that most nonparticipants ever know) focuses on what outsiders *think* it all means. Having no way to conceptually separate consensual corporal punishment from violence, for example, many outsiders confuse the two. A complex, dreamlike phenomenon is slapped with a powerful buzzword, distorted, and rendered one-dimensional. S/m is consensual; violence is not. Nonconsensual, violent, or abusive behavior in a relationship is s/m's opposite, since it is characterized by lack of choice and communication, while s/m emphatically requires both.

Some feminists who are justifiably angry at gender inequality (the kind of power that isn't exchanged but *wielded*) are sensitive to any manifestations of power imbalance in a relationship, even when it's temporary and negotiated. A woman wouldn't want to give up power to a man or even another woman, they say, if she hadn't internalized harmful, socially-imposed roles. But what's not feminist about a woman empowering herself to explore her innermost erotic fantasies? What about the legions of men who want to bottom, either to women or to each other? And what about the female experience of topping?

No explanation of the real dynamics of s/m seems to affect this analysis, even when the results include a heightened sense of empowerment, sexual satisfaction, and self-esteem. The feminist critique of s/m suffers from the same myopia as the conservative one—an entrenched refusal to let preconceived notions of acceptable sex expand to acknowledge what people are really doing.

Many s/m players note that the sharpened communication skills they've attained from playing, along with the heightened sense of personal boundaries and limits that s/m play often helps them discover, make them less likely than the average person to be involved in abusive relationships. People who engage in vanilla (non-s/m) sex, including feminists, have a lot to learn from their s/m-playing neighbors with regard to communicating about desire and limits.

S/m culture has evolved to allow people who are interested in divergent sexual behavior to meet, and to teach people safe ways to conduct the variety of arcane games that many s/m aficionados favor. From the technology of whips and paddles, genital safe-sex techniques, and how to safely tie up a partner, to the art of bringing an emotionally overwhelmed person back to herself again, the s/m community has developed manuals, groups, and classes to learn skills necessary for unusual kinds of play. Contrary to their public image as scary, kinky thrill-seekers, most s/m players are warm, intelligent, loving, tolerant, and committed to their community and their erotic craft.

Twelve years have passed since the first relationship in which I experienced my submissive dreams made flesh. Today I know that if my then-love and I had had more information about how to stay emotionally safe, the conflicts between our feelings in and out of bed might have been easily resolved. Like any young person stumbling into sexual awareness, I started without all the data.

I began by meeting people who acknowledged they played s/m. They were a motley bunch, mostly outwardly unrecognizable as practicing "perverts," but some so in love with s/m's thrill and rebellion against the conventional that they wore it on their sleeves. Mostly they were dear and friendly. As a novice I was treated with respect, and let me observe and learn as long as I wanted before including me.

I found my current sweetheart three years ago and knew when I met him that s/m and dominance/submission would be integral to our play—without that he wouldn't have inspired the deep passion I now need and expect with my partners. It is part of how I express and receive love now: to delight in ritualized games of belonging. Helplessly bound and taken, I feel at the height of my erotic powers, which may sound paradoxical, but one measure of my sexual power is how vulnerable and receptive I can be, how much passionate and masterful attention I can receive. My vision taken from me by a laced-up velvet hood, I am both supremely objectified and taken to another plane of sensual awareness, with every physical sensation twice as powerful because I don't see it coming. Ironically, it is my own *subjective* consciousness that is paramount. Blindfolded, I must trust him to care for me, and reality dissolves into his touch and the sound of his voice. I dress provocatively for him and my gift is his response. Objectification—creating myself as an object of desire—is a pleasure for me when I solicit and control it.

He takes me over his knee to "punish" me for some sin or slight we have contrived together, and I go from seductive wiggling to fear to tears and catharsis. I can replay childhood emotions and give them an adult finale, reassured that I am more loved and stronger than I ever felt as a child. Sometimes I go beyond the place of struggle and "pain" and float on a sea of endorphins, aware that I have bypassed the point where previously I had to call my safeword and ask him to stop. Sometimes in play I wear a collar that means I am his, devoted to his pleasure, and I find it as satisfying as any new bride finds her wedding ring. In every case, from ritualized dominance to intense physical sensation, I know my lover is devoting all his attention to me and to the experience he is creating for and with me. His reward is my response and my emotional and physical engagement. And when the scene is over—his mastery and my submissiveness tucked away with all our other sex toys until we want to play with them again—we respond to each other as intensely as equals as we do when we've assumed our roles.

And sometimes he devotes himself to me, dressing and behaving to please me—for we, like many, perhaps most, participants in s/m, exchange roles sometimes. (Often s/m players, expecially those who are experienced, have no real role preference; they value equally each type of play.) This is the hardest part for many outsiders to comprehend. It's one thing if we *must* act out these erotic compulsions, they think. But the prevalence of *switching* insists that our behaviors are *chosen*.

In sex, especially, people tend to pathologize things outside their experience. If they are not doing it, people seem to reason, it must not be a good thing to do. Yet human erotic diversity involves a stunning rainbow of possible turn-ons, and if it were socially acceptable for us to share these differences with each other, we would see how many versions of arousal and pleasure-seeking there are. Instead, we are pressed to keep our erotic desires secret, even from ourselves. We are encouraged to think of diversity as dangerous. Almost everyone steps into the fantasmagoric world of their sexuality quite alone, and it's a wonder, given the lack of support and permission for what we find there, that we all don't slam the door and run screaming back to the familiar. Some do just that, and for them the erotic is forever tinged with danger. For many others, the erotic world is a lonely one, where "normal" sexual behavior carefully acted out fences us off from the alluring visions, acknowledged but never explored, of our fantasy life.

I cherish s/m because participating in its intense rituals tells me that I have begun to break down my wall of fear about my own (and others') sexual possibilities. It breaks down other fears as well: that I am not in control, of either my sex or my life; that I will not be listened to by my partners or have my limits respected; that I do not even know what my limits are. This is the heart of the matter as regards my involvement with s/m: I get to explore the continuum of power and powerlessness with partners I choose because I trust them and communicate well with them. This trust allows the possibility of vulnerability, surrender, and profound intimacy. The emotional power and catharsis of this can scarcely be described. Unlike my earliest experiences of unsettling intimacy, I now know that I have the capacity to communicate and set limits around my most powerful feelings. I don't always feel like playing s/m games with my lover, nor does he with me. But our partnership will always be an s/m partnership because of the intensity and bonding we've accessed through that play.

Most important of all, I am now able to be honest about my desires. For me, being authentic about my sexuality leads to a greater authenticity in all things. To be able to reject the notion that we must all be sexually uniform is as central to my sense of self-worth as any other thing because I know, and you do too, that we are all unique—many waves in a great erotic ocean.

Tee Corinne

DREAMS OF THE WOMAN WHO LOVED SEX

The Woman in Love met Desire in the French Quarter, at a party, with wine and cheese and art. Desire sat at the distant end of the courtyard, wearing white: hat, slacks, jacket, shirt open at the neck. The shadows both illuminated and obscured her. She smoked, gestured lazily, sipped a tall, frosted drink. Delicate, graceful women came and went from where she lounged, casual, observant.

The Woman in Love saw Desire as if from a long way off, down a tunnel, under water, like a beacon glowing in the shelter of the late afternoon.

"Who's that woman?" she asked her friends.

"Stay away from her, honey," the first replied. "She's trouble. Too smart for her own good."

"Too hot for her own good, you mean, don't you? Women always leaving their men for her, even when she doesn't want them."

"Right. She's not interested in settling down. Not that one. She's a writer, a Yankee, a reporter. Works for the *Times-Picayune*. Supposed to be from a good family. They pay her to stay away. You know the kind."

The Woman in Love didn't know, had never met the likes of her before but was certain, at that moment, that she wanted to know her, know more about her, touch and kiss and hold that lean, fine-boned body against her own.

The Woman in Love moved to the brightly lit portico and stood where her profile could be observed as she studied the paintings hanging there. She stood, hoping to be noticed, tingling with anticipation, expectancy. Someone brought her a drink. An old love lightly kissed her neck in passing, told her she looked beautiful. Having lost herself in conversation, The Woman in Love's awareness would return abruptly to the hazy white figure moving, ever closer, at the edges of her vision.

The Woman in Love's heart beat loudly as Desire moved near, touched her shoulder lightly and asked, in a voice felt before it was heard, "Would you like to dance?"

The room shivered. "Magic," the Woman in Love thought. "Magic is very near."

"Yes, thank you, I'd love to dance." The Woman in Love turned and faced Desire for the first of many times. She faced the woman's angular face and steady, sweet eyes. An explosion of spices, remembered pleasures, filled her mouth.

Desire brushed a lock of hair from the forehead of the Woman in Love, leaving the ghost of her fingers lingering, pulsing. Desire's hand, warm, settled at the Woman in Love's waist, gently guiding her through the foyer, among the other guests, the potted palms and ferns, the fringed and shaded lamps.

Finding a room where dancers swayed to recorded music, Desire opened her arms and the Woman in Love stepped forward, sliding one hand around Desire's neck, another settled in her outstretched hand. The Woman in Love was aware of her own breathing, the other's warmth, many perfumes like blooming flowers, cinnamon, the heavy thudding music, her nipples hardening against the fabric, the subtle give of the other's breasts, Desire's cheek moving against her own.

"You smell like the women in Paris," Desire said.

"Chanel No. 5. An old lover sends it every year, perfume and chocolates and roses for my birthday."

"Are roses your favorite flower?"

"No, gardenias."

They circled and turned, broke for drinks, returned to dance close, their heat rising. The Woman in Love shook a little in her excitement, thinking, "This is too fast, too much. I'm not sure I'm ready for her, for passion or love, attraction or lust to pull me from my work." She imagined herself consumed by flames.

"I saw your paintings in the front room," Desire said. "*Grief* and *Summer*. I liked them very much."

"Thank you," the Woman in Love said, lowering her head, remembering the oil of a woman dressed in black, her mother, raging at death that stole her dreams, that soon would steal her life. The Woman in Love thought more thankfully of the second painting, *Summer*, women lovers with flowers in their hair.

"I've seen your work before," Desire said, touching the Woman in Love's chin, drawing her back to the party. "At the James Gallery. A large oil of a woman reading, two women on a bench, some self-portraits."

The Woman in Love stopped dancing, pleased and startled. She smiled fully into the face of Desire, into Desire's eyes.

"You mentioned Paris. Have you been there?" the Woman in Love asked.

"Yes."

"To the Louvre?"

"Yes."

"Is the *Winged Victory* as beautiful as photos make her seem?"

"Yes. Very grand and sexual."

"Maybe I'll visit her someday." The Woman in Love felt shimmery, noticed the smell of cloves, of paprika, of steamed bay leaves.

They danced several slow, final turns of the room before the Woman in Love decided to leave, wanting to think, to savor the remembering, to catch her psychic breath, to reconstruct her understanding of her self.

They wove a trail between friends and strangers, working slowly through the amber light, intimate odors, cardamom and mint, Desire's hand resting lightly on the Woman in Love's hip.

At the door they exchanged addresses, phone numbers, agreed to meet again, perhaps later in the week. Desire held the hand of the Woman in Love for a long time, studying her as if she were a work of art. Desire lifted the fingers of the Woman in Love and pressed them to her lips, that old engaging gesture.

"I'm being courted," the Woman in Love thought, "and I am charmed."

The kiss dissolved. They said goodbye. The Woman in Love walked toward the river, feeling the evening full across the close-walled streets. She smelled the red bean and rice smells, the gumbo and crab, crawdaddy and shrimp. Jasmine bloomed. Somewhere a tenor sax slipped along the hot, damp, slow-moving air. She felt at home here, listened to scattered, distant conversations, music from the strip joints, sailors' whistles, horns tooting, laughter, a lean fiddler playing a high, wailing, cajun tune.

Before returning home she stopped for coffee, chickory-spiced, light with cream. She ate beignets, the light pastries dissolving against her tongue. Absently, she licked the powdered sugar from one finger after another, thinking of the way Desire had kissed her hand, the feel of her cool lips, warm breath. She remembered Desire's hand, light and firm against her back, leading her. Thrill and fear seemed poised, balanced.

She went home, pushed through the wrought iron gate, crossed the narrow, bricked courtyard and climbed, dreaming, to the third floor. Lingering outside her door, she leaned against the balustrade, shook her head to clear and settle thoughts which drifted out across the treetops and into lighted rooms where a voice behind her shoulder asked, "Do you want to dance?"

Taking a deep breath, the Woman in Love acknowledged that she had run from Desire. Turning, she entered her nest, dropped her clothes into the hamper, crawled between old and loving sheets and reached for her groin.

"I want her," she thought. "Want her," she sang quietly as her fingers worked their magic, her hips began to roll, her back to arch.

"Want her, want her," as she slowed rushing excitement, prolonged imminent joy.

At dawn, Desire knocked on her door, smiling ruefully, holding a gardenia.

"I couldn't sleep," she said.

They lay together late into the day. Desire held the Woman in Love. They held each other, rocking, talking, the sheets electrified, their hair in disarray.

They held each other that day and for many nights thereafter. Desire touched the Woman in Love demandingly, with leg and hands and tongue. The air filled with drifting odors: nutmeg, garlic, lemon, mustard, licorice, molasses, thyme.

In quiet times the Woman in Love thought, "Somehow, surely, this will enrich my work, will resonate in depth through all my future imagery. Please."

At other times she didn't think at all.

"Run off with me," the Woman in Love begged and Desire refused, following her own road into the future.

"I'll forget you," threatened the Woman in Love, but she never did.

The Woman in Love married for sex and comfort and shortly began taking lovers: women and very young men. Her husband adored her, drew life from the fires that burned within her, loved her genius for creative solutions.

"They say my father could repair a car with a hairpin," she would say, but of course that didn't explain her abilities. For generations, though, her family had been good with their hands.

Safely married, obsessed by the past, the Woman in Love began painting the hands of Desire, working sometimes from memory, sometimes from photographs. Although many of the canvasses were realistically rendered, some were colored by passion: green in the shadows, brilliant reds, purples, cadmium edges.

> *Exhausted, in the late afternoon, the Woman in Love dreams she's weaving through bamboo forests, toes squishing in warm mud, wandering among the eucalyptus, sniffing, open-mouthed, inhaling, running through fields of mint: peppermint, gingermint, Egyptian mint, spearmint, apple mint, catnip, lemon balm, pennyroyal.*
>
> *She runs, the Woman in Love dreams, running, smelling, embracing odoriferous day.*
>
> *As evening comes over her, it overcomes her, lowering her onto soft plants, crushed leaves oiling her body. She lifts her hips into the face of evening, combing her fingers through her own hairs, claiming her pleasure in her womanly birthright, exposed, exalted, understood.*
>
> *Awakening slowly to the entering evening, the Woman in Love runs her hands over her own body, reclaiming the real from the dream. Conscious now, she remembers the hands of Desire, inhales slowly, feeling the cool hands move over her, another awakening, memory encoded in all her surface cells. . . .*

Beloved fingers, spread across blue denim, flat against the table, felt at night, unseen; the Woman in Love recalls the hands of Desire, longs for them, ripens for them.

> *She dreams she is a fruit tree within the beloved's land, an apple tree, pruned, cleaned of parasites, rich with fruit turning bright in the summer heat. She dreams her feet are roots sunk deep, drawing water from the unseen stream.*
>
> *Her only need in life is to ripen, to grow, sustain, survive. The beloved's fingers move over her, caress her bra, remove dead branches, leaves.*

The tree of the Woman in Love sways in a lazy breeze, glistens with morning dew, traps moonlight in her veins. She sings whispering songs praising the wind, the light, the heat, the night of rest, the slow surge of passion waking the fog-cloaked dawn.
"Eat me soon," she tells her love. "Eat me soon."

Desire found the Woman in Love living in suburbia, teaching college, married still.

"Shall I go away?" Desire asked, holding herself quietly.

"No," the Woman in Love whispered. "I never did forget."

Swimming at midday in cool water, against the flow, between boulders, Desire smiles at the Woman in Love, tickles her with her toes, races her from shore to shore. Desire pulls her bodice down and squeezes the nipples of the Woman in Love, squeezes and molds her breasts, kisses her with a probing demand, a wanting that will not be stilled. Desire pulls the Woman in Love into the sand and reaches inside her suit, inside her body, pushing her want forward. The Woman in Love pushes back to meet her, to match her, to open to this mating so sun-wrapped, thrust upon her, so longed-for and feared and revered. Coming, she loses contact with all but the radiating sensations centered in her groin, in her ass. Her breath, withheld, she now expels and rocks and burrows into her lover's shoulder, into her lover's breast.

She dreams she is walking through a tunnel constructed of barrel arches. The woman beside her is tall, angular, softened at the edges. They stride in unison, in slow motion, up and down like carousel horses. Sounds form a rolling sea around them. The liquid gathers between her legs, begins its movement downward.

At that shimmering moment when they reenter sunlight, as the sounds rapidly shatter, compelling sensations race outward along her thighs. She feels herself to be both women, inside both women's bodies. The Woman in Love breathes deeply. Both women sigh.

Arriving home late one night, the husband of the Woman in Love confronted her with "What would you do if I asked you not to see her any more?"

"Leave you," she said.

The Woman in Love returned from the beach alone, bringing polished bones of wood, blue lupine, pebbles filled with light.

Desire met her halfway with small, hungry kisses, smiles, touches as soft as moth wings.

"I've decided to leave my husband," the Woman in Love said, whispered, sighed.

"Not because of me, I hope," Desire replied.

"No. No. Because of me."

Through winter and following spring they love:

When you touch me, when I respond, joy unfolds.

You have become my text, my love; your body, your words. I have bound your letters into a volume I carry with me, read at night before I sleep, at dawn before I move into the day.

Your love is a fine spray misting my movements, mellowing my colors, lightening what might have been despair. Where your hands have been, I am yours, and your hands have been everywhere. Your words enter my soil like rain. Your memory. Oh love, your memory takes me suddenly, wrenches me from this world into a fairy tale where I am loved the way I always wanted to be.

The Woman in Love dreams and rubs her body against the other's, soft and accessible. She dreams of prairies, wheat fields waving along her torso, streaming in the wind. She wakens to find her hand between the other's legs. Caressing, she imagines she is the first lover there, that they are sixteen-year-olds upstairs at her parent's home, holding each other, undressed, their imaginations excited. Everything is new, intense, iridescent. . . .

Desire awakens her with coffee, trails fingers along her body, tells her hunger in the touch of her palm. The Woman in Love responds with ardor, pelvis rising without conscious thought. The lover darts her tongue inside, taps excitement's pulse, teasingly withdraws, sustains, intensifies, releases. . . .

Sweet anticipation, rising warmly into her awareness, the Woman in Love moved on, wiping her past out behind her for shorter or longer periods of time. Opening herself to the world, the Woman in Love reached out with her attention, her intelligence, her curiosity. Time became immodest, a luxury she squandered exuberantly.

Anticipation awakened her, awakened in her, became the subtle tempo underneath her days.

The memory of Desire, going other places, living other lives, the memory of Desire whispered softly to her, a breeze among the cotton-woods, the cypress, jade and acacia trees. The memory of Desire winked at her from small, starry wildflowers, comforted her when loneliness seemed real. . . .

The Woman in Love met Desire again in London, sitting in a pub, slim, graying, full of stories. They returned to her flat, undressed almost shyly, excited still. Beneath the sheets they continued talking, touched slowly, hesitantly, joked about their mouths being dry.

When the Woman in Love buried her face in the other's shoulder, the hands of Desire were freed to move over her, opening her again.

"So long," she said. "It's been so long since we've been together, since it's been like this for me."

That first coming together, again and again, over distances beyond her imagination, compelled awe. The adequacy of a cheek, a touch, became fire and hunger, sweat and love.

The Woman in Love moaned.

The Woman in Love sighed.

Desire raged and washed over her. This time they both came.

In the morning the Woman in Love woke first, turned to kiss her lover, found her quiet and still. The Woman in Love feared morning would take what the night had given, touched her lover's shoulder lightly and willed herself returned to sleep. She dreamed of beaches, of walking alone on windswept ocean beaches, looking for someone.

She dreams the wind is blowing off the water, reaching through her clothes, drawing her hair from her face. Morning explodes, coral and flushed, exposing multiple horizons. Gulls flash and circle, calling to her, teasingly, to join them. She lifts from the sand, elongating her body, stretching her muscles, reaching out.

Soaring higher, she wants to thank the birds, the morning, but finds she cannot speak. The rosy gilt-edged hands of day encompass her, wrap around her, turn her, mold the furry ravine between her legs. Behind the dreamer's dream eyes, novas explode, the day breaks in two, freeing shooting stars across a velvet sky. The dreamer gasps and twines her fingers in the heliotrope hair of day. An early breeze kisses her cheeks, flutters a curtain lightly across her face. Stretching, she soars again, slides and turns, coupling with the wind.

Nearing Desire, excitement rises, circles within her torso,

242

whistles in her head. Dreaming, she crashes into the other's shore, rolls and turns across her beaches, kites and dips along the other's bony spine.

Desire erupts into a twilight sky to meet her, flowing down her own sides, winking, fiery. Warm breath, lava-flecked, encases her extended body, claiming her.

The Woman in Love awakened to find herself enfolded. Oh, those body smells, warm touch, firm hands. "Oh, god," said the Woman in Love. "Thank you, god," she said and looked into the other's eyes, liquid, calm and close.

They ate oranges in Valencia and bathed in the sea.

In Barcelona they lived in a small, cool, white room; wandered among the flower vendors until, aroused beyond propriety, they returned to their room and drank each other's bodies, breathed each other's smells.

Their honeymoon lasted as long as they needed. When their work drew them back to America, they returned, alone, together.

John Preston

How Dare You Even Think These Things?

The first story I remember writing was a medieval fantasy. A handsome lord rode through his domains examining the serfs who worked the land, stripped to the waist, their masculine beauty open to his evaluation. He was going to claim one of them for his bed, asserting his *droit du seigneur* to fulfill his lust.

I wrote the story on a ruled pad while sitting on the porch of our house and I still remember, over thirty years later, the sun's warmth on my groin as I scribbled out the tale of power and sex. I can't remember whether I fantasized myself as the lord or his peasants. I suspect it was probably both. I have always used my pornography to inquire into my own sexuality more than I have tried to capture a single point of view. Even then, pornography, for me, was exploration.

I left my work out on the table while I went to the kitchen to get a drink. When I came back to the porch, I found my grandmother reading my writing. She looked at me with fury and disgust. *"How dare you even think these things?"* she yelled at me. Then she tore the small, amateurish manuscript to shreds.

No one in our house ever mentioned the incident afterward. I didn't write fiction again for years.

My mother gave me a great gift when I was in high school. I wrote an English term paper on conformity. It was the 50s and suburban America didn't appreciate rebelliousness. To make it worse, I had likened the price I had to pay for acceptance from my peers and my teachers to prostitution.

My instructor and the school administrators pointed to that word and accused me of writing pornography. They told my mother that she would have to come to the school and meet with them to discuss the disciplinary problem I was creating.

That afternoon, my mother sat in the principal's office and listened meekly as he ranted about my insubordination. I had been born when my mother was quite young. She was only in her early thirties at this time. She'd grown up in the same town that we lived in. She'd gone to the same school and had the same English teacher and had known the principal and guidance counselor during her own student days. My mother is a large woman, but she seemed as small as one of my classmates as she listened to them all agree about the dangers that I represented:

How dare he even have these thoughts?

To my surprise, and to the others' shock, my mother suddenly sat up straight in her chair, clutching her purse, and looked the rest of the adults in the eye, one by one. "You will not do to my son what you did to me. You will not tell him what to think."

She was the person most stunned by her own statement. She slumped back in her chair, exhausted. But she finished her speech: "My son will not be punished for what he's written. He's here to learn how to think, not what to think. You will do nothing to him. I've read his paper. I'm proud he could express himself so well."

Then she stood up and we went home. Once there, she went to bed with a cold compress on her head, a migraine pounding in her temples.

She would never tell me what had happened in her own school days, but it obviously had taken an enormous amount of strength for her to face the living demons of her adolescence. I learned then, from my mother's example, that courage could be costly. I also knew that I'd never been more proud of her.

When I look at pictures taken of me in my adolescence, I'm always stunned by how attractive I was. I didn't feel it. Some message I'd received told me I was repulsive; who I thought I was then had nothing to do with the photographic images I can hold in my hand today. I knew I was strange and that my strangeness was something others thought was despicable. It was, in fact, so abhorrent that I didn't even know its name.

Rumor told me that there were horrible men who loitered in bus stations. They were to be avoided at all times. Somehow I translated that gossip into something else: I should go to one of these places and find those men. They were waiting for me; they had something to tell me.

When I was no more than fifteen, I made up some excuse to go into Boston alone. I sat on a cold bench in the lobby of the Greyhound station and waited there until someone found me.

My escort proved to be a traveling salesman from Hartford who was out on the town after drinking too much champagne at a concert at Symphony Hall. He was tipsy enough to brazenly invite me up to his room at the Statler Hotel, on the other side of Park Square.

I remember—and I remember this *vividly*—sitting on the edge of his bed while he undressed, having only been able to take off my shoes and a single sock. "I've never done this before," I told him.

He sneered at me. Teenage boys who sold themselves in Park Square always claimed innocence, I'd learn later, hoping to drive up their price. But finally he listened to me carefully enough to realize I was telling the truth.

I have always been astonished by what happened after that: he proceeded to give me a complete sex education, including play-by-play illustrations of all the possible acts two men could perform. I sucked him; he sucked me. I fucked him; he fucked me. I ate his ass; he devoured mine. All through this action, he delivered a running commentary on how it should be done and with what discretion, and how to find my own partners.

Most of the talk was affirmative, but there were also very practical warnings. I was cautioned away from men who would offer a young man drugs that could turn into a trap. I was told how to identify syphilis chancres and other signs of disease that might threaten me. I was encouraged to use a condom if I had even the slightest doubts about the risk involved.

(He even had rubbers in his wallet and gave me a step-by-step demonstration on how to put one on, first illustrating the procedure on himself and then making me put a condom on my own cock, to show him I'd learned my lesson well enough.)

When I got older, I studied sexual health at a major university and eventually joined the staff of the school's program in human sexuality. I later worked for one of the largest and most prestigious sex information and education organizations in the country. I met with Masters and Johnson; I visited with staff from the Kinsey Institute; I shared meals with the leading sexologists of our times.

I have never heard such a brilliantly clear and helpful sex education lecture as the discourse that traveling salesman from Connecticut gave me on his bed in that hotel room. I have always thought it was one of the great blessings of my life.

I eventually found the written word about sex in the books by a man who wrote as Phil Andros. By the time I found those books, I already had the basic information down. Now I needed the mythologies of the world I was entering. I needed to know more about how others had built their lives around these facts; I needed to know the tales that would give them meaning; I had to learn to consider myself beautiful.

The kind of exciting and often hard sexuality Andros wrote about was what I wanted to experience, or, often, it reflected what I had actually gone through. I could only find his books in the sleaziest porn stores, but I used to scour their racks looking for his by-line.

Many years later, in the 70s, after I had started to write pornography myself, I discovered Phil Andros's real identity. He was Samuel Steward, once a protégé of Gertrude Stein's. I tracked down an address for him in Berkeley, California, and arranged to visit him.

Steward was in his sixties by the time I found him. We spent days together, just talking about his life and his experiences. I learned all about the charmed circle of writers and artists who had gathered around Stein and Alice B. Toklas. I also heard Steward's stories of handsome young sailors and street-smart laborers who'd inhabited his sexual world in Chicago, where he'd spent most of his adult years. With each story, Steward could usually bring out some memento as an illustration.

Steward had looked around at his life as a young man in the 20s and decided that the world was only going to give him loneliness in his old age. The silence within which he lived offered him no evidence of any other possibility. He defended himself against that isolation by compulsively cataloguing his adventures, not only by writing about them for his public but also by keeping an exhaustive journal and by accumulating an incredible collection of memorabilia. (His greatest prize was a lock of Rudolf Valentino's pubic hair, which sits, encased in glass, in a shrine at the foot of his bed.)

Steward felt he had written his pornography too soon. No one would publish it but the smallest and, often, the trashiest companies. After a few years, he abandoned the work and retreated into his personal archives.

He hadn't seen that his pornography was changing the landscape in which it was happening. Many young men like myself were reading his adventures and were finding a mentor. Those once disdained, then out-of-print books had become collectors' items, passed hand to adoring hand by those of us who were the vanguard of gay writing, as it would come to be understood.

I wasn't the first young man to find him. I remember being enchanted by his description of one other—a porn star, as I recall—who would bicycle over the Bay Bridge from San Francisco to Berkeley to spend time with Sam and offer his adored body as an homage to the pioneer. Far from being abandoned, Steward was spending what he thought were to be his last lonely years receiving the adulation of a small but vital company of fans.

(Later, the cult that grew up around his writings would lead publishers to reissue most of his books. They were no longer hidden in cheap stores but were candidly displayed in the stacks of the new gay bookstores that were opening, bringing the written words of the gay experience to anxious readers.)

All this was the more astonishing to him because he had never expected to live this long; he'd had tremendous health problems. He described waking up every morning and pinching himself to see if he was still alive. He wouldn't plan for anything beyond that day, and, when each dawn arrived, he claimed it as a gift from the gods, something he hadn't expected to ever experience.

I knew that Steward had also been a tattoo artist at one time. I pleaded with him to come out of his retirement and mark me. I wanted put upon my own body a signal that the unspeakable was being uttered, that the things that should never be thought were coming true.

Sam arranged for the use of a friend's salon in San Francisco. We met in the storefront in the South of Market district. He drew on my chest the design he created for me: a quill dipping into an inkwell that became a pink triangle.

I spent a lot of time searching out the world of pornography. It wasn't the only literary country to which I journeyed, but it was always my favorite.

A few years ago, May Sarton was to be the guest of honor at a fund-raising dinner being held in Boston. I was asked if I would escort her to the function. Ms. Sarton was frightened of being in the city alone, especially after dark. She would be staying with old acquaintances in Cambridge. I agreed to pick her up and drive her across the Charles to the hotel where the function was being held.

There was a driving rainstorm that night and I got lost in the twisting streets of the university city, but I eventually found the correct address and had a lovely talk with the poet as we traveled down Memorial Drive. She'd seen some of my writing and liked what she'd read. We both had cats and we talked endlessly about them.

We got to the hotel and went into the cocktail reception being held for the honorees. A flock of lesbians surrounded Ms. Sarton with pure adoration.

That didn't surprise me; her reputation, especially among women readers, was very well established. What did startle me was that a group of gay men began to gather in line to greet me. I assumed, since we were all in our tuxedos for the big night, that these men wanted to meet me because of my essays, or perhaps some of the softer books I'd written, the ones that even May Sarton could admire. I thought they might have heard of me because of my reputation as an activist; the dinner was to benefit a political organization. But I was wrong.

One by one the men—the supposed elite of the new gay world—came up to me and confessed to me their most intimate secrets. I heard graphic descriptions about their sexual habits. I learned just where they read my pornography and just how long they could hold off having an orgasm while they did it. I realized that only a few years earlier, these men would never have dared say these things. They wouldn't have congregated together at a gay gathering. Only a few years earlier, they would have been invisible.

I listened to all of this come from the mouths of men who had won political office all through New England. It came from the mouths of men who owned large businesses. It came from the mouths of men who had used my books to explore the territory of their masturbatory fantasies with the help of the characters from my books. They knew Mr. Benson personally; they'd had sex with Pedro; they dreamed of the arrogant youths I'd found on the streets of Boston.

All the time I was smiling to myself. We were standing, after all, in the same hotel in which I'd lost my virginity with my Hartford salesman. It had been renovated and given a new name, but it was still the place where he'd taught me how to say the words of sex out loud. I wondered if he wouldn't be very proud of me now, listening to how much I'd passed on his lessons to these men.

> Will someone please talk about our children? They are being deprived of sex and love. What will happen to a generation that lives without those miracles?
>
> COLLEEN DEWHURST

When AIDS struck, the first messages from the bureaucracies were demands for abstinence. I knew it was a disastrous strategy. Gay men who had grown up having to reclaim their bodies from the prohibitions of medicine and politics weren't going to listen to those "authorities."

But my sexual health training told me just how dangerous this epidemic was. Things did have to change. But it would have to be the role of the pornographer to retell the tales and transform the terrain of our fantasies.

I called together a group of pornographers and created with them a volume of safe-sex stories, trying to stake out new paths for our readers. Later, I found a man who was using his body to give strip shows around the country, interspersing his lewdness with lectures on how safe sex could be fun. I used him to write a book, a guide to the new land.

Some people have credited the massive outpouring of new erotica, of which my work was only a part, with saving lives. Gay pornography can do that. It has that tradition. I remembered that both Sam Steward and my traveling salesman had talked about the dangers of hepatitis (does anyone remember hepatitis?) and other sexually transmitted diseases. We could learn from their lessons. Pornography saved lives in other ways as well. It gave us words to communicate our feelings. It broke some of our most bitter isolation from one another. It created dreams and hope.

I'd thought that one of the rewards I'd get as a pornographer would be simple sex. It happened, not nearly as often as I wished it might, but those men did find me occasionally.

One of them lived in Boston, a hundred miles from my home in Maine. He would call me up and beg me to let him visit, or to at least see him when I went down to the city. He'd describe which of my pornographic books contained those adventures he wanted to have.

I finally agreed. We made a date. Then the tone of the conversations changed. He knew that I'd taken a test for HIV antibodies. He wanted to know my status.

What difference did it make? I asked. I had written the books on safe sex; he claimed to practice protection in his own encounters. We didn't have to know such things; our pornography could exist without risk.

But he pushed and shoved. The information I held was new to me, and it was tender, but I gave in to his insistence. I told him I was positive.

We were modern urban gay men, he assured me. That was no problem.

Our telephone courtship had been long-lasting and intense. When we met for dinner, it picked up immediately and we talked about our closest fantasies over good glasses of wine. But as the meal ended, and the time came to leave, supposedly for his apartment, he began to withdraw. It was so real that I actually thought the wall against which he sat was moving backward, away from me.

I said something blatant about my expectations. He proclaimed shock. Of course he hadn't meant that. This was just an escapade for him, a chance to meet a pornographer in the flesh. He had never intended to put his body on the line, not into my hands.

I sat there and realized what was happening. Put on the spot, he wasn't going to have sex with a contaminated pornographer. I told myself: this is how they're all going to act, if I tell them.

How dare I even think these things?

I had another dinner with a modern straight couple not long after my aborted assignation. I'd learned not to discuss my own infection. I talked instead about the work I was doing with people who were living with AIDS. In the conversation, the subject of their sexual longing came up. The woman in the couple screwed up her face in loathing: "How can they expect anyone to touch them that way?"

How dare I even think these things?

Public health officials are obsessed by "noncomplaint carriers," those people who have tested positive for HIV antibodies but who continue to show up in clinics with other sexually transmitted diseases. A calamity needs villains. The government officials see an army of Patient Zeroes descending on Maine to kill off innocent victims.

(Isn't that redundant, I ask: "Innocent victims?" How can a victim be guilty? I'm ignored.)

If people had decent sex education, they'd know how to protect themselves, I point out. We need to provide people with better information.

"We can't!" some of the bureaucrats respond. "That would be pornography!"

But if you don't, you're leaving people out there undefended.

"Gay men can provide their own educational materials," I'm told. Over eighty percent of the people who have contracted AIDS in the state of Maine have become infected through homosexual acts. The state doesn't fund any safe-sex material for the gay population.

But it's not just the state. This is the most common phone call I receive these days:

"Did you know that _____ was in the bars last night?"

"So?"

"He has AIDS!" (Or, "He's HIV positive!" Or, "I saw him at the clinic the other day!") "They shouldn't let him in. The bar owners have an obligation to protect us!"

"You have an obligation to protect yourself."

"He'll give all of us AIDS!"

"He's told me he's only having protected sex."

"But everyone should know that he's infected! No one should sleep with him."

Or me.

The lepers are defiling the temple! Cast them out!

How dare you even have these thoughts!

My body rebelled, before my spirits were healed, after I learned that I was HIV positive. I came down with a bacterial prostate infection, something that had nothing to do with my HIV infection.

"When was the last time you had an orgasm?" my doctor asked me.

"Days." Then I admitted: "Weeks."

She looked at me carefully and said, "I'd have a very hard time if I had to go that long without sex."

I didn't say anything.

Then she explained that the prostate contains a pool of fluids that become stagnant if they're not ejaculated during sex. They become a welcoming breeding ground for bacteria. I had to flush out my system. I had to have sex, of some kind.

Anne Rice describes pornography as a place where people visit; it's not a place where one lives. I've always loved that perspective, it helps me understand my role as a pornographer. I'm a tour guide helping strangers see the landscape of our erotic potential. "This isn't the time to stop writing pornography," she says. "This is the time when erotica is all the more important."

I sat in front of my VCR and watched erotic tapes, one after another, trying to get myself back into the now-forbidden area of pornography.

At first I could only jerk off in the most mechanical fashion. What was wrong with me? I had once claimed all of this for myself, and now I was a shunned outcast from a land I had helped to create.

But of course. My pornography had been full of details about the glory of men's cocks. I had pulled them out of their pants and I'd looked at them with adoring scrutiny. I'd taken images from aboriginal rites and declared men's semen to be the means through which lessons could be transferred.

With the news of my own infection, I was in such shock that the pornography I'd created became, in my own mind, the actually physical place where disease had passed into my body.

I had to work to climb back. First, I had to make my pornographic videotapes a place I could visit. Then I began to look at the devastation of my imagination, how much my own infection had altered the way I approached pornography.

I usually create pornography the way other people consume it. I sit at my machine and I write it until I'm so turned on I can't stand it, and then I rush to find a comfortable place where I can pull out my cock and then tease myself to an orgasm. Or else I find some fantasy so compelling that I cannot ignore it. Those times, my dick is already so hard I usually can only type a page or two before I have to come, and sometimes I just shoot while I'm writing out the images.

Some of my pornography—not all of it but much of it—has been a retelling of actual events. As I saw the risk of the kinds of sex I once practiced become malevolent—and this happened before I understood that I myself was infected—my pornography moved to a more fantastic arena, one where pleasure remains without danger.

I created a world where proud men existed for one another's entertainment, where physical endurance was a norm but cruelty wasn't permitted. This world, The Network, was a place where no one was put at risk. It was the safe haven for my pornography during the epidemic.

I had left The Network when I learned of my infection. Slowly, over the weeks following that visit to my doctor, I rediscovered The Network's contours and fell in love once more with its citizens. They were moving, in my imagination, to an even more sacred place, one where they understood they were guardians of holy lands, where their duty was to keep the flames of erotic desire burning.

Readers want these explorations. The pornography I create sells well; it's talked about; there are new men on the phone wondering about the places I'm describing. But the rest of the world doesn't seem to want this material. Apparently trying to appear good and clean, book publishers move away from anything written about gay sex other than self-help manuals. A window opened in publishing during the time of gay liberation and sexual revolution. There were writers willing to promote our pornography as something important, and there was a time when publishers were willing to risk accepting that. Now the window is slamming shut. The pornographic word is being erased.

I ended one book I wrote about The Network with: "And the Master's Journals Will Be Continued." The editor had crossed out that line and had scrawled on the manuscript: "Not here they won't." It took three years to find another publisher willing to see a volume about The Network into the bookstores, and he's been fired by the conglomerate that has since bought the house.

The experimentation that had driven so much of the gay press is dying, or dead. Most gay periodicals that had once been journals of pornography, the places where I and my peers learned our craft, are now owned by one straight male businessman. Occasionally an editor at *Mandate* or one of the other magazines this man owns will try to create meaningful space in which a pornographer can work, but the lack of concern or care the publisher shows for this work is so intense that the effort never lasts.

And writers are abandoning this landscape as well. One editor has told me that over half of the manuscripts his publishing house receives—and it's been one of the major suppliers of gay literature over the past years—are set in the just recent past, obviously to justify sexual actions that couldn't happen safely today. Looking at our world and the way we are now, and looking at this world with its full erotic capability, is something too many writers have proved incapable of doing.

A writer like myself—one who can move across the boundary and live in a nonpornographic place—is put under great pressure to leave that world behind now. There are hints that I shouldn't continue to ruin my reputation, but the lure is often more subtle; the rewards for writing nonpornography during a time of AIDS aren't a mistake.

The ways that my road maps can reach people are being blocked; the words I write are written now without any real expectation that they can be published, or that they can be published in any form that isn't humiliating to me. While my pornographic books sell as well as any others I write, I'm paid a tenth as much for them. There's no way, now, to support oneself as a professional writer by creating pornography.

(And what will people think of my pornography now, anyway? Now that they find out I'm infected? *How dare he even think these things?*)

The avenues to writing about sex are closing. The boundary of what the world will accept as our pornographic vision is narrowing, at least in print.

Now I discover that we're reverting to an oral tradition, as though we must move the lines of our struggle back to some place from which we thought we'd escaped. The bookstores exist through which a reader can find a writer, but they become useless as fewer and fewer decently written pornographic works find their way through the new barriers and into print.

That doesn't mean people aren't looking for pornographic mentors. I now sit in my apartment in Portland and receive younger men who come to me and ask me to talk about what has gone on. They know about risks and infections, and they understand the need for caution, but they still want to know about the world of pornography.

I sit with them and tell them about the old days and show them the old books and magazines and answer their questions. "What was it like to go to a bathhouse?" "Did you really go to the Mineshaft?" "Was The Saint as glorious as they say?" "How does leather feel on your naked skin?" "Will those days ever return?"

And I see in their eyes the vision of pornography, and the hope that it will still be valued. *How dare they even think these things!*

James Broughton

AT BECK'S MOTEL ON
THE 7TH OF APRIL

At Beck's Motel on the 7th of April
we went to bed for three days
disheveled the king size sheets
never changed the Do Not Disturb
ate only the fruits of discovery
drank semen and laughter and sweat

He seasoned my mouth
    sweetened my neck
    coddled my nipple
    nuzzled my belly
    groomed my groin
    buffed my buttock
    garnished my pubis
    renovated my phallus
    remodeled all my torso
until I cried out
until I cried
        I am   Yes
        I am your   Yes
            I am   I am   your
            Yes   Yes   Yes

Ron Koertge

THIS IS FOR EVERY MAN WHO LICKS

This is for every man who licks
his shoulder during solitary sex,
rubs his beard against the stripey
deltoid muscle or bites himself hard.

This is for the woman who at the body's
buffet touches her breasts one at a
time then reaches for the place
she has made clean as Mother's kitchen.

Masturbation should be as exciting as any
heavy date: have a drink first, lay out
some poppers, open that favorite book
to the most shameful passage because
without blessed shame nothing is
as much fun.

And please don't jump up afterwards
and rush for the washcloth like all
the relatives were on the porch
knocking, their hands hot from
casseroles and a cake with God's
name on it.

Rather lie there, catch your breath,
turn to yourself and kiss all the nimble
fingers, especially the one that has
been you-know-where, kiss the palms
with their mortal etchings and finally
kiss the backs of each hand as if
the Pope had just said that you are
particularly blessed.

7

EROTIC TRANSCENDENCE AND SELF-DISCOVERY

INTRODUCTION: PART 7

According to Judeo-Christian ideology, the world of eros, the body, and human sexuality is essentially the domain of the devil. In this worldview, the realm of the physical is base, a beastly distraction from spirituality—from the high, mental, hallowed pursuit of God and the good, ethical life. We are told that the more we open ourselves to the influence of eros, the more we listen and respond to the dictates of the body, the more we enjoy and pursue our sexual natures, the farther we stray from moral rectitude, spirituality, and emotional well-being.

The writing in this section argues that precisely the opposite is true. It argues that the erotic world, honored and freed from the stigmas of guilt and the forces of suppression, can be a powerful path toward both spiritual transcendence and psychological self-discovery. It calls on us to stop trivializing the erotic/sexual world as we so often do, as if sex involved nothing more than sensory stimulation, ego gratification, and the pursuit of orgasm.

That there is more to sex than the heady pursuit of carnal pleasure may be hard to accept in the wake of the sexual explosion of the 60s and 70s, when relatively safe, reliable birth control combined with feminism, psychedelics, and the movements for gay, lesbian, and bisexual liberation to release us suddenly from some of our heritage of sexual repression and fear. But the pieces in this section suggest that it is precisely our failure to recognize the depth and complexity of erotic engagement that underlies much of our current sexual dissatisfaction.

In the heady time of so-called free love, when sex and sensuality overflowed the banks of previous restriction and became available to all who chose to immerse themselves in those waters, we seemed collectively to want nothing more than to gobble as much erotic experience as we could. We were, after all, starving beings emerging from forty (or fifteen hundred) years in the desert into a world of green jungles bursting with exotic fruit. It was an exciting moment in the cultural history of American sexuality, and an important first step in freeing ourselves from the claustrophobic properties of the 50s—the monolithic, white-picket-fence, clean-and-tidy, asexual suburbanism of the postwar economic miracle.

But even as we feasted on the multiplying erotic delights we discovered at every turn, even as we gloried in our power to transcend political, cultural, and sexual conventions long considered sacrosanct, we began to come up against the limits of the path we were on. In Hegelian terms, the new synthesis started to generate its antithesis. The crest of the wave was moving faster than the base and there were cliffs directly ahead. Woodstock gave way to Altamont; LSD to speed; SDS to the SLA; the delight of freely pursuing sexual pleasure to feelings of sexual emptiness and dissatisfaction, even before herpes and AIDS came along.

We had released the pressure of decades of sexual inhibition, but there was more to the picture than simply having more sex, having sex with more partners, having sex with less guilt and more information, having sex with significantly less pregnancy and disease, or having sex in previously prohibited ways (with your mouth, with your ass, with a vibrator, with a dildo, or with people of your own gender). Jumping into the sexual rabbit-hole as innocent as Alice, we found ourselves facing underground kingdoms we could not have expected and did not know how to interpret.

Much as we would like to believe that we can jump in and out of erotic and sexual encounters as easily as we can jump in and out of a shower, a movie, or a subway, the experience of being sexual in full, rich, powerful ways inevitably engages an entire range of complex issues, emotionally and spiritually. This can be problematic, because many people now want to be sexual more often and with more partners than they want to engage intimately, let alone relationally, or spiritually.

But these deeper energies are integral aspects of erotic experience, no matter how diligently we try to reduce sex to the simple pursuit of physical pleasure. Whenever we play with erotic energy, we engage both emotional and archetypal forces that have their roots in the very heart of who we are as human beings, in how we define ourselves and relate to the world around us. Entering fully into the erotic world necessarily raises issues and feelings, for example, around our (usually unfulfilled) infantile desires to be nurtured and held, our prenatal memories of being at one with another human being, around ego dissolution and the blurring of interpersonal boundaries, and around surrendering rational control of our behavior. Erotic connection inevitably raises all the issues related to intimacy—the desire to be close to someone else, the fear of becoming lost or smothered, and all the past yearnings, fulfillments, wounds, and disappointments we have experienced in this regard. Being sexual raises issues of our worthiness to receive love or pleasure, as well as when and how we want, or don't want, to extend these ways of caring to another.

As we go deeper into the emotions freed by deep erotic experience, we are often brought face-to-face with anger, passion, even rage, which we may find embarrassing or disturbing. We find ourselves dealing with issues of power (how much power we are willing to allow ourselves to have in the intimate presence of another, how much interpersonal power we feel we can handle responsibly), and of trust (how much we are willing to bare ourselves to another, to let ourselves be seen in our emotional nakedness and confusion, to put our well-being in the hands of another). Going still deeper, erotic experience takes us down to basic feelings about the existential balance of order and chaos (ultimately to our feelings about life and death), and even to a quality ofexperience that many describe as direct contact with the divine.

The nine pieces in this final section offer a wide variety of perspectives on the possibilities for transcendence and self-discovery through erotic expression. They range in focus from the psychological to the spiritual, from the personal to the religious. Former Carmelite Kevin Regan begins by offering his vision of sexual union as "the finest prayer a married couple can offer to God." Challenging the Christian tradition of separating erotic from spiritual exploration, Regan notes the similarities between prayer and sexual love, urging us to pursue the religious experiences of surrender, intimacy, and the willingness to confront the unknowable through the flesh, instead of in opposition to it.

From a very different perspective, sexual philosopher and explorer Marco Vassi discusses sexual experience as a means of exploring the very meaning of life. He calls the attempt to pursue enlightenment through disembodied mental activity a decidedly male perspective, perhaps a consequence of male spiritual teachers defining as inferior an embodied, feminine way of engaging the world. Tantric teacher Margo Anand takes us into precisely this body-centered, Eastern spiritual perspective with an overview of the four-thousand-year-old Tantric tradition that explicitly engages sexuality as a path to spiritual enlightenment.

Robert Moore and Douglas Gillette examine the male archetype of the lover as both the sensual embodiment of play and shameless display, and as the source of male spirituality and mysticism. They contrast the dimension of man as lover with the other male archetypes of warrior, magician, and king. Similarly, Robert Bly extrapolates from his personal experience to speak of making love as an essential way of calling the soul back into the body.

Editor Sy Safransky muses on the interaction of eros and love, on the importance of erotic interpersonal melting as a means of both discovering oneself and of transcending the limits of the self. Moving into more specifically sexual territory, writer/healer Deena Metzger speaks of sexuality as a path that leads to the heart of life itself, where all forms are represented simultaneously—the plant form, the animal form, the forms of light, the violence that tears us open and throws us into the core of our essential selves. Poet and songwriter Leonard Cohen testifies to the power of contacting another person's vulnerability and pain through the experience of touch; and Lenore Kandel's "Eros/ Poem" is a final, unbounded song of praise to many-faceted young Eros, "child of the gods, who loves only beauty and finds it everywhere."

Kevin Regan

THE PRAYER OF CONJUGAL LOVE

Sexual union is the finest prayer a married couple can offer to God. As an expression of God's love, it creates unity and joy which are the surest sign of God's presence. As an expression of the couple's love for each other, it is the clearest affirmation that love is their vocation, a call to build God's kingdom. With such power to realize God's presence, one wonders why there is so little written about conjugal love as prayer. This is especially puzzling given the multitude of books on centering prayer, charismatic prayer, holistic prayer, liturgical prayer, the Jesus prayer, and biblical prayer.

The answer is initially found in the Church's persistent prejudice against the body with a consequent fear of integrating the body, with all of its fleshy passion, into Christian spirituality. On another, more subtle level, the habit of neglecting conjugal love as a form of prayer is an expression of a deep-rooted fear: the fear of mystery. We live in a society which deliberately doubts and systematically rejects the presence and therefore the importance of mystery. Due to a pseudoscientism and an isolated rationalism, we intentionally exclude the paradox of mystery, of sacrament from the dynamic of our everyday lives. We have chosen to live in fear with doubt and anxiety as our constant cohorts rather than to face the tumultuous ferocity of mystery. We flee from mystery for we can neither measure nor control it. We run away from the change mystery may bring about in us, the assumptions it would force us to abandon, from the uprooting it would demand of us, if we integrated it into our lives. Our desire to escape the mystery which is within and without has placed our lives in jeopardy. We think we fear loss of freedom, fear the Russians, or fear war, but the reality we fear more than all the nuclear warheads, more than all the enemies real or imagined, is the reality of love and the surrender love demands. The Church, which is the guardian of the sacramental way of living, has failed to respond to the challenge.

It is no wonder that one of the most predominant characteristics of our age is impotence. Not that we are without power, but that we experience ourselves individually and collectively as powerless. The results of our impotence are everywhere present. We have sex as a constant stimulus for our egos, but sex without love and therefore without consequence. We have an abundance of food, yet millions go hungry. We need housing and shelter, medical care, energy to heat our apartments and homes, and still we have massive unemployment. We have the largest population in the history of our planet, yet are paralyzed by loneliness. We have arsenals of weapons never equalled in destructive power, yet no security. We have only the old, bitter fear which continues to breed more and more weapons. We are impotent. We are afraid. We fear love. We have forgotten how to dance. We need desperately to hear the music of the divine conductor, to give up our old role as disembodied spirits and become full-blooded lovers, ecstatic prayers. Conjugal love points the way.

Not long ago my wife and I explained to a newspaper reporter that our opposition to paying war taxes was rooted in our love, that is, in our sexual union. This was the real story: the willingness of a couple to face jail and separation because of their love, their desire to defend the living. However, the depth and mystery of our love story offered too great a challenge, and it scared the reporter off. He wrote instead about banal confrontations between ourselves and the Internal Revenue Service.

Had he pursued the real news, the reporter would have discovered it is love's character to transform ordinary people from people of fear into people of hope, and to empower them to face even the most menacing fears. Good news indeed! It is in this power to transform that conjugal love and sexual union are most characteristic of prayer, that they are at once so inviting and so threatening.

Sexual love transforms, as does prayer, not through violence or the promise of immediate results, but through gradually deepened intimacy. Like a new wine that matures and blossoms in aroma and taste and color with slow, faithful attention to the aging process, so too sexual union gradually transforms anxious sweethearts into whole-bodied, full-spirited lovers. The key to a joy-filled sexual embrace is like the key to all joy-filled prayer. It is surrender. To the degree you love, you give yourself over to the other. You sacrifice all defenses and release the ego into the care of the other. You become totally vulnerable; thus love is a threat. But without becoming vulnerable you cannot love; without surrender there can be no intimacy. It is at the point of surrender that the vocation to the married life and to the celibate life meet and support one another.

Prayer unites us with God in a unique union, though shared by many; this is equally true of sexual embrace. It is truly a climbing inside the other. There results a knowledge of self and of the other which no one else has. It is in the security of this union that the depth and center, the heart of our own identity, appears and disappears. This is the pivotal moment when we know ourselves as loved not only by our immediate lover, but through her or him by God. This experience cannot be clung to or contained, rather it springs up to be realized in the freedom and security of love, to disappear again until a similar experience of attentiveness, forgetfulness, and purity is present. No attempt to repeat or hold on to the experience will succeed. Any reenactment is impossible. Should one make such an attempt, the result will be total frustration at facing a false image created by the mind, a projected illusion. Much of society's preoccupation with sex today is a chasing after illusions motivated by a desire for genuine intimacy but without the willingness to risk being vulnerable. Much of the nudity which fills our movie screens is a false image of the true nakedness which would bare both body and soul, revealing hidden fears and dread, but also the soul's power of acceptance, its rich resources of forgiveness and healing. Our willingness to reduce sexuality to the physical is an infantile attempt to know ourselves and each other without involving those powers that make us human and which raise our sexual union to the level of intimacy.

Sexual union, like all prayer, realizes our poverty, our absolute need for each other. In sexual union we discover that wholeness of being is a gift which, although sought by us, demands a complete letting-go into the care and embrace of the other. It is this act of surrender which is the married couple's celebration of the paschal mystery, the dying and rising of Christ. It is also an anticipation of individual and planetary dying and rising in Christ. It is in the act of surrender, when one chooses to become totally open and vulnerable, that the affirmation of faith in life beyond death is actualized. For without such faith, surrender would be conditional. It is worth repeating that this act of surrender into the hands of another without knowledge of the consequences or outcome is at the heart of both the married and celibate state. Through this action of total exposure, of reaching out and letting go, of giving and receiving, penetration and acceptance become one action teaching us again and again who we are and who God is.

Intimacy then is not conceived, as in the past, as freedom from the flesh; rather we are transformed and elevated into God's full-grown children by freedom through the flesh. It is not, therefore, a holy act to abstain from sexual union in order to discipline the body and during this time to offer prayers to God. Rather, it is the function of sexual union in conjugal love to celebrate the fullness of the Incarnation, God in our flesh. It is the purpose of conjugal love to realize the Spirit's life-giving action not in moments of planned abstinence, but in the spontaneous ecstasy of sexual embrace at the point of sexual union.

In a world which views its accomplishments, its goals, its vision of reality, its technical achievements as ends in themselves, as idols, sexual love invites us as lovers to go beyond society and the self, to stand outside the self, to experience the world from a unique vantage point, to discover what is lasting and what is temporary. Sexual union is mutual surrender to the mystery at the heart of human life and married love. It is the realization that we are not, for all our technological prowess, the center of the universe: God is the center everywhere present with no circumference.

It is precisely in realizing God as the center of the universe that sexual union is an act of profound worship and praise. It is as worship and praise that the life of celibacy and the life of conjugal love bear witness to a transcendent God, a timeless kingdom. For sexual union to become sacramental it must be transformed by Godly love. For the solemn promise of celibacy as a life dedicated to service of others and love of God to be fruitful, it must be eminently human. Thus there will be neither marriage nor giving in marriage, for the fullness of love in the kingdom will be realized equally through marriage and the celibate state. All will then echo the Spirit's voice, "Set me as a seal on your heart, as a seal on your arm. For love is strong as death, jealousy as relentless as the grave. The flash of it is a flash of fire, the very flame of the Lord himself. Love no flood can quench, no torrents drown."

Marco Vassi

BODHI IS THE BODY

Enlightenment has been almost exclusively a man's game. Women have been considered at best irrelevant and at worst ruinous in the quest for truth. In less hypocritical times, this was stated openly by the priests of all the major religions; today the notion has gone underground, but is more pernicious for just that reason.

This insight came to me, as many of my most acute visions do, while I was fucking. To describe what she and I did, the feelings which flowed, the passions that informed our behavior, would not be to the point. What takes place between a man and a woman when they return to the *source* is far deeper than language. We fucked and we made love; we did both, shifting from an activity in which two individuals act upon one another, to a movement of a single entity that no longer distinguished among its parts. The night was a reality with the quality of a dream, and hummed with that singular vibration of union, where subjective and objective interpenetrate like the blue and red of yin and yang.

The violet ecstasy of those hours entered me with all the significance of a childhood imprinting. As I lay in her arms, her body an undulating density of corduroy coils, the smells and sounds and texture of our dance conjured a realm of awareness in which the chains of time were shattered.

And with apparent incongruity, a line from an old book came into my consciousness: "When one is ready, the teacher will appear."

I was at a stage where I had been doing a particular kind of work, using Gurdjieffian methods of self-observation, paying attention to the physical aspects of my being—posture, gesture, facial expressions, the sound of my voice, movements. Without any effort at changing myself in a given direction, I adhered simply to the discipline, and the work had begun to show a result. I was beginning to find many facets of my existence clarified, and doorways to so-called higher states were opening. Questions which had tortured me were seen through, and debilitating habits fell away. No decisions were involved; the process of self-observation made all things obvious.

Concurrently, I wondered from time to time whether some master would pop up one day to take me by the hand and lead me to realms of knowledge closed to ordinary mortals. But it was not until I spent that night with Julia that the basic prejudice which lies at the root of so many schools of enlightenment flashed in all its dimensions. Something about the concept of esoteric wisdom had long bothered me, and now I could see what it was: in its continual focus on a condition removed from day-to-day life, most of the supposedly spiritual literature had dropped women to the status of hindrance. Without being stated in so many words, it was assumed that no woman could ever be a teacher, or if one were, she would have to operate in the capacity of a man's role.

As we took to one another's arms and legs and eyes and I was infused with a stinging alertness, I saw that she was giving me, at that very moment, lessons about the meaning of life that were as profound as anything any teacher or master had ever talked about. From terror to bliss, all the modes of being triumphed between us. She was providing me with the completion without which all verbal knowledge is fatuous mumbling. While I had vaguely been expecting a bearded and robed Indian expatriate, the truths I was so hungrily seeking were pressed tightly against me, in the shape of a mouth against my mouth, and a vortex of energy which called me into the hot, wet center of her body. Singing and sweating the wondrous song of sex, we were joined in full intimate contact with the living embodiment of our primary reality as human beings.

"All this," I thought, "through contact with a woman. All this, through the vehicle of sex."

In a very important sense, my life had been a struggle to come to terms with women, beginning, of course, with my mother. In doing that I was, without articulating it as such, defining what it meant to be a man. I had spent many years in the boundless stretches of homosexuality, and despite the treasures I had found there, saw that that style of life, if followed exclusively, was for me ultimately sterile. It did not, by itself, replenish the juices I needed to sustain me.

With women, I had practiced a judicious promiscuity, and even when I lived with a woman for any length of time, I could not appreciate her as anything but a minor incident in my life. I was infected with the thought that someday I would meet a teacher, a man, who would show me the way. It took many years of work and the help of a woman therapist to point out that *the man I was looking for was myself.*

Like so many of my generation, I ransacked the wardrobe of Eastern thought for answers, and found the same spectrum available as in the West, couched in different terminology. It went from folksy wisdom to obscure mystifications and occasionally, as in Ch'an Buddhism, a perfectly penetrating truth. But for all the value of these aphorisms and instructions, none of those hundreds of thousands of words helped fill the very real hole in my psyche. The greatest help I received from the East was the assurance that I wasn't the only one facing the thorny problems of living by attempting to contact the vibration of universal consciousness. The greatest damage done by my foray into Oriental attitudes was the perpetuation of the notion that enlightenment is a state which precludes, or ignores, continuing relationship with women.

The following story exemplifies this attitude in perhaps its mildest form. A Zen master and his disciple were walking along and came to a stream where a woman stood by the shore, not wanting to wet her robes in crossing. The master picked her up and carried her across. He and the student continued for several miles and the disciple finally burst out, "It is against all our teaching to have anything to do with women, and yet you picked her up in your arms." The master snorted, "I put her down at the far end of the stream, but you, it seems, have been carrying her in your mind all this way."

The story is used to point up the process whereby we are trapped by conceptual thought, and as such is a salutary tale. One is very prone to admire the old monk for his greater "humanity." But several questions are raised, such as, "What sort of teaching is it that treats women as a species of psychic lepers, to be avoided at all costs?" And, "What sort of society is it in which a woman comes to view herself as so inept and frail that she can't cross a stream by herself?"

Here one gets into the trickier question of whether there is something in the nature of woman that is intrinsically disruptive to a man's peace of mind. God knows, any man who has become involved with women has certainly been tempted to quit their company forever and choose monastic seclusion as a viable alternative. But if peace of mind has to be bought at the price of the exclusion of half the species from meaningful social intercourse, then one must call into doubt any so-called higher state of consciousness available only under that condition.

Putting aside the contention of the sexual nihilists that men and women are inherently damaging to one another's well-being, the cause for such a split between male and female is to be sought in conditioned attitudes toward the problem. There are certainly times when a man must be alone, and times when he must be in the exclusive company of other men. But to raise such a cyclical psychological process to the level of a permanent and laudable condition, and then to bolster it with ideological argument, is pathological.

In the West, beginning with the Pauline misogyny, women have been held by official Christian spokesmen to be little better than slaves, and the sex with which they tempt men has been considered the most cunning work of the devil. To counterbalance this, the Church raised Mary to the status of supervirgin, making her equally unreal. Popes have blessed armies with holy water, sending them happily off to slaughter, and then promulgated laws which condemn teenagers for necking. I don't know why I expected anything better from the East. Stupidity is not the special province of any hemisphere or nation or creed. As in any given sampling of any portion of humanity, there are a few who have attained wholeness in this area, and the rest stumble along in different stages of waking sleep, using more or less satisfying rationalizations to hide their basic fear.

Enlightened men may choose, for their own reasons, to remove themselves from the company of women. In our time, Thomas Merton comes to mind. Others, equally fulfilled creatures, may not. Alan Watts is an example. It is when the private solution of a strong man is turned into a rule for others to live by that the damage is done. I knew a woman who was capable of total orgasmic release. She had no problem with the quibble as to whether orgasms are clitoral or vaginal. When she came, she came entirely, from her toes to her brain, shivering, bursting, melting, burning, climaxing fully. She began to study with a hatha yoga teacher, a sweet old man who had founded an institute and culled a following from several thousand of the disenfranchised young of America. His mastery of the asanas was unquestioned, and his desire to help humanity was sincere. Yet, he managed to insinuate such an atmosphere of ethereal pseudo-spirituality that his students saw giving up sex as a mark of progress toward some mystical goal. The woman, her eyes possibly blinded by the thick haze of incense which hung over the institute, lost sight of the fact that yoga is primarily a process for keeping the body strong, the mind clear, the heart capable of loving. She rejected sex, and commenced to spend much of her time in a trance-like state which she identified with cosmic calm. Half a year later, she was utterly dispirited, and despite the regularity of her new-found habits, she had let slip the *elan vital,* that spark of vivacity which is the sign of the sexually alert person. With the revivifying power of the orgasm denied her, her body no longer thrilled with energy. She lost her zest for living and became an automaton.

This is not to denounce yoga, but the imposition of a poorly understood worldview on a set of exercises. Nor is there anything necessarily wrong with celibacy. There are circumstances in which celibacy is the natural order of things. A person who loses a mate, for example, may not be able to fuck for a long period of time. This is simple biopsychology. Or a person may be jaded through sexual overstimulation, and will need some time to lie fallow. Or a person may come to a point at which sex ceases to operate through the genital channels. And, of course, there is, with age and wisdom, a gradual refinement of the uses of sexual energy altogether.

These are all organic processes. But to make an *a priori* value of celibacy and to claim that to stop fucking will bring one closer to God or enlightenment is, categorically, a pathological defense on the part of a person who is sick in his or her sex, and is reaching for the most grandiose rationalization by which to defend that perversion.

I returned to my own experience to find what was true for me. This much I knew: to fuck a woman that I care for, and to melt into orgasm with her, subsumes all that is fine in life. In fact, I found that unless all the rest of my life was in order, I was not free to partake of that sublime experience. The orgasm is *the* life-enhancing process. From its physiological function of discharging tension and toning the organism, to its biological function of improving the quality of children that are born, to its spiritual function of putting one in touch with higher forms of energy, it contains all the keys anyone might want. Sex is a complete activity, bringing all the fragments into a whole, operating as the most subtle and immediate communication between human being and human being. It acts resoundingly to affirm the pulse of life; in its contractions and expansions, it *is* the pulse of life itself. How on earth, I wondered, could anyone view it as anything but a central factor in a person's attempts to live most fully?

It did not take long to see that such an attitude arises through the failure of teachers and so-called holy men to come to terms with their feelings about women. Seemingly, they have not been able to deal with their fear, their confusion, their loathing, their need, their desire, their hidden worship, of women. With a shift that has become the mark of our history, they separated the genders in their own context, and made enlightenment a preserve for men only, in the same way that the Catholic Church has decreed that no woman is good enough to hold the consecrated host in her fingers. Those women who did try to crash the gates became grotesques, like St. Theresa, with her scorching visions of angels piercing her bowels with flaming spears, and Madame Blavatsky, who could out-think, out-curse, and out-maneuver any man who came into her vicinity, and won her theosophical spurs over the heads of men who were thrillingly eager to feel her psychic lash across their metaphysical buttocks. But such women only underscore the hidden thrust of the sacred teachings, the one sentence that lies at the core of all major religious systems: that one cannot learn anything from a woman that is of any real value on the road to enlightenment, and that any sexual contact with women is at best a distraction from the process of seeking truth.

Although he never addressed himself to the problem directly, it was Wilhelm Reich who most forcefully, among men, cut through the obfuscation. It was his observation that when the life energy which flows through us is blocked, distorted, or "armored" as a result of growing up in a particular civilization, total orgasmic release is impossible. So far as I know, he was the first to differentiate betwen mere ejaculation for the male, or clitoral/vaginal stimulation for the female, and the full vegetative rush of complete orgasm. In a condition of orgastic impotence, the person will manifest one of two basic characterological states: fascism or mysticism. Either there will be a softening of the sense of self, in which the person loses all awareness of boundary; or there is a hardening, in which rigid boundaries become the central aspect of the lifestyle. One need not be too sophisticated to see that these are indeed the ruling modes of social life in the world today. The governments and official institutions are almost totally fascistic in their machine-like quest to impose conformist order on all human beings, while the masses of people stagger around in an obscurantism relieved only by their vague mystical yearnings, their hope for salvation from above.

To extrapolate from that vision to the topic at hand, it is necessary only to point out that what has been denied to women is the acknowledgment that they are teachers of life *in their very bodies.* Very few women I have known have possessed this awareness of their own biological efficacy. The sickness of mankind has been the overwhelming importance placed on discursive thinking, to the detriment of the life processes at large. Women, who instinctively understand the severe limitations of conceptual thought, have not only been relegated to second place, but have been forced to deny their immediate perception of the true hierarchy of value. When a woman says in scorn and sorrow, "You only want me for my body, don't you?" neither she nor the man she addresses usually has any inkling of the profundity of the insight contained in that question.

For what the man wants is to *feel his own body*, and it is with practically automatic tropism that he reaches to a woman, to sense his palpable reality by embracing a person who is fully alive inside herself. Those women who have attained this awareness form the heart of the current phase of women's perpetual struggle for liberation. But these very women then refuse to serve as psychological wet nurses, to be available to men who are still allowing themselves to be transmogrified into robots.

What men need right now, more than anything, is the ability to *be aware of their own feelings.* And the only men who, as a self-identified group, are freeing themselves to feel are gays. There is a strong argument to be made for the notion that homosexuality should be the general sexual form of the future, with heterosexual unions forming a minority, but even if that were so, historical intransigence is unlikely to allow it. The majority, the heterosexuals who run the machines of civilization, will most likely grow more and more alienated from their animal sensibility, men becoming plastic automatons and women continuing to trudge behind, and produce either a world of grey uniformity or the next and utterly cataclysmic war.

To know oneself as a body is more important, at this moment in history, than to read the words of all the wise men who have ever lived. The enlightenment game, as it is classically played, has degenerated to a pathetic masturbation, fit only for men who are still seeking their lost fathers and afraid to accept the sexuality of their mothers. It is ironic that yoga has become such a fad, for the sense of the word is "to join," giving the idea of union. But the union most naturally available to us, the coupling in the sexual act, is losing its healing function. To deny this embrace, or to turn it into a sensual pastime, or to base it on ideas of conquest, *is to kill a real chance to understand what life is all about.* For if in our time a man and a woman cannot experience sex except as a symbol, then total insanity is upon us.

Any process of enlightenment which degrades the fact of the body by rejecting sex is perverse. Any teacher who does not realize and admit the nature of women, as bodies, into his teaching, is a neurotic charlatan. If Adam and Eve do not find a way to get it together, the species will not survive.

The notion that women and sex have been excluded from the area of seeking truth might seem an overstatement, but consider the common prejudice which keeps most of us from wondering whether Buddha continued fucking after his satori. The legend has it that after he became enlightened, his wife became a nun. And what of Jesus? What mammoth insensitivity is involved in presuming that he had nothing to learn in the arms of Mary Magdalen? Did Meher Baba fuck? Did Krishnamurti fuck? These questions seem blasphemous. Yet why should that be if we were not so conditioned to believe that holiness and wisdom are incompatible with sexuality, that an enlightened man will no longer have intimate contact with a woman's body?

In the act of fucking, a woman can teach a man lessons of life he cannot find in any book or in the rigamarole of any sect. If only he knows how to read them. If only she is aware of them herself. A man who cannot learn from a woman, a naked woman vibrantly alive with the pure passion of living, is no longer human, no matter how elevated his station or glorious his rhetoric.

On that night with Julia, I felt that realization with a sense of homecoming. There, in the cock and cunt, in the heat and patterns, in the movement and stillness, in the sound and silence, in the pervasively private moments when male and female join to become a single entity, is the key to our search for meaning.

Margo Anand

THE TANTRIC VISION

Sex is first of all a matter of energy. The more energy you have, the more blissful you can be, and the better sex becomes. If you mobilize your energy and express it more fully, you can experience orgasm as an *energy event* that can be learned and duplicated independent of the sexual context. Once you have learned how to experience orgasm as an energy event outside the sexual context, you feel empowered to take responsibility for your own well-being in sex. You know that the true source of your pleasure lies not in your partner but within yourself.

You can then learn to contain the energy, relax into it, and expand it. Ecstasy happens to you when you stay relaxed and aware in high states of sexual or nonsexual arousal. You can experience this state with or without a partner, for long periods of time.

This is not, as one may experience in ordinary sex, an alternation between arousal and relaxation, but a simultaneous *resonance* between them. You allow the energy to rise to higher and higher levels while at the same time relaxing into the excitement, letting it spread through the body and containing it for longer and longer periods. You generate high levels of sexual arousal that are followed, just before the point of orgasmic release, by complete stillness of mind. At the same time, you relax certain muscles, breathe deeply and slowly, and apply other simple techniques that transform the nature of your orgasm. This prepares you for a full-body orgasm, which depends on the body's ability to vibrate beyond conscious control. Instead of a localized genital release, you experience a prolonged series of subtle, continuous, wavelike pulsations that spread through the body, resulting in the impression that you are melting into your partner.

In this state, the orgasmic sensations are no longer exclusively dependent on genital interaction but are often perceived as an altered state of consciousness. Unlike the short peak of genital orgasm, what you feel is not a reflex act that leads to a sudden and uncontrolled release of energy, but a deep letting-go that is reached through a consciously controlled practice. As the energy between your bodies melts and merges, sexual communion becomes an experience of deep intimacy.

Most lovemaking is very dynamic. You move vigorously, and you breathe hard, building up sexual passion until you explode the energy outward in a final release. In contrast, the orgasm of the brain resembles the smooth, endless gliding of a kite in the wind. This orgasm greatly stimulates the brain cells and creates a bridge between the right and left hemispheres, fusing the intellect of the left hemisphere with the intuitive faculties of the right. It is this fusion that creates the experience of ecstasy, in which body, mind, heart, and spirit all participate.

Our culture has lost the understanding that sexual energy is a physical expression of spiritual power. In truth, the desire to unite sexually with another human being is a reflection of an underlying spiritual need to experience wholeness and complete intimacy, transcending the individual's sense of separateness and isolation. It is a need to return to the original source of creation, to the oneness we experienced in our mother's womb and, beyond that, to a oneness within the self. Sexual union without this sacred element, carried out only for the sake of pleasure, is commonly thought to be enough to satisfy our needs. But it rarely does, and then only fleetingly. With the sacred element added, it is possible for us to experience a connection with the life force itself, with our deepest creative impulses.

When the sexual force is considered to be a purely physical, instinctual drive, it is often misused and becomes associated with personal power—the dominance of one gender over another—and conquest. Deprived of its sacred dimension, sexual energy is repressed and eventually directed against life itself. This, in turn, results in disrespect, disease, abuse, rape, and other forms of sexual violence.

Negative social conditioning about sex inevitably creates fear, and this fear is passed from generation to generation by well-intentioned agents such as parents, teachers, and religion. In early childhood most of us absorb condemnatory attitudes about sex without even becoming aware of the process. This conditioning cripples our spontaneity, our expression of sexual vitality, our pleasure, and our ability to love and honor one another.

When people think of Tantra, they often think of celibate monks and yogis and, therefore, the suppression of orgasm. This is a misconception, implying that the attainment of ecstasy is based on the denial of one of life's most enjoyable activities. Indeed, it is out of the seed of lovemaking that the flower of ecstasy grows. Another popular view is that Tantra resembles a sexual orgy and promotes hedonistic indulgences.

In fact, Tantra is a middle path. It is neither indulgence nor repression. It teaches you to look directly into your sexuality so that you can understand, experience, and transform it rather than being either antagonistic to or enslaved by sex.

Tantra was born in India around 5000 B.C., through the cult of the Hindu god Shiva and his consort, the goddess Shakti. Shiva was worshipped as the embodiment of pure consciousness in its most ecstatic state, and Shakti as the embodiment of pure energy. The Hindus believed that through uniting spiritually and sexually with Shiva, Shakti gave form to his spirit and created the universe. Tantra, therefore, views the creation of the world as an erotic act of love. The joyful dance between Shiva and Shakti is reflected in all living beings and manifests itself as pleasure, beauty, and happiness. This, in Tantra, is the nature of the divine, the root of all that exists.

Tantra originally developed as a rebellion against the repressive, moralistic codes of organized religions and the ascetic practices of the Brahmins—the Hindu priesthood—particularly against the widespread belief that sexuality had to be denied in order to attain enlightenment. *Tantra* means "weaving," in the sense of unifying the many and often contradictory aspects of the self into one harmonious whole. *Tantra* also means "expansion," in the sense that once our own energies are understood and unified, we grow and expand into joy. Always a rebellious and nonconformist approach that challenged taboos and belief systems, Tantra branched out and influenced not only the Hindu but also the Taoist and Buddhist traditions. Tantra influenced Western religious history through the ecstatic cult of the Greek god Dionysus around 2000 B.C.

The great mystics of the Tantric tradition scandalized mainstream society and were often condemned and persecuted. The style of their teaching is characterized by what the Tibetan Tantric tradition calls *crazy wisdom,* a process in which the teacher uses paradoxical stories, seemingly absurd questions, and unexpected behavior to tease, jolt, startle, and provoke people to drop conventional attitudes and embrace the whole spectrum of life, with no contradiction between the sacred and the profane, the spiritual and the sexual.

One of the most extraordinary Tantric mystics was Saraha, who lived in India around the ninth century. Respected in his day as a great scholar and philosopher, he shocked everybody, so the legend goes, by becoming the consort of an enlightened Tantric woman teacher. They lived together in a cemetery, dancing and singing with such contagious ecstasy that everybody who arrived to bury the dead lost their sadness and became enraptured and enlightened. Through him, it is said, the king and queen of the land became enlightened, and eventually the whole kingdom entered a period of great joy and peace.

The Tantric vision *accepts everything*. There is nothing forbidden in Tantra. Everything that a person experiences, regardless of whether it is usually judged as good or bad, is an opportunity for learning. For instance, a situation in which you feel sexually frustrated is not viewed negatively in Tantra, but as a teaching.

In Tantra there is no division between what is good and what is bad, what is acceptable and what is unacceptable. For instance, Tantra, as I understand it, places no moral judgment on your sexual preferences. In Tantra the focus is not so much on with whom you do it but rather on how you do it. Hence, Tantra can be practiced by anyone who is attracted to this path.

The Tantric vision is one of wholeness, of embracing everything, because every situation, whether pleasant or unpleasant, is an opportunity to become more aware about who you are and how you can expand your capacities. And this provides a great opportunity for integrating all aspects of yourself, including those parts that you may normally reject or hide. This vision also recognizes that within each adult human being there is a natural, unspoiled, childlike spirit who can openly and innocently explore unfamiliar territory. The innocence of this spirt remains intact and represents our natural capacity to enjoy life, to love, to play, and to be ecstatic.

Because Tantra believes in wholeness, it embraces opposites, seeing them not as contradictions but as complements. The concepts of male and female therefore are not set apart, forever divided by a gender gap, but are viewed as two polarities that meet and merge in every human being. Tantra recognizes that each human being, whether man or woman, has both masculine and feminine qualities.

What this means is that by discarding our gender stereotypes, we can expand our sexual identities tremendously, honoring the polarity in ourselves that until now has been largely ignored. In Tantra the man can be encouraged to explore his soft, receptive, vulnerable, feminine aspects. He can slip out from beneath the weight of his male responsibilities, stop performing, and relax, taking his time in sex, making love without a specific goal, allowing himself to receive while his partner initiates. For her part, the woman can explore her masculine dimension, recognizing that she is capable of dynamic leadership in lovemaking, taking the initiative, creating new ways of guiding, teaching, and giving herself and her partner pleasure. The man does not give up his masculinity, nor does the woman abandon her femininity. They simply expand their potential to include the other polarity.

In Tantra, when the male and female polarities merge, a new dimension becomes available—the sense of the sacred. When the sacredness of sexual union is felt, it is possible to experience your connection to the life force itself, the source of creation. This connection lifts your consciousness beyond the physical plane into a field of power and energy much greater than your own. Then you feel linked, through your partner, to everything that lives and loves. You feel that you are a part of the great dance of existence; you feel one with it.

Tantra views sexual union not only as sacred, but as an art. Interestingly, the Sanskrit root of the word *art* means "suitably united." To become Tantrikas, practitioners of Tantra, lovers were required to be versed in a multiplicity of skills, such as conversation, dance, ceremony, massage, flower arrangement, costumes and makeup, music, hygiene, breathing, and meditation, among others.

When we learn the erotic arts in this way, a deep healing of our sexuality takes place. The sex act is not a hurried and tense affair, fraught with the dangers of disease (transmitted by partners who do not take time for thorough preparations), but a safe and healthy exchange between partners who respect and know each other intellectually, emotionally, and sensually before they enter into sexual union. This is what is urgently needed today: a playful, loving, and comprehensive perspective on sex that makes it safe and ecstatic at the same time.

According to Tantra, sex is first a matter of energy, and Tantra views energy as the movement of life. Within the human body, energy is continuously in motion. For example, the nucleus and electrons of an atom have characteristic vibratory movements and rhythms. The same goes for the molecules, cells, and organs of the human body. Each cell in the body pulsates rhythmically, and so do the heart, diaphragm, intestines, lungs, brain, and many other physiological components. The vibrations from these rhythmic movements generate bioelectrical currents that stream continuously through the whole body. They also generate energy fields that surround the body, and our moods and emotions generate specific vibrations that alter these energy fields as well.

One of the deepest insights of Tantra is that the human body is a single energy phenomenon. At one end of the spectrum, at the physical level, this energy is expressed as the sex drive. At the other end of the spectrum, at the level of the nervous system and the brain, energy is experienced as ecstasy. The sexual drive is instinctual, raw, unrefined energy. This same sexual drive can be transformed and refined into ecstasy. It is one energy manifesting itself in different ways. Sexual energy is therefore to be accepted and respected as the raw material, the crude oil, from which the high-octane fuel of ecstasy is produced.

It is said that the earliest Eastern mystics obtained their first glimpses of spiritual enlightenment at the moment of orgasm. Indeed, many people know that orgasm can temporarily transport them to a state of rapture. For a few seconds the mind becomes devoid of thought, the egocentric view of life disappears, and we step outside of time into the timeless *now* of bliss. So sex, to the early mystics, was the very source of the religious experience, as it can still be today, given the right attitude and conditions. Some aspects of the Tantric attitude are these:

Learn self-love. Love begins at home, with loving yourself—not self-centered indulgence, but the ability to trust yourself and listen to your inner voice, the intuitive guidance of your own heart. Loving yourself means that you realize that you deserve the experience of ecstasy. Loving yourself also means that you are not willing to compromise or settle for less than you really want, especially in sex. Trying to love another when you do not love yourself does not work. You end up feeling possessive, jealous, and dependent. By contrast, when you really begin to love yourself, you become a magnet, attracting the love of others.

Yet you don't need others to feel whole. Love becomes a state of being. Out of your own sense of abundance, you want to share and celebrate—you are grateful to receive and to give. This is freedom, the basis of true partnership.

Drop guilt. Guilt goes very deep, below our conscious thoughts. For centuries organized religions have used guilt about sex as a subtle way of manipulating and exploiting people, and the recent liberalization of sexuality has not yet succeeded in erasing this cruel legacy.

Enjoy spontaneity. We have a tendency to trust experts, methods, and techniques while denying our own spontaneous feelings. Life is a great mystery. Give yourself the freedom to respond to the new and unfamiliar. Trust your own originality. Explore your own natural, original, unique ways of making love.

Cultivate pleasure. Our culture has trained us to believe that we don't really deserve pleasure, that cultivating leisure is selfish, that giving pleasure is more honorable than receiving it, that having fun is wasting time—a distraction from more important matters. When we do allow ourselves to receive pleasure, we give ourselves conditions such as, "I should give him something in return for all this pleasure I am experiencing"; "I am taking too much of her time"; or "I shouldn't show how much I enjoy this, or he'll think I'm a whore!"

Discover meditation. By sitting in a position of relaxation and stillness, focusing your attention inside and deepening the rhythm of your breathing, the busy chatter of your thought gradually settles. As your mind quiets down, you are able to direct more attention to your feelings and sensations, expanding your ability to experience pleasure. Heightened awareness of body, heart, and mind allows higher, more intense levels of pleasurable experience. By quieting the mind, meditation also allows freshness and innocence to return to the act of lovemaking.

Give up goal orientation. You cannot *will* ecstasy. You can simply prepare the right conditions for ecstasy to happen to you. This is why so many Western lovers are frustrated in their attempts to experience ecstatic sex. They strive to achieve it through willpower and control, whereas it is actually a question of creating very intense experiences that are immediately followed by relaxing and letting go.

Allow surrender. Surrender is an essential aspect of Tantra. There is, however, a lot of confusion about what surrender means. People are suspicious of this term, which they equate with loss of free will and personal power. In fact they are confusing surrender with submission, which is a passive attitude that implies giving up responsibility for one's behavior. True surrender is a conscious choice made from free will. It means opening your heart and trusting the person you are with.

Robert Moore and Douglas Gillette

THE LOVER IN HIS FULLNESS

The Lover is the archetype of play and of *display*, of healthy embodiment, of being in the world of sensuous pleasure and in one's own body *without shame*. Thus, the Lover is *deeply sensual*—sensually aware and sensitive to the physical world in all its splendor. The Lover is related and connected to them all, drawn into them through his sensitivity. His sensitivity leads him to feel compassionately and empathetically united with them. For the man accessing the Lover, all things are bound to each other in mysterious ways. He sees, as we say, "the world in a grain of sand." This is the consciousness that knew long before the invention of holography that we live, in fact, in a holographic universe—one in which every part reflects every other in immediate and sympathetic union. It isn't just that the Lover energy *sees* the world in a grain of sand. He *feels* that this is so.

A young boy entered psychotherapy at the insistence of his parents, because, as they said, he was very *strange*. He was, they said, spending too much time alone. What this boy reported, when asked about his supposed strangeness, was that he would go on long walks in the forest until he found a secluded spot. He would sit down on the ground and watch the ants and other insects making their tortuous ways through the blades of grass, the fallen leaves, and the other tiny plants of the forest floor. Then, he said, he would begin to feel what the world is like for the ants. He would imagine himself as an ant. He could *feel* the sensations of the ant as it climbed over the pebbles (to him, huge rocks) and swayed precariously on the ends of leaves.

Perhaps even more remarkable, the boy reported that he could feel what it was like to be the lichen on the trees and the cool, damp moss on the fallen logs. He experienced the hunger, and the joy, the suffering and the satisfaction, of the whole animal and plant world.

This boy was, in our view, accessing the Lover in a powerful way. He was instinctively *empathizing* with the world of things around him. Perhaps he *was* really feeling, as he believed he was, the actual experiences of those things.

We believe that the man accessing the Lover is open to a *collective unconscious,* perhaps even vaster than that which Jung proposed. Jung's collective unconscious is the unconscious of human beings as an entire species and contains, as Jung said, the unconscious memories of all that has ever happened in the lives of all the people that have ever lived. But if, as Jung suggested, the collective unconscious appears to be limitless, why stop here? What if the collective unconscious is vast enough to include the impressions and sensations of all living things? Perhaps, indeed, it includes what some scientists are now calling *primary awareness* even in plants.

This idea that there is a universal consciousness is reflected in Obe Wan Kanobe of the *Star Wars* series, who is deeply sensitive to and empathic toward the whole of his galaxy and feels any subtle changes in *the Force.* Eastern philosophers have said that we are like waves on the surface of this vast sea. The Lover energy has immediate and intimate contact with this underlying *oceanic* connectedness.

Along with sensitivity to all inner and outer things comes passion. The Lover's connectedness is not primarily intellectual. It is through feeling. The primal hungers are felt passionately in all of us, at least beneath the surface. But the Lover knows this with a deep knowing. Being close to the unconscious means being close to the *fire*—to the fires of life and, on the biological level, to the fires of the life-engendering metabolic processes. Love, as we all know, is *hot,* often "too hot to handle."

The man under the influence of the Lover wants to touch and be touched. He wants to touch everything physically and emotionally, and he wants to be touched by everything. He recognizes no boundaries. He wants to live out the connectedness he feels with the world inside, in the context of his powerful feelings, and outside, in the context of his relationships with other people. Ultimately, he wants to experience the world of sensual experience in its totality.

He has what is known as an aesthetic consciousness. He experiences everything, no matter what it is, aesthetically. All of life is art to him and evokes subtly nuanced feelings. The nomads of the Kalahari are Lovers. They are aesthetically attuned to everything in their environment. They see hundreds of colors in their desert world, subtle nuances of light and shadow and shades of what to us are simply browns or tans.

The Lover energy, arising as it does out of the Oedipal Child, is also the source of spirituality—especially of what we call mysticism. In the mystical tradition, which underlies and is present in all the world's religions, the Lover energy, through the mystics, intuits the ultimate Oneness of all that is and actively seeks to experience that Oneness in daily life, while it still dwells in a mortal, finite man.

The same boy who could imagine himself as an ant also reported what we could see as the beginnings of mystical experience in his account of a peculiar feeling he had on certain occasions at a YMCA camp one summer. Once a week, the campers would be roused from their beds late at night and trekked along obscure forest paths in the pitch blackness to a central clearing, there to watch a reenactment of ancient Native American songs and dances. This boy said that often, as he was snaking his way along behind the other boys from his cabin, he would have the almost uncontrollable urge to open his arms wide to the darkness and to fly into it, feeling the trees tear through his spiritual body with no pain, just a feeling of ecstasy. He said he felt like he wanted to be one with the mystery of the dark unknown and with the threatening yet strangely reassuring night forest. These kinds of sensations are exactly what the mystics of the world's religions describe when they talk about their urge to become One with the Mystery.

For the man accessing the Lover, ultimately everything in life is experienced this way. While feeling the pain and the poignancy of the world, he feels great joy as well. He feels joy and delight in all the sensory experiences of life. He may know, for example, the joy of opening a cigar humidor and smelling the exotic aromas of the tobaccos. He may also be sensitive to music. He may feel exquisitely the eerie thrumming of the Indian sitar, the swelling of a great symphony, or the ascetic thunk of an Arab clay drum.

Writing may be a sensuous experience for him. When we have asked writers why so many of them feel that they have to smoke when they sit down to their typewriters, they have told us that smoking relaxes them by opening up their senses to impressions, feelings, the nuances of words. They feel deeply connected by doing this with what they call "the earth," or "the world." Inside and outside come together in one continuous whole, and they are able to create.

Languages—the different sounds and the subtle meanings of words—will be approached through the Lover's emotional appreciation. Other people may learn languages in a mechanical way, but men accessing the Lover learn them by feeling them.

Even highly abstract thoughts, like those of philosophy, theology, or the sciences, are felt through the senses. Alfred North Whitehead, the great twentieth-century philosopher and mathematician, makes this clear in his writings, at once technical and deeply feeling-toned, even sensual. And a professor in higher mathematics reported being able to *feel,* as he put it, what the "fourth dimension" is like.

The man profoundly in touch with the Lover energy experiences his work, and the people on the job with him, through this aesthetic consciousness. He can *read* people like a book. He is often excruciatingly sensitive to their shifts in mood and can feel their hidden motives. This can be a very painful experience indeed.

The Lover is not, then, only the archetype of the joy of life. In his capacity to feel at one with others and with the world, he must also feel their pain. Other people may be able to avoid pain, but the man in touch with the Lover must endure it. He feels the painfulness of being alive—both for himself and for others. Here, we have the image of Jesus weeping—for his city, Jerusalem, for his disciples, for all of humanity—and taking the sorrows of the world upon himself as the "man of sorrows, one acquainted with grief," as the Bible says.

We *all* know that love brings both pain and joy. Our realization that this is profoundly and unalterably true is archetypally based. Paul, in his famous "Hymn to Love," which proclaims the characteristics of authentic love, says that "love bears all things" and "endures all things." And so it does. The troubadors of the late Middle Ages in Europe sang of the exquisite "pain of love" that simply is an inescapable part of its power.

The man under the influence of the Lover does not want to stop at socially created boundaries. He stands against the artificiality of such things. His life is often unconventional and *messy*—the artist's studio, the creative scholar's study, the "go for it" boss's desk. Consequently, because he is opposed to *law,* in this broad sense, we see enacted in his life of confrontation with the conventional the old tension between sensuality and morality, between love and duty, between, as

Joseph Campbell poetically describes it, "amor and Roma"—*amor* standing for passionate experience and *Roma* standing for duty and responsibility to law and order.

The Lover energy is thus utterly opposed—at least at first glance—to the other energies of the mature masculine. His interests are the opposite of the Warrior's, the Magician's, and the King's concerns for boundaries, containment, order, and discipline. What is true within each man's psyche is true in the panorama of history and cultures as well.

Robert Bly

THE HUMMING OF EROS

The image I like best, very honestly, is that [eros is the] humming in the beehive that keeps the whole thing together. Eros is not abstract; you can feel it in your body. It takes all the parts of your body and it brings them together. It's like a glue. And sometimes, after you make love, there will be that kind of humming. Your arms finally feel connected to your body and your legs feel connected, and your heart feels connected.

I remember the first time I made love I felt my soul come right down into my body afterwards. Wasn't that a joining! Where had it been before that time? I don't know. But it was eros that brought it down into the body, and I could then be with it.

So I learned at that moment that you must never make love only once because making love the first time is just to call your soul down, and get rid of some sperm. Then, be sure to wait. . . . You wait a little while, and then the second lovemaking is the one that she was really asking for the first time, because your soul will be in it this time. And the third time is even better: two souls in it then.

So that's something you learn: that eros is there to bring things together, and women are really tired of being made love to by men whose souls are up around the moon somewhere.

Sy Safransky

Some Enchanted Evening

My friend Ron is in California now, making movies or waiting tables; we never write and I don't know when I'll see him again. But I'll always remember something he once said, which was one of the most honest things I've ever heard a man say. "The only time I'm happy, really happy," Ron said, "is when I'm in a woman's arms."

I know, I know. . . . There are men about whom this isn't true at all, or so it seems, men who are happy only when they're making money, men for whom happiness is found only in another man's arms, men who are devoid of passion for anything or anyone, because their heartache is too great or because their hearts were never broken—yes, men to whom women are no more important than poetry to a rock. Or so it seems. But I wonder whether this kind of indifference isn't always a lie, whether it doesn't mask the greatest need. There's a howling in all of us. Some admit it; others say it's the wind, and shut the window, and go to sleep. But in their dreams everything they touch screams.

What have I ever craved more than a woman's arms? To be up half the night, talking, laughing, making love—have I ever been closer to heaven? The bed becomes your church; you pass the collection plate back and forth until you've given too much, then your poverty becomes your gift: your tears, her tears—I mean, when it's right, who can tell laughing from crying? And though, in days or months or years to come, you'll swear you were fooling yourself, you weren't, it really happened: in the midst of all that fluttering, between the spilled wine and the giggling and the breathless kiss, your hearts billowed out like great white sails, and above you for a moment hovered the dove.

For a long time, I disparaged romantic love, even as I yearned for it; better, I said to myself, to long for true love, total selflessness without thought of return, saintliness. Better to crave God's embrace than a woman's embrace. What is romance, after all, but a golden chain that winds first around the heart, then around the neck? What sweeter lie do we whisper to ourselves than that another person can save us? The truth is they do, for a while—days or weeks or months, even years. But eventually we find out that no one can save us from ourselves. The realization is stunning, like seeing a photograph of the earth taken from space. How mysteriously alone we are! How tempting to imagine that if we're loved our loneliness will be dispelled.

Yet here I am, celebrating with champagne and flowers my second anniversary, with my third wife. My conceit, lustrous as her skin in the flickering candlelight, is that I've finally learned something about love. She's been married before, too: in the lines around her eyes, I trace the scars, but when she smiles, the pain is transfigured; I trust her pain, and what she's learned from it, and the light in her eyes—how can I not trust that? It's a beacon to me, a refuge; more than four walls can ever be, it's home. Am I a man in love, which is to say, as big a fool as God has made? A friend, asked if she trusts eye contact, says, "I trust it foolishly."

If I've learned anything, hasn't it been how little I've learned? Norma and I sip our champagne; a breeze from the window slaps the candle, and my memory, like a breeze, calls up other nights, other eyes, other women I've lived with and loved—how with each, I built a temple of hope, and placed upon the altar the unclaimed future, with the sunny side up; how our hands and tongues and lives wound around each other as effortlessly as morning light filling a room; you could no more separate us than take the blue from the sky. Yet here we are, in the long night of disbelief we were sure would never follow: we're together no more. With each, in turn, the tears became a rain, the rain became a river, and we are rushed down the waters of life with about as much control as a barrel.

In the movie *Last Tango in Paris* there is a heart-rending scene which evokes, for me, the impenetrable mystery of loving someone: why two souls, different as sky and sea, are called from opposite ends of the universe to make together a home, a life.

The estranged wife of Paul (Marlon Brando) has killed herself. Alone with her, in the funeral parlor, Paul contemplates her lifeless body upon its bed of flowers, her face set in a smile that is nearly beatific—a death mask which betrays his memories of her as in life she betrayed him, as they betrayed each other, with bad decisions, indiscretions, broken vows. He curses her, vilely and furiously—it is shocking; we expect, foolishly, something different for the dead—and then, suddenly, he begins to cry, his hatred dissolving into remorse and longing and grief, as time itself dissolves, and she is again his darling, his tender love, the one he reached for across the aeons, and who reached for him, and then let go, and now has let go for good. "A man can live for two hundred years," he weeps, "and never understand his wife."

Is it the women I haven't understood, or myself? The need to love and be loved—how much of it really had to do with them, their individual temperaments, charms, braininess, magic, their faces so ordinary and so adored? What have I looked for in their eyes but a truer reflection of myself? How passionate I've been, in pursuit of life through these other lives. What a devotee of desire! But not merely of the honey breasts and milky thighs, not merely of tastes tasted, the stuttering tongue appeased—but desirous, most of all, for desire itself. I've been hungry for hunger. I've come before my women like a starving man to a banquet table laden with everything delicious and suddenly within reach, and sat there scowling, insisting that someone feed me, feed me with a smile, with her hair brushed back just so, with nothing else on her mind, with undying devotion to my hunger, my awful hunger. No one could do it right, at least not for long. And so we hurt each other, terribly—I, convinced I was starving; they, convinced my appetite was grotesque, for sex, for sorrow, for sympathy, but mostly for the party not to end. My need, finally, was to keep alive the possibility of deliverance, no matter that I knew, deep down, that no one would deliver me this way. To give up the yearning for a woman to save me was terrifying, because it meant facing an ancient anguish my heart just couldn't bear. To give up the promise of love—the dizzying romance that someone else could meet my needs, fill my emptiness, still the howling—would mean acknowledging just how profound my pain was. To be lost, like a child, in my memories of childhood, to be drawn deeper and deeper into that maelstrom of grief—no, anything but that. Better the bruised look, the turned back, the slammed door. Better the quixotic search for the next shapely savior. But, of course, it would happen again. We seek our completion in the strangest ways, but seek it we must. We reenact the old hurts, we summon forth the ghosts of Mom and Dad and resurrect for them a new body, a new face, a voice with just a hint of the old, and we bid them to sit down beside us, here at the banquet table, and beg them once again to feed us, please, and please, this time, with a little love.

The truth is, there are no love substitutes. There's love, and there's everything which masquerades as love, all those diamonds that turn out to be glass: the world's prizes, and the prizes of the flesh, and the prizes of the spirit, too, so that God became the one I turned to when the fairy tale sputtered and the night came on: God as Mom, God as Dad, a God as distant and unattainable as the painful memories I used God to mask. But did it really matter whom I knelt before? What I worshipped was my own longing, what I loved was what I was able to get.

My children sometimes play a game called "Opposites," in which everything you say is the opposite of what you mean; they are learning, as they grow older, that most of us speak that way all the time. Every time I've said, "I love you," hasn't it been a lie? What I loved was *the way I felt* when a woman talked to me, when I thought of her, when her sunlight slid across the big dark barn of my heart after a night of rain. I loved the end of storm and loneliness, the clouds opening.

But this is like loving the postman because he brings you a letter you wrote to yourself a long time ago, in a time before time when you were whole, and love was as natural as breathing, and you hadn't yet bought the lie that you needed someone else's approval to be complete, that enchantment resided in another's eyes, not yours, that security needed to be sought, that you could find yourself in someone else! Deep within us that knowledge still throbs, in our heart of hearts, the heart that can't be broken, where the words *God* and *love* and *truth* are not distant signposts but closer than two bodies can ever be—closer than her hair, dark and storm-tossed the way I like it, splayed across my face; closer than her breath, smelling of me, and mine, of her, mingling above us; closer than her secret wish, whispered in my ear, for a finger here, and mine, for a tongue there, blazing like fire and going up like smoke; yes, closer than memory and regret; closer than that. Closer than my mother a thousand miles above me, bending down to pick me up; closer than my father at the door. Closer than close—where the tyranny we call love is seen for what it is: our human prison, to which we've fashioned the lock, and the key, and forever go on confusing the one with the other, and always in the name of love.

Have I learned a thing or two? Knowing what something isn't, isn't the same as knowing what it is, but it's a start. Some humility about love is a start. I start with what is dead in me, what hungers for the kiss of life, what wants to live in astonishment—not *through* but *with* a woman—and I acknowledge how difficult this is: did I say difficult, or impossible?

For example, I learn to leave my wife alone. For someone as unsure as I of his self-worth—longing for the kind word, the hand-out, the pressing of flesh on flesh—this is no small accomplishment, and often I fail, but then I get the chance not to blame her for my pain. Of course, it's always more complicated than that, for there's her pain, too. Does she rub my wounds with the balm of a little lie? If I realize what she's doing, do I merely get angry, or do I have to consider why? Do I, like a blind man, give her my hand, to run across her hidden face, so I might know her darker features, her fear? Do I lose myself in sympathy, or judgment—or reach through to real compassion? Do I stay the distance, or jump the wall—love her, or write a poem about love gone astray?

I have a desk drawer full of poems, for my exwives; for the other women I've lived with; for the women I've known briefly, and slept with once, or known no less intimately for never having touched them; for friends who, had we cared less for each other, might have been lovers, and lovers who cared enough to become friends. Knowing that my love is nine-tenths lie, I say I love them still, that they're here with me on this anniversary night as the men Norma has loved are with us, too, that if togetherness is mostly illusion, so is separateness, and that everyone we've loved, however imperfectly, has left their mark on us, and we on them.

I fasted for a week before our wedding day, to "purify" myself, but by the time the ceremony started I was more dizzy than pure. I promised Norma the sweet air of me, but knew I'd deliver the meat. No angel touched me as I nervously recited the vows—which, two years later, seem both practical and preposterous: either you need volumes to get you through the hard times, or nothing so much as silence.

We lift our glasses and gaze at each other romantically, before one or the other of us breaks the spell with a wink. We both know what an absurd yet touching drama this is: this marriage rooted in human frailty and conceit but rooted, too, in God's will. Yes, we know—until the next awful moment when we forget, and have to struggle against the amnesia drawn before us like the darkest of curtains. The grief becomes our bond. Grief, joy—one turns to the other quicker than you can say, "How was your day?"

And who's to say which is more love's measure? I didn't know I'd fallen in love with Norma until the first time I saw her cry. Through my tears and hers, which no lover's hand can stay, I'm falling still: through our shared loneliness, gathered into our hearts like a wild bouquet, then hurled away; through the sounds our bodies make, rolling together like chords; through echoes of pleasure. . . .

One moment we're "in," the next moment we're "out" of love; we agree, over the flickering candlelight, that we can scarcely say which serves us better. The pain of love always leads us down to a deeper, more compassionate love—but who can remember this? Who can bear the pain of love for what it is: the heart's unbearable treasure?

Deena Metzger

THE WORK TO KNOW
WHAT LIFE IS

At night, when you were in my body, when you were the tree giving breath to the night, I took it in. We lay there, your mouth open against mine with the breath going back and forth. I said, "This is the Amazon. I want to grow dark as a jungle with you, to feed all the myriad birds, to give off air to breathe." We lay together, dark woods feeding the universe, you breathing into me; I, taking your breath, holding it in my body, saying, "Life, Life, Life."

I wanted to be a plant form. I wanted to laugh under you like grass, to bend and ripple, to be the crisp smell, to be so common about you, to be everywhere about you, to house the small and be there under your body when you rolled there, where I was.

I wanted to be the animal form. I wanted to howl, to speak the moon language, to rut with you as the August moon tipped toward roundness and the blood poured out of my body. I held your penis that had plunged into me, and afterwards my hands were red with my own blood. I wanted to paint our faces, to darken our mouths, to make the mark of blood across our bodies, to write "Life, Life, Life" in the goat smell of your hands. You carried it all day on your fingers, as I carried your pulse in my swollen cunt, the beat repeating itself like a heart. My body had shaped itself to yours, was opening and closing.

I wanted to be the forms of light, to be the wind, the vision, to burn you like a star, to wrap you in storm, to make the tree yield. I wanted to drown in your white water, and where your fingers probed I wanted to hear each pore cry out, "Open, Open. Break Open! Let nothing be hidden or closed."

I wanted to be all the violences opening, all earthquake and avalanche, and the quiet, all the dawns and dusks, all the deep blues of my body, the closing and opening of light. I wanted to be the breath from the lungs of the universe, and to open your mouth with a tongue of rain, to touch all the corners and joinings. And when you entered me, when I heard you cry, "Love me, love me, love me with your mouth," I wanted to enter you with everything wet and fiery, to enter you with breath until you also called out and called out and called out, "Life, Life, Life."

Leonard Cohen

Beneath My Hands

Beneath my hands
your small breasts
are the upturned bellies
of breathing fallen sparrows.

Wherever you move
I hear the sounds of closing wings
of falling wings.

I am speechless
because you have fallen beside me
because your eyelashes
are the spines of tiny fragile animals.

I dread the time
when your mouth
begins to call me hunter.

When you call me close
to tell me
your body is not beautiful
I want to summon
the eyes and hidden mouths
of stone and light and water
to testify against you.

I want them
to surrender before you
the trembling rhyme of your face
from their deep caskets.

When you call me close
to tell me
your body is not beautiful
I want my body and my hands
to be pools
for your looking and laughing.

Lenore Kandel

Eros/Poem

Praise be to young Eros who fucks all the girls!
Only the gods love with such generosity
sharing beatitude with all
Praise be to Eros! who loves only beauty
and finds it everywhere
Eros I have met you and your passing goddesses
wrapped in a haze of lovelust as true as any flower
that blooms its day and then is lost across the wind
I have seen your eyes lambent with delight
as you praised sweet Psyche's beauty with your loving tongue
and then have seen them sparkle with that same deep joy
as other tender ladies lay between your hands
Praise be to Eros! who can hoard no love
but spends it free as water in a golden sieve
sharing his own soft wanton grace
with all who let his presence enter in
faithless as flowers, fickle as the wind-borne butterfly
Praise be to Eros, child of the gods!
who loves only beauty   and finds it
everywhere

EPILOGUE

We call it the real world: the world of things and deeds, appointments and careers, earning a living and cleaning the house, going on vacation and going to the movies. This is where we turn when we need to feel solid ground under our feet. This is what we think of when we need to reaffirm that there is something basic and immutable, something solid and unchanging that can provide a primal sense of stability and continuity.

We all need stability in one form or another. It is a matter of simple emotional survival. We need fundamental principles around which we can define an ordered, reasonably predictable universe. Without organizing principles everything becomes random, meaningless, uncertain. To avoid this sense of meaninglessness, this sense of existential chaos, we have been taught to turn to the world of reason, the world of conscious direction and control. We call this, unambiguously, *the real world,* as if any other way of finding direction, setting our course, defining ourselves and the world around us were mere illusion.

But, as this book hopefully shows, there is another world that lies beneath the rational world we acknowledge as real. It is a world of tremendous significance and power, no matter how consistently and ferociously we try to discredit it as insignificant, delusional, or ephemeral. True, we can think this world beneath the world into nonexistence; we can rationalize it to such an extent that it disappears before the dissecting power of our minds. But even as we think it away, we continue to *feel* both its power and its primal authenticity. We may not be able to *see* it, but we cannot stop *sensing* it. We may not be able to categorize or define it, but we remain aware that something is moving around down there, just beyond sight, just beyond consciousness, something in the shadows just beyond the reach of the firelight, beyond the glare of the city lights. Perhaps we are intrigued by what we sense out there/down there/in there, seductive and elusive. Perhaps we are frightened by it. Perhaps both.

This world that we know exists, beyond the boundaries of science, mind, and reason, is what this book addressed as the world of eros. It is indeed a world of immense power and potential—potential for tremendous life, energy, and personal growth when engaged with clarity and awareness; potential for great danger, confusion, and harm when entered carelessly and unconsciously.

As we have seen, the erotic world is one we have been taught to disrespect and fear so thoroughly that most of us have lost all but the most fragmentary ability to honor, trust, or vividly experience its many manifestations. Discovering the colors and shapes of our erotic existence—who we are and who we want to become as erotic beings—something that should be a natural, intuitive process of personal growth, becomes in our erotophobic culture, a difficult and confusing project of emotional and spiritual archaeology. We must dig through imposed layers of containment, control, fear, and misunderstanding just to experience fully what was originally as available to us as moving and breathing, to reclaim the erotic impulse that is one of the most basic, life-affirming aspects of being human.

Hopefully the essays, stories, personal statements, and poems of this book provide some assistance in that process, some encouragement, some insight, some new perspective to help unravel the erotic tangle we find all around us. Grappling with the wonders and mysteries of eros is one of the basic adventures of being alive. Eroticism is not the sort of issue we ever really understand or fully resolve in our lives. But we stand at an unusual point in the history of Western erotic culture, when this whole aspect of life is being addressed and debated publicly as never before, probed and explored with tremendous passion and potential. It is not an overstatement to say that the issues around sex and eros are as fundamental as any other in these times—psychologically, culturally, socially, even politically. Much will depend on whether we, as a nation, as a culture, and certainly as millions of individuals, choose to essentially embrace Eros and all the possibility that he represents, or once again fearfully attempt to banish him to the shadows of our lives.

CONTRIBUTORS

MARGO ANAND has studied with many Tantric masters and conducts sexual ecstasy workshops in Europe and the United States. She is the author of *The Art of Sexual Ecstasy*.

LONNIE BARBACH, PH.D., is a clinical faculty member of the University of California, San Francisco, and the author/editor of *Pleasures: Women Write Erotica; Erotic Interludes: Tales Told by Women; For Yourself; For Each Other; Women Discover Orgasm;* and *Going the Distance: Secrets to Lifelong Love*. She lectures internationally on relationships and sexuality.

JOHN BERGER is well known as an art critic, novelist, and film scriptwriter. His books include *A Painter in Our Times; About Looking; Ways of Seeing; Art and Revolution; The Success and Failure of Picasso; The Sense of Sight; Pig Earth; Once in Europa; Lilac and Flag;* and *G*, which was awarded the Booker Prize in 1972.

ROBERT BLY is a poet, storyteller, translator, and worldwide lecturer. His poetry has won many awards, including the National Book Award. His numerous books include *Iron John: A Book About Men; Loving a Woman in Two Worlds; The Light Around the Body; American Poetry;* and *News of the Universe*.

SUMMER BRENNER is the author of several books of poetry and fiction, including *From the Heart to the Center; The Soft Room;* and *Dancers and the Dance*. Her work has appeared in *Deep Down: The New Sensual Writing by Women* and *Up Late*.

SUSIE BRIGHT is the author of *Susie Sexpert's Lesbian Sex World*, editor of *Herotica: A Collection of Women's Erotic Fiction*, co-editor of *Herotica 2*, and former editor of *On Our Backs* magazine. Her writing has appeared in such periodicals as *Esquire, Elle, Forum, Image,* and *Outlook*.

JAMES BROUGHTON has produced twenty books and as many independent films. His most recent books are *Ecstasies; Graffiti for the Johns of Heaven;* and *Special Deliveries: New and Selected Poems*.

CAROL CASSELL, PH.D., is past president of The American Association of Sex Educators, Counselors and Therapists, and was the first director of the Planned Parenthood Federation of America's Department of Education. Her books include *Straight from the Heart* and *Swept Away: Why Women Confuse Love and Sex*.

GRETA CHRISTINA describes herself as a thirty-year-old, white, gay-and-lesbian-identified bisexual baseball fan. Her essays, columns, features, and reviews have appeared in *On Our Backs* and the *San Francisco Bay Times*.

LEONARD COHEN is well known as a poet, novelist, songwriter, and singer. He describes himself as "a visceral romantic," "a hero in the seaweed," and "on the lam." His books include *The Energy of Slaves; Beautiful Losers; Selected Poems; 1956–1968; The Favorite Game;* and *Parasites of Heaven*.

TEE CORINNE is a lesbian photographer and writer whose books include *Dreams of the Woman Who Loved Sex; Intricate Passions; The Sparkling Lavender Dust of Lust; The Poetry of Sex: Lesbians Write the Erotic;* and *Riding Desire*.

E.E. CUMMINGS, at the time of his death in 1962, was probably the most widely read poet in America after Robert Frost. He was born in Cambridge, Massachusetts in 1884 and lived most of his life in Greenwich Village and Madison, New Hampshire.

BETTY DODSON has been a public spokesperson for self-sexuality for nearly two decades. She has taught thousands of women and men through her Bodysex Workshops and through her ground-breaking books, *Liberating Masturbation* and *Sex For One*. She is also a noted artist who has had several exhibitions.

ROBERT T. FRANCOEUR is Professor of Human Embryology and Sexuality at Fairleigh Dickinson University, a Catholic priest, and a Fellow of the Society for the Scientific Study of Sex. He is the author of twenty books on human sexuality, including *Hot and Cool Sex; Eve's New Rib;* and *Becoming a Sexual Person*.

NANCY FRIDAY is the author of many bestselling books, including *My Secret Garden; Forbidden Flowers; Men in Love;* and *My Mother/My Self.* Her most recent book is *Women on Top*.

DOUGLAS GILLETTE is a mythologist, artist, pastoral counselor, and cofounder of the Institute for World Spirituality. He coauthored *King, Warrior, Magician, Lover* with Robert Moore.

ALLEN GINSBERG was born in 1926 in Paterson, New Jersey. His many books of poetry include *Howl & Other Poems; Kaddish & Other Poems; Reality Sandwiches; Planet News; The Fall of America; Mind Breaths;* and *Plutonian Ode*.

NAN GOLDIN is a photographer whose work explores the themes of gender identification, sexuality, relationships, and alienation. Her best-known work,

The Ballad of Sexual Dependency, exists as a book, a live multimedia presentation, and a videotape that includes over seven hundred images and a sound track.

RICHARD GOLDSTEIN is an executive editor of *The Village Voice.* He writes on issues of sexuality, culture, and politics. He is the author of *Reporting the Counterculture.*

JAMES JOYCE was born at Rathegar, a suburb of Dublin, in 1882 and was educated at Jesuit schools in Ireland. He left Ireland in 1904 and spent most of the remainder of his life abroad, chiefly in Trieste, Zurich, and Paris. He died in 1941.

LENORE KANDEL is a poet whose erotic writing has been well known since 1966, when publication of *The Love Book* resulted in international praise, controversy, and two much-publicized obscenity trials. She is also the author of *Word Alchemy; An Exquisite Navel; A Passing Dragon;* and *A Passing Dragon Seen Again.*

RACHEL KAPLAN is a performer and writer living in San Francisco. She is a regular columnist for *Frighten the Horses* magazine.

CAROLYN KLEEFELD is the author of three books of poetry: *Satan Sleeps With the Holy; Climates of the Mind;* and *Lovers in Evolution.*

MARTY KLEIN is a licensed and certified sex educator, and the author of *Your Sexual Secrets* and *Ask Me Anything: A Sex Therapist Answers the Most Important Questions for the '90s.*

RON KOERTGE is the author of fifteen books of poetry, including *Life on the Edge of the Continent; The Father-Poems;* and *Cheap Thrills.* He has also published two novels and has written a script for the television series *Hill Street Blues.*

ROLLO MAY is a practicing psychoanalyst and a training and supervising analyst at William Alarson White Institute of Psychiatry, Psychoanalysis, and Psychology. His many books include *Freedom and Destiny; The Meaning of Anxiety; Psychology and the Human Dilemma; Power and Innocence; The Courage to Create;* and *Love and Will.*

DEENA METZGER is a poet, novelist, playwright, and therapist whose work involves the relationship between eros and peacemaking. Her books include *The Woman Who Slept with Men to Take the War Out of Them; Tree; Skin: Shadows/Silence; Looking for the Faces of God; The Axis Mundi Poems;* and *What Dinah Thought.*

HENRY MILLER was born in 1891 in Brooklyn, New York. He spent many years in Paris where he wrote his best-known novels, and later moved to Big Sur and to Pacific Palisades, California, where he died in 1980. He was elected to the National Institute of Arts and Letters in 1958.

ROBERT MOORE is a psychoanalyst and professor of psychology and religion at Chicago Theological Seminary. He also teaches at the C. G. Jung Institute in Chicago. He coauthored *King, Warrior, Magician, Lover* with Douglas Gillette.

THOMAS MOORE practices archetypal psychology in New England. He is the founder and director of the Institute for the Study of Imagination, author of *The Planets Within* and *Dark Eros: The Imagination of Sadism,* and editor of *A Blue Fire: Selected Writings of James Hillman* and *Care of the Soul.*

JACK MORIN is a psychotherapist in private practice and a teacher of courses in human sexuality. He is the author of *Men Loving Themselves* and *Anal Pleasure and Health.*

JOAN NELSON is a sex therapist in private practice in the San Francisco Bay Area. She is also a chaplain of the American Humanist Association.

ANAÏS NIN is best known for her *Diary,* which has been called one of the outstanding literary works of this century. Her other books include *House of Incest; Winter of Artifice; A Spy in the House of Love; Delta of Venus; Little Birds; In Favor of the Sensitive Man and Other Essays;* and *D. H. Lawrence: An Unprofessional Study.*

CAMILLE PAGLIA is associate professor of humanities at Philadelphia College of the Performing Arts, University of the Arts, and the author of *Sexual Personae: Art and Decadence from Nefertiti to Emily Dickinson.*

JOHN PRESTON is the editor of *Hometowns,* author of *The Big Gay Book,* and former editor-in-chief of *The Advocate.* His erotic novels include the Master series and *Mr. Benson.* His essays and reviews have appeared in such periodicals as *Harper's, The Advocate, Drummer,* and *Semiotext(e).*

CAROL A. QUEEN is a San Francisco writer, sex educator, and sexuality activist. Her work has appeared in *Taste of Latex, Frighten the Horses, Spectator, On Our Backs, Bi Any Other Name, Herotica 2,* and *The Realist.* She is a member of the training staff of San Francisco Sex Information.

KEVIN REGAN teaches social morality at a Catholic high school in Rhode Island and is a counselor in private practice. He is married, the father of two college-age children, and the author of *Prayer Services for Adolescents: 21 Themes.*

MICHAEL RUBIN is the author of five books including *Whistle Me Home; In a Cold Country;* and *Unfinished Business,* and editor of *Men Without Masks.* His stories have appeared in *Redbook, Cosmopolitan, Family Circle, Antioch Review,* and *Kenyon Review.* He died of AIDS in November 1989.

HELEN RUGGIERI is the editor of *Uroboros* magazine. Her books include *Concrete Madonna* and *The Poetess.*

SY SAFRANSKY is the editor of *The Sun: A Magazine of Ideas.*

SCARLET WOMAN is the assumed identity of a middle-aged San Francisco therapist who describes herself as a poet, craftswoman, feminist, mother, leatherdyke, killer femme slut. Her writing has appeared in anthologies by Joan Nestle and Pat Califia.

ANNE SEXTON was born in Newton, Massachusetts in 1928. Her many books of poetry include *Love Poems* and *Live and Die,* which was awarded the Pulitzer Prize. Her poems have appeared in such periodicals as *The New Yorker, Harper's, Hudson Review, Partisan Review,* and *Poetry.*

DAVID STEINBERG is an author, editor, and publisher of sex-positive erotic photography and writing. He has been active in the California and national feminist men's movements for the past fifteen years, leading workshops on men's roles, fathering, male sexuality, and "Pornography, Erotic Imagery and Sexual Fantasy." He is the co-creator of *Celebration of Eros,* a multimedia erotic theater presentation that has toured nationally since 1985. His other books include *Erotic by Nature: A Celebration of Life, of Love, and of Our Wonderful Bodies; Fatherjournal: Five Years of Awakening to Fatherhood; Beneath This Calm Exterior; Welcome, Brothers: Poems of a Changing Man's Consciousness; If I Knew the Way . . . ; Yellow Brick Road: Steps Toward a New Way of Life; Doing Your Own School;* and *Working Loose.*

SALLIE TISDALE is the author of *The Sorcerer's Apprentice; Harvest Moon; Lot's Wife;* and *Stepping Westward: The Long Search for a Home in the Pacific Northwest.* She writes frequently for *Harper's, The New Yorker, Esquire,* and other magazines.

CAROLE S. VANCE is the editor of *Pleasure and Danger: Exploring Female Sexuality* and a contributor to *Caught Looking: Pornography, Feminism, and Censorship.* She is a feminist theorist and activist who teaches sex and public policy at Columbia University School of Public Health. She is a founding member of FACT (Feminist Anti-Censorship Taskforce).

MARCO VASSI, "one of the old bolsheviks of the sexual revolution," worked as a writer, teacher, psychotherapist, and as a translator of Chinese. Author of sixteen books and hundreds of articles, essays, and stories, he was widely acknowledged as one of the foremost erotic writers in America before his AIDS-related death in 1989. His books include *The Stoned Apocalypse; The Gentle Degenerates; The Erotic Comedies; Lying Down: The Horizontal Worldview;* and *One Hand Clapping.*

MICHAEL VENTURA is the author of *Shadow Dancing in the U.S.A.* and *Night Time, Losing Time,* and co-author with James Hillman of *We've Had One Hundred Years of Psychotherapy & the World's Getting Worse.* He writes frequently for the *L.A. Weekly.*

GORE VIDAL's many written works include plays, short stories, essays, and such novels as *The City and the Pillar; Julian; Burr; Duluth; Myron; Kaliki; At Home;* and *Myra Breckinridge.* He received the American Book Critics Circle Award for criticism in 1982.

PAULA WEBSTER is a New York anthropologist and writer. She is the author of *Bound by Love: The Sweet Trap of Daughterhood.*

ELLEN WILLIS is a staff writer at *The Village Voice* and is the author of *Beginning to See the Light,* a collection of essays on culture and politics. She has been a feminist activist since 1968 and was cofounder of the original Redstockings.

BARBARA WILSON is the author of *Miss Venezuela,* a collection of short stories, and six novels, including *Cows and Horses* and *Gaudi Afternoon.* She is cofounder and copublisher of Seal Press.

PERMISSIONS AND COPYRIGHTS